Gender, Labour, War and Empire

Gender, Labour, War and Empire

Essays on Modern Britain

Edited By

Philippa Levine
Professor of History, University of Southern California, USA

and

Susan R. Grayzel
Associate Professor of History, Department of History, University of Mississippi, USA

First published 2009 by
PALGRAVE MACMILLAN

Palgrave Macmillan in the UK is an imprint of Macmillan Publishers Limited,
registered in England, company number 785998, of Houndmills, Basingstoke,
Hampshire RG21 6XS.

Palgrave Macmillan in the US is a division of St Martin's Press LLC,
175 Fifth Avenue, New York, NY 10010.

Palgrave Macmillan is the global academic imprint of the above companies
and has companies and representatives throughout the world.

Palgrave® and Macmillan® are registered trademarks in the United States,
the United Kingdom, Europe and other countries,

ISBN-13: 978-0-230-52119-3   hardback
ISBN-10: 0-230-52119-3   hardback

This book is printed on paper suitable for recycling and made from fully
managed and sustained forest sources. Logging, pulping and manufacturing
processes are expected to conform to the environmental regulations of the
country of origin.

A catalogue record for this book is available from the British Library.

Library of Congress Cataloging-in-Publication Data
Gender, labour, war and empire : essays on modern Britain / [compiled
    and edited by] Philippa Levine, Susan R. Grayzel.
      p. cm. – (Genders and sexualities in history)
    Includes bibliographical references.
    ISBN-13: 978-0-230-52119-3 (alk. paper)
    ISBN-10: 0-230-52119-3   (alk. paper)
      1. Great Britain–Social conditions–20th century. 2. Women–Great Britain–
    History–20th century. 3. Great Britain–Colonies–History. 4. Great Britain–
    Race relations–History–20th century. 5. Great Britain–Foreign relations–
    20th century. 6. Civilization, Modern–British influences. I. Levine, Philippa.
    II. Grayzel, Susan R.
    DA566.4.G435 2009
    941.082–dc22   2008030085

10   9   8   7   6   5   4   3   2   1
18   17   16   15   14   13   12   11   10   09

Printed and bound in Great Britain by
CPI Antony Rowe, Chippenham and Eastbourne

For Sonya,
Colleague, Friend, Mentor

Contents

Acknowledgements

The editors wish to express their gratitude to Geoff Eley, Catherine Hall, Connie Hamlin, and Michael Strang for their early assistance, Kali Israel for her invaluable encouragement and aid, and all of the contributors for their fine work and willingness to share in this labour of love. Sue Grayzel wishes to thank the history department of the University of Mississippi for its financial support, Nikki Bourgeois for her assistance with the index, Joe Ward for his moral support, and above all, Philippa Levine; in addition to being tremendous fun, it has been intellectually satisfying and a genuine privilege to be her collaborator. Philippa Levine would like to thank, most especially, Sue Grayzel, model collaborator and good friend, with whom it has been a profound pleasure to work. Also, thanks to Curt Aldstadt, who as ever, reminded me that the singular pleasures of the academy have some pretty decent rivals out there. My life would be the poorer without him. The University of Southern California has been as generous an employer as one can imagine, and I thank the university for time off and for research funding.

Notes on Contributors

Elizabeth Buettner studied under Sonya Rose at the University of Michigan. She is Senior Lecturer in History at the University of York (UK). Her publications include *Empire Families: Britons and Late Imperial India* (2004), which was the joint winner of the Women's History Network Book Prize for 2004. She was shortlisted for Young Academic Author of the Year in the *Times Higher Education Supplement* Awards in 2005.

Becky E. Conekin is Senior Research Fellow & Course Director for the MA in the History & Culture of Fashion, the London College of Fashion. Her PhD (1998) was supervised by Sonya Rose and Geoff Eley. Her publications include: *The Autobiography of a Nation: The 1951 Festival of Britain* (2003) and as co-editor, *Moments of Modernity* (1999), and the special 10th Anniversary issue of *Fashion Theory* dedicated to *Vogue* magazine (2006).

Dennis Dworkin teaches British and Irish history and cultural theory at the University of Nevada. His recent publications include *Class Struggles* (2007) and "Intellectual Adventures in the Isles: Kearney and the Ireland Peace Process", in Peter Gratton and John Panteleimon Manoussakis (eds) *Traversing the Imaginary: Richard Kearney and the Postmodern Challenge* (2007).

Geoff Eley is Karl Pohrt Distinguished University Professor of Contemporary History at the University of Michigan, Ann Arbor. He is the author of *Forging Democracy: the History of the Left in Europe, 1850–2000* (2002) and *A Crooked Line: From Cultural History to the History of Society* (2005); and co-author with Keith Nield of *The Future of Class in History: What's Left of the Social?* (2007). He has also published widely in German history of the nineteenth and twentieth centuries. He is currently writing a general history of Europe in the twentieth century.

James Epstein teaches at Vanderbilt University, and is author, most recently, of *In Practice: Studies in the Language and Culture of Popular Politics in Modern Britain*. He is presently working on a study of Britain and Trinidad in the age of revolution.

Laura L. Frader is Professor of History at Northeastern University and a Senior Associate in Residence at the Center for European Studies, Harvard. Her most recent books include, with Sonya O. Rose (eds) *Gender and Class in Modern Europe* (1996); with Herrick Chapman, *Race in France* (2004); and *Breadwinners and Citizens. Gender in the Making of the French Social Model* (2008).

Martin Francis is the Henry R. Winkler Associate Professor of Modern History at the University of Cincinnati. He has published widely on the histories of politics, gender and war in twentieth-century Britain. His most recent publication is *The Flyer: Men of the Royal Air Force and British Culture, 1939–1945* (forthcoming).

Susan R. Grayzel is Associate Professor of History at the University of Mississippi. She is the author of *Women's Identities At War: Gender, Motherhood, and Politics in Britain and France during the First World War* (1999), which was awarded the British Council Prize in 2000, and *Women and the First World War* (2002), a global history.

Philippa Levine is Professor of History at the University of Southern California. She is author, among other works, of *The British Empire: Sunrise to Sunset* (2007) and *Prostitution, Race, and Politics: Policing Venereal Disease in the British Empire* (2003).

Alice Ritscherle is an Assistant Professor of History at Stony Brook University. Her research, to date, explores the ways that memories of World War II informed British racial politics and responses to immigration between 1945 and 1968.

Harold L. Smith is Professor of History at the University of Houston-Victoria and a Fellow of the Royal Historical Society of Great Britain. He is the author of *The British Women's Suffrage Campaign 1866–1928* (2nd ed., 2007), co-author of *Minnie Fisher Cunningham: A Suffragist's Life in Politics* (2003), and editor of *British Feminism in the Twentieth Century* (1990).

Penny Summerfield is Professor of Modern History at the University of Manchester. She has written widely on the social and cultural history of the Second World War, notably, with C. Peniston-Bird, *Contesting Home Defence: Men, Women and the Home Guard in the Second World War* (2007) and *Reconstructing Women's Wartime Lives: Discourse* *and Subjectivity in Oral Histories of the Second World War* (1998). She is currently working on a project with support from the Leverhulme Trust, entitled "The Popular Memory of the Second World War in British Society 1945–1970".

Angela Woollacott is Professor of Modern History at Macquarie University, Sydney. She is the author of *On Her Their Lives Depend: Munitions Workers in the Great War* (1994); *To Try Her Fortune in London: Australian Women, Colonialism, and Modernity* (2001); and *Gender and Empire* (2006). Current projects include two co-edited anthologies on transnational lives; a study of three iconic 'Australian' women performers, race and modernity in the early twentieth century; and a new research area exploring cultural understandings of the political changes in mid-nineteenth century Australia in imperial context.

List of Illustrations

1
Introduction

Philippa Levine and Susan R. Grayzel

I.   Why Gender, Labour, War and Empire?

The title of this volume, "Gender, Labour, War and Empire", reflects
some of the more important issues on which modern British historians
have chosen to focus in the last two decades. Moving away from political narratives, recent studies of modern Britain have connected the
metropole and the colonial hinterlands, placed Britain in larger comparative and transnational frameworks, and re-examined the milestones
of the modern era – industrialization and total war for instance. Such
interventions have done so in innovative ways that expand traditional
interpretations, so as to encompass a greater diversity of experiences
and offer a more inclusive vision of modern Britain. In gathering together the essays that follow, we have sought both to contribute to these
developments and to acknowledge the significance that scholarship on
labour, gender and war have had on those studying and teaching
modern Britain and its empire. We also intend this volume as a tribute
to the work of Sonya O. Rose whose contributions to these areas in
modern British history have been of considerable significance.

The transformation of British labour history began with E. P. Thompson's *The Making of the English Working Class* a half century ago. Ever
since, historians have been drawing upon his insights about class as
both process and relationship, and on his insistence on reading a broad
range of cultural productions as historically significant. The later incor-
poration, begun in the late 1970s, of gender analysis radically reshaped
our understanding of how both the working and middle classes came
into being. The work of Leonore Davidoff, Catherine Hall, Deborah
Valenze and, of course, Sonya Rose has alerted us to the gendered division of labour and the limits of dividing the world simplistically into

1

public and private spheres.[1] The linguistic turn has likewise brought about a richer sense of identity, experience and agency as contested and relationally constructed. As studies of Britain have further broadened to include imperial aspects not only as a separate category of study but as integral to understanding the nation itself, the reading of class as universal as well as all-encompassing has virtually disappeared. A more nuanced understanding of class connects it with other sources of identification: gender, nationality, ethnicity and race.

In a similar vein, what we might call the 'imperial turn' has productively questioned not only the contours and meaning of British imperialism, but – as in the case of the influential work of Antoinette Burton – the forging and definition of the nation-state itself.[2] Vigorous debate over just how tightly meshed the metropole and the colonies have been has underscored a good deal of the work on the British Empire that has appeared in the last fifteen years or so.

Where the imperial history of an earlier age emphasized diplomatic doings, official policy and, sometimes, resistance to it, the 'new imperial history' has turned rather towards a cultural reading of empire. Not surprisingly, questions of gender have played significantly in this new approach as historians have taken critical notice of the frequent imbalance between men and women in colonial arenas. Rather than reading this phenomenon as merely descriptive and obvious, historians such as Barbara Bush, Catherine Hall and Kathleen Wilson have convincingly demonstrated the profound effects of sex ratios in determining the colonial experience for both colonized and colonizer. We might further note that feminist historians have been in the forefront of the trend that has called for bringing colonizer and colonized into the same analytic frame, and in insisting that influence moves in both directions, and indeed across colonies, and not just outward from the metropolitan centre.

Critical to these new approaches to imperial history has thus been a growing insistence on the mutuality of British and colonial history. Though not without their critics, proponents of this position argue that activities and ideas in the colonies had as much effect on the course of domestic British history as the centre did on them, and that further, cross-colonial currents were also of considerable importance. This challenge to a 'top-down' history which saw policy imposed from London on largely tractable colonies as the primum mobile of imperial experience took its inspiration in part from the class-inflected social history of the 1970s and in part from post-colonial theory.

In this greater attention to the interplay between colony and metropole, historians have begun to examine more critically both state-sanctioned violence as a necessary feature of the colonial enterprise, and the particular significance of colonial wars. The imperial expansion that so characterized the nineteenth century also meant renewed and more sustained violence in the colonies. The conduct of various imperial constituencies during the Boer War, for example, reveals how claims to national identity could be recuperated by women seeking their own rights or conversely by a state trying to harness women to the imperial project, as Anna Davin, Laura Mayhall and Paula Krebs have suggested in differing ways.[3] The challenges to liberal notions of Britishness posed by the conduct of this "far away" war – the existence of concentration camps and of war waged against civilians – affected both growing critiques of imperialism and a resurgent patriotic nationalism.

Locating warfare as a phenomenon that must be addressed beyond the battlefields has further reshaped the study of nineteenth and twentieth-century Britain. At least since the publication of Paul Fussell's *The Great War and Modern Memory* in 1975, investigations of the effect of total war on identity and memory have fundamentally altered the history of Britain at war.[4] A growing literature on the two World Wars has expanded our notion of the terrain upon which war was waged and the ways in which military conflict must be understood culturally as much as politically, economically or even socially. Historians and cultural critics of the First World War such as Joanna Bourke, Adrian Gregory, Nicoletta Gullace, Samuel Hynes and Daniel Todman have provided ever more nuanced investigations into the ways in which war was imagined as well as experienced, remembered as well as recorded, by women as well as men.[5] Key cultural studies of the Second World War such as Angus Calder's *The Myth of the Blitz* and Peter Stansky and William Abraham's *London's Burning* have shed light on how and why the story of Britain's "finest hour" was constructed both during and after the war.[6] Scholars investigating women and gender in wartime have illuminated the profound extent to which gender shaped both the experience and the memory of war.[7] Just as the history of British imperialism can no longer be seen wholly as a male narrative and experience, it is no longer possible to write women out of the history of war and warfare. Other works have put Britain's involvement in the total wars of the twentieth century in imperial and comparative contexts; as a result, our understanding of the myriad ways war has shaped individual imperial subjects, as well as the nation, has been greatly enhanced.[8] An increasing attention to the role played by colonial soldiers and of the burden shouldered by Britain's colonies in wartime has further challenged Eurocentric readings of the two wars in productive ways.

Victory in the Second World War did not lead to a purely triumphalist nationalism, of course. Profound social and cultural changes ushered in by the postwar welfare state and by the processes associated with decolonization further complicated notions of Britishness. The postwar era was not neatly "post-colonial", and nor did class lessen as a dividing line in British society. Recent works on the Mau Mau rebellion in Kenya have suggested that ceding control of African colonies was fraught.[9] International incidents heralding Britain's loss of control over its "sphere of influence", whether in the Malayan Emergency of the late 1950s, the Suez Crisis of 1956 or Rhodesia's UDI almost a decade later, in conjunction with the increasing presence of what were called "New Commonwealth" immigrants in the British Isles themselves, provoked intense discussion of who belonged to, and in, the post-imperial nation.[10] As a result, both Britain and Britishness are now seen as contested in ways that open up the field to fruitful new avenues of inquiry.

II.   New ways of thinking about gender, labour and war in Imperial Britain

Given these major and rich developments, defining Britishness and the scope of modern British history has become increasingly complicated, but at the same time offers new opportunities to meet the intellectual and political challenges that accompany the changing nature of this scholarship. Tellingly, many of the chapters in this collection engage with the methodologies of cultural history, paying close attention to language, representation and such objects of mass culture as political rallies and demonstrations, fashion magazines and, in particular, cinema, that most modern of cultural practices.

Contributors to an influential collection of essays published in 1999, *Beyond the Cultural Turn* – including those who work on Britain (such as Sonya Rose) – have argued for the importance of seeing how cultural practices intertwine with social ones in historically contingent settings.[11] It is no longer enough to speak of plural cultures and to acknowledge the constructed nature of cultural texts. Many of the essays that follow read cultural sources as core indicators of the status of national identities and belongings. All of them engage to differing degrees with new modes of inquiry into the very nature of Britishness.

The volume begins with an essay by Denis Dworkin on regendering class, an exploration of the remaking of the history of the British working class through the lens of gender scholarship. Through a careful analysis of the work of Sonya Rose, Dworkin illuminates the significant changes labour history has undergone since E. P. Thompson's ground-breaking work of the early 1960s. Dworkin demonstrates the debt its continued vitality owes to gender historians, particularly those willing to combine social and cultural approaches.

The next several essays in the book focus our attention on labour in the British empire in several of its earlier, key phases, using detailed case studies and a comparative focus. James Epstein's contribution offers a close reading of colonial rule in Britain's first imperial age, when labour was a fundamental aspect of colonial policy, and questions of free versus slave labour were politically central both at home and in the colonies. Epstein's work investigates how Caribbean colonialism at the moment of abolition could be imagined without slaves. Schemes to provide agricultural labour for Trinidad relied on pre-existing assumptions about the character of both imperial subjects and non-British labourers: Scottish Highlanders, Africans and the Chinese. As Epstein concludes, the continuation of indentured migration made the goal of establishing "free labour" on the island untenable, and "the stark opposition between slave and free worker which abolitionists had embraced as a necessary fiction proved unsustainable in the post-Emancipation world".[12]

The essay by Philippa Levine on the racial dimensions of regulating prostitution, offers a comparative analysis of governmentality and the control of women's bodies. She combines an analysis of gender with the imperial debates over racial and sexual control. Like other comparative work on gender and sexuality, this essay demonstrates that there was no single strategy for regulating "dangerous classes" of women, but that local conditions and assumptions invariably shaped the management of female sexuality. Nonetheless, and significantly, what seldom differed was the belief, among government officials, politicians and others, that such control was vital to the maintenance of political stability, whether in colonial or domestic settings.

Angela Woollacott's study of the colonial actress examines how race and modern notions of the exotic shaped the growing respectability of colonial women's bodily and performative display in early twentieth-century London. Woollacott investigates the experiences of Australian women actresses working in London as a form of "imperial careering", and argues that for "colonial women, the growth of theatre as an empire-wide industry opened up travel opportunities and access to the metropole".[13] Centred on the ways in which London functioned as an imperial metropole, Woollacott looks at a diverse group of white settler women and their complex relations and associations to that cultural centre.

Together, these essays frame labour and sexuality as constant and long-term problems for the British imperial state in three contrasting arenas. These three markedly different kinds of labour – coerced (slavery), liminal (sex work), and performative (actresses) – highlight the often close link between work and sex, and the always gendered nature of labour transactions, themes consistently central in the work of Sonya Rose, as Woollacott specifically reminds us. Traditional labour histories of the modern period invariably made the factory worker – and the male factory worker, at that – the central axis on which labour analysis turned. This concentration on groups routinely excluded from consideration by labour historians until relatively recently heralds a distinct change in the field, one in which Sonya Rose's *Limited Livelihoods* (1992) played a key role. A broader definition of what constitutes work, which can encompass unwaged work, work outside the legal economy and workers not readily identifiable as proletarian has deepened and developed the contours of labour history in valuable ways. These essays are both informed by and aim to push forward these developments, with their shared emphasis on innovatively rethinking "labour".

The next section of the volume focuses on the Second World War, turning to what many have argued was twentieth-century Britain's defining moment. Three case studies illuminate key political, social and cultural aspects of wartime Britain, and a fourth essay investigates its postwar representations. As was true of earlier wars and imperial conflicts, the exigencies of this war created opportunities for recasting notions of citizenship and national belonging, and several of the chapters in this section focus on the way in which women and gender centrally shaped this process.

The first of these, Harold L. Smith's essay on British feminism during the war, offers an analysis of the cross-party Woman Power Committee and its wartime reform efforts. Smith demonstrates both the achievements and limitations of feminist efforts to shape public policy regarding women in the labour force and at home. With the introduction of conscription for women helping to reshape debates about women's wartime labour, questions of equal sacrifice and equal pay came to have new resonance. Feminist demands that women be treated equally with male labourers had little effect. Enduring gendered assumptions that women's central contribution was still to be found within the home clearly governed state and union thinking.

Nonetheless, interest in what women at home might and should contribute to a wartime state permeated popular culture. As the following chapter by Becky E. Conekin, on how British *Vogue* responded to the war demonstrates, even fashion – or perhaps especially fashion in the era of rationing – could be enlisted for the greater good. Conekin tracks the substantial transformation of the editorial content of Britain's most significant mainstream fashion magazine during the war, uncovering a "more complicated and heterogeneous" display of ideal femininity than one might first assume. In part, this was due to the role of the magazine's official war correspondent, photographer Lee Miller, and her key role in disrupting expectations about women and the representation of war by placing herself in the line of fire.

As Conekin points out, artifacts of wartime popular culture, such as those we see in British *Vogue*, sought to maintain an uneasy balance between reflecting the needs of "ordinary" life and acknowledging that these now took place in extraordinary times. In doing so, as is the case with Grayzel's and Summerfield's reflections on wartime and postwar film, this essay belongs to the kind of cultural history that carefully contextualizes and takes seriously the ephemera of daily life in a time of conflict. Such materials – especially cinema – a deeply shared, public experience, as Summerfield reminds us, can act as "vectors of memory". They do more than reflect a cultural moment: they shape how traumatic experiences come to be understood.

In another analysis of popular culture, Susan R. Grayzel demonstrates the significance of civilian, especially women's, morale, through an examination of the literary and cinematic versions of *Mrs Miniver*, which offered iconic images of women at war. The maintenance of morale became another kind of labour assigned to women and as the discussion of Struther's prewar and wartime writings reveals, one that they frequently embraced. Grayzel also explores the sharply conflicting American and British reactions to the film that was made from the bestselling text in 1942, a work praised for its veracity across the Atlantic and attacked at home, although its popularity remained unaffected. Despite these attacks, the enduring power of Mrs Miniver as a feminine icon encompassing a universal experience of stoicism under fire remains almost undiminished, having become a kind of shorthand for the popular memory of the women's war.

This section concludes with an essay by Penny Summerfield on remembering the Second World War, that further explores cinematic representations of the war and, in particular how different constituencies laid claim to the war's legacies in 1950s popular cinema. Summerfield highlights the ways in which these films celebrate the self-control and "stiff upper lip" which served as a "powerful signifier of what it meant to be British" in a way that conveniently elided claims to Britishness by those of the "wrong" class, race or gender.[14] Throughout the 1950s, then, popular cinema helped ensure that the public memory of the war focused on a particular narrative emphasizing British justice and the rectitude of the British empire.

The book's final section addresses two intertwined phenomena: the psychological and cultural aftermath of World War Two and the effects on Britain of its loss of empire. Martin Francis uncovers how the war was reimagined in the 1950s as a means to reassert racial and social hierarchies now being vigorously challenged in both colony and metropole. He shows the potency of the RAF's heroic legacy during the Rhodesian UDI, a legacy that erased the contributions of colonial and especially non-white flyers to the war effort. The emphasis on Rhodesian leader Ian Smith's wartime service served to bolster a certain image of the RAF pilot, one whose loyalty to the British empire was unquestioned. As this essay so powerfully demonstrates, "memories of the anti-Nazi struggle and the twilight of empire are irretrievably linked, at the levels of both the real and the fantasized" with clear implications for the ongoing use of RAF pageantry in spectacles of commemoration and celebration.[15]

The two essays that follow likewise focus on postwar concerns about race. Alice Ritscherle's contribution examines the imperial backdrop for debates about citizenship and the cultural foundations of Britishness during the 1960s by examining metropolitan reactions to the political crisis in Southern Rhodesia (Zimbabwe) in 1965–66. Like Francis, Ritscherle views Rhodesia's UDI and the political crisis it evoked as pivotal for postwar Britain. As her analysis shows, Smith and UDI's "metropolitan supporters recast meanings of the 'People's War' for British political culture, aligning its memory with the defence of right-wing politics and nationalist chauvinism, rather than social democratic or egalitarian values".[16]

The question of what values meant in terms of postwar notions of sexuality appear in Elizabeth Buettner's consideration of the publicly-voiced anxiety provoked by questions of interracial sex in postwar Britain, a time of increased immigration. She examines popular media representations of courtship and marriage across the colour line to conclude that: "Britain's early postwar offer of citizenship to persons from the colonies and Commonwealth regardless of race provoked immense anxiety about the effects this might have within the domestic spaces of the nation and the homes within it".[17]

The final essay by Geoff Eley, on how the national past was imagined in the "Heritage Films" of the years 1980–1995, brings the analysis of post-imperial Britishness to the end of the twentieth century.

Effectively deconstructing the films of Ivory, Merchant and Jhabvala, Eley shows how these films reinscribe "'tradition' as the central good of the national past" at a heightened moment of anxiety about the wholeness of this same past.[18] Eley's analysis of the work done by heritage films to create a nostalgic and stable vision of Englishness in a post-imperial world underscores the continued centrality in British culture of many of the themes engaged in the essays in this volume, and in the work of Sonya Rose: ethnicity, gender, class relations, and national identity. The erasure of conflict and the creation of a refuge so acutely described by Eley as the central conceits of this genre surely serve as an argument for why work such as that offered here, and so boldly and brilliantly insisted upon in Rose's own work, continues to be a vital counter to the blunting tendencies of nostalgia, erasure and willed forgetfulness.

Taken as a whole then, the essays in this volume contribute to the ongoing disruption of older master narratives concerning Britain's rise and fall as an industrial and imperial power. Instead, and in myriad ways, they shed light on the contested nature of class identity by showing how attention to gendered and often marginalized forms of labour can fruitfully complicate the story of modernizing Britain. In a slightly different register, the explorations of the gender politics and the cultural representation of the Second World War deconstruct this essential national experience of Britain's twentieth century. The essays on postcolonial or decolonizing Britain further dissect and help lay to rest an uncontested and unitary sense of Britishness in the twentieth century. "Gender, Labour, War and Empire" may serve as a shorthand for modern Britain, but all of these subjects deserve even deeper excavations that we hope these essays invite.

III.   Conclusion: Sonya Rose and modern British history

The topics covered by these essays are also ones to which Sonya O. Rose, to whom this volume is lovingly and respectfully dedicated, has made a major contribution. Rose's monographs, *Limited Livelihoods* and *Which People's War?*, in particular, have done much to transform the field of modern British history, with their many keen insights into gender, class and the permutations of national and imperial identities during wartime, especially the critical moment of the Second World War. Her contributions to labour history in Britain are particularly well explored in the essay by Denis Dworkin, who finds Rose exemplary in her ability to bridge "social and cultural approaches – cultural Marxist and

poststructuralist perspectives" on class. Laura Frader's afterword, meanwhile, examines Rose's impact on the history of gender.[19] As previous
work by Frader and Rose defines it, gender forms "the basis for social
exclusions and inclusions and constitutes inequalities in power,
authority, rights, and privileges".[20] Sonya Rose's work on gender and
class in the nineteenth century and on gender and sexuality during
twentieth-century total war vividly demonstrates this.

All of the essays collected here – some by those who had the good
fortune to study with Sonya Rose or to count her as a mentor, others
by scholars influenced by her substantial contributions to modern
British history – engage with a series of inter-related themes central to
the study of modern Britain and its empire. In choosing to name this
collection "Gender, Labour, War and Empire" we endeavoured not
only to highlight subjects of interest to Rose, but also to demonstrate
their centrality to a thorough understanding of modern British history.
These four topics are deeply connected to one another – as Rose well
knew – for to strip histories of modern Britain of any one of them is to
impoverish our broader understanding. Further, as Rose herself might
argue, the category of gender remains a central one for understanding
all of these other topics. As Rose points out in *Limited Livelihoods*,
"gender is a pervasive symbolic system which inheres in *all* social relations [emphasis added]".[21] Changing labour practices and policies, the
experience of total war, and the expansion and subsequent decline of
the British empire were all phenomena where gender more than mat-
tered: where it was, in critical ways, definitive. Whether we wish to
understand the imperatives of battle, the character of different modes
of imperial rule, or how work skills are defined and valued, an appreciation and understanding of gender relations – the construction of
masculinity and of femininity – is critical. It is thanks to Sonya Rose,
among others, that trends in modern British history continue to affirm
this central insight.

Notes

1 See Leonore Davidoff and Catherine Hall, *Family Fortunes: Men and Women
   of the English Middle Class, 1780–1850* (Chicago, 1991), Sonya O. Rose, *Limited
   Livelihoods: Gender and Class in Nineteenth-century England* (Berkeley, 1992),
   Deborah Valenze, *The First Industrial Woman* (New York, 1995).
2 Antoinette Burton, "Who Needs the Nation? Interrogating 'British' History",
   Journal of Historical Sociology 10, no. 3 (1997): 227–48.
3 Paula M. Krebs *Gender, Race, and the Writing of Empire: Public Discourse and
   the Boer War* (Cambridge, 1999); Anna Davin, "Imperialism and Motherhood", *History Workshop Journal* 5 (1978): 9–65; Laura E. Nym Mayhall,

"The South African War and The Origins of Suffrage Militancy in Britain, 1899–1902", in *Women's Suffrage in the British Empire. Citizenship, Nation, and Race*, ed. Ian Christopher Fletcher, Laura E. Nym Mayhall, and Philippa Levine (London, 2000), 3–17.

4 Paul Fussell, *The Great War and Modern Memory* (Oxford, 1975).

5 See among others: Joanna Bourke, *Dismembering the Male: Men's Bodies, Britain and the Great War* (Chicago, 1996); Susan R. Grayzel, *Women's Identities At War: Gender, Motherhood, and Politics in Britain and France during the First World War* (Chapel Hill, 1999); Adrian Gregory, *The Silence of Memory: Armistice Day 1919–1946* (Oxford, 1994); Nicoletta F. Gullace, *The Blood of Our Sons: Men, Women and the Renegotiation of British Citizenship during the Great War* (New York, 2002); Samuel Hynes, *A War Imagined: The First World War and English Culture* (London, 1990); Daniel Todman, *The Great War: Myth and Memory* (London, 2005); Jay Winter, *Sites of Memory, Sites of Mourning: The Great War in European Cultural History* (Cambridge, 1995).

6 Angus Calder, *The Myth of the Blitz* (London, 1991); Peter Stansky and William Abrahams, *London's Burning: Life, Death and Art in the Second World War* (Stanford, 1994).

7 Penny Summerfield, *Women Workers in the Second World War* (London, 1984) and *Reconstructing Women's Wartime Lives* (Manchester, 1998); Lucy Noakes, *War and the British: Gender, Memory and National Identity* (London, 1998); see also the essays in Christine Gledhill and Gillian Swanson, *Nationalising Femininity: Culture, Sexuality and British Cinema in the Second World War* (Manchester, 1996), Antonia Lant, *Blackout: Reinventing Women for Wartime British Cinema* (Princeton, NJ, 1991); Phyllis Lassner, *British Women Writers of World War II* (Houndsmills, 1998); Gill Plain, *Women's Fiction of the Second World War: Gender, Power and Resistance* (Edinburgh, 1996).

8 See among others Sonya Rose's own contribution, *Which People's War? National Identity and Citizenship in Wartime Britain, 1939–1945* (Oxford, 2003).

9 Caroline Elkins, *Imperial Reckoning: The Untold Story of Britain's Gulag in Kenya* (New York, 2005) and David Anderson, *Histories of the Hanged: The Dirty War in Kenya and the End of Empire* (New York, 2005).

10 Jayne O. Ifekwunigwe, *Scattered Belongings: Cultural Paradoxes of "Race", Nation and Gender* (London, 1999); Yasmin Alibhai-Brown, *Imagining the New Britain* (New York, 2001), also Kathleen Paul, *Whitewashing Britain: Race and Citizenship in the Postwar Era* (Ithaca, 1997).

11 See Victoria E. Bonnell and Lynn Hunt, "Introduction", in their *Beyond the Cultural Turn: New Directions in the Study of Society and Culture* (Berkeley, 1999) and Sonya O. Rose, "Cultural Analysis and Moral Discourse: Episodes, Continuities, and Transformations", in *ibid*.

12 See chapter by Epstein.

13 See chapter by Woollacott.

14 See chapter by Summerfield.

15 See chapter by Francis.

16 See chapter by Ritscherle.

17 See chapter by Buettner.

18 See chapter by Eley.

19 See chapter by Dworkin and afterword by Frader.

20   Laura Frader and Sonya Rose, "Introduction", *Gender and Class in Modern Europe* (Ithaca, NY, 1996), 20.

21   Sonya Rose, *Limited Livelihoods. Gender and Class in Nineteenth-Century England* (Berkeley, 1991), 9.

Part I

Labour, Sex and Race:
The Problem of Modernity

2
Remaking the British Working Class: Sonya Rose and Feminist History

Dennis Dworkin

Introduction

Although I've known Sonya Rose for several years, we don't have the kind of relationship that usually forms the basis for a contribution to a festschrift, typically comprised of essays by students, friends and close colleagues.[1] Rather my essay is based on an appreciation of and respect for Rose derived from my work on the cultural Marxist and feminist traditions of British labour and working-class history to which Rose has contributed.[2] I've recently published a book, *Class Struggles* (2007), an intellectual history and survey of debates on class since the nineteenth century, its primary focus being on scholarly and intellectual work from the last twenty-five years.[3] In it I devote most of a chapter to the work of feminist historians of Britain, among the most innovative scholars who have grappled with the relationship between class and gender. In the chapter's final section, I discuss recent efforts to rewrite the history of the British working class in terms of gender, focusing on the contributions of Anna Clark, Carolyn Steedman and Rose. In the present essay I build on the arguments made there, situating Rose's work in relationship to the major intellectual and political debates in labour, social, and cultural history and Marxist and feminist theory since the 1970s. A close reading of Rose's work cannot but fail to produce admiration for the scope of her intellectual engagement and for her generosity towards intellectual positions with which she finds herself at odds. Critically engaged in fields often characterized by crippling polarization and divisions, she has developed positions that draw on multiple perspectives, some of which have been signified as being incompatible. In doing so Rose mapped out new directions for labour history. She charted a path that sought to overcome the antagonisms between social and cultural approaches – cultural Marxist and post-structuralist perspectives – antagonisms that have been an important component of historiographical debates in recent years.

In crucial ways Rose follows the path paved by Leonore Davidoff, one of her close friends and mentors.[4] Rose, like Davidoff, is an American feminist scholar whose work focuses on Britain (although, unlike Davidoff, she has lived most of her life in the United States rather than in Britain). Also like Davidoff, Rose explores the historical relationship between class and gender from a historical perspective and the training of a sociologist. I would not be surprised to find that many readers of Rose's historical work are unaware that she has a background in sociology, as her work exudes a historian's sensibility. Rose held an appointment at the University of Michigan in Sociology as well as History. But it is not only her institutional credentials in sociology that are important. Her background in that field is apparent in the debates in which Rose has engaged, and it manifests itself in the ease with which she moves between theoretical discussions, on the one hand, and primary sources on nineteenth-century English workers – her major historical interest as a labour historian – on the other. While many historians struggle with expressing, sometimes even admitting to, the theoretical dimension of their work, Rose has written about it. She has produced critical overviews of the development of feminist and labour history, focusing on their connection to ongoing debates in history, cultural studies, historical sociology and feminist theory. My treatment of feminist historiography in *Class Struggles* is indebted to Rose's historiographical and theoretical essays, as they comprise valuable representations of the intellectual landscape of the last fifty years.[5] Here I treat these essays as quasi-autobiographical reflections, revealing Rose's own intellectual growth, development and preoccupations. They help shed light on the context of her historical scholarship, notably her major study of British working-class history, *Limited Livelihoods: Gender and Class in Nineteenth-Century England* (1992).

The quintessential worker and the creation of separate spheres

Sonya Rose's historical scholarship on the nineteenth century is rooted in what she described in 1992 as, "more than two decades of intensive scholarship on the subject of women and work that challenges the gender-blind assumptions embedded in traditional sociological and historical scholarship".[6] Yet if her historical work is rooted in a critique of mainstream labour and working-class history, it is likewise indebted to the historiographical revolution of the 1960s and 1970s that came to embody this "traditional" approach. The new labour history focused on working-class culture and politics, particularly the industrial workers and skilled artisans of the nineteenth century, and stressed the centrality of class consciousness and struggle. This class-struggle model was used to describe the process whereby skilled artisans became class conscious in the attempt to resist transformations in the labour process that threatened to reduce the value of their skills and make them into proletarians. This conception of history was greatly indebted to the inspiring example of E. P. Thompson's *The Making of the English Working Class* (1963), which aspired to recover the history of the working class from the bottom up within a materialist and cultural Marxist understanding of society and history. Thompson acknowledged that class was founded on exploitative relations of production. His emphasis, however, was on class consciousness: how these relations "are handled in cultural terms: embodied in traditions, value-systems, ideas and institutional forms".[7]

Socialist-feminist historical scholarship grew out of the emergence of second-wave feminism and the cultural and political milieu of the sixties and seventies, but it was influenced by an older generation of Marxist historians, especially Thompson. For Rose, as for other feminist labour historians of this second wave, the new working-class history and especially Thompson's rendering of it had "enriched our understanding of working-class formation". As she remarked of Thompson: "His analysis of working-class culture and political activism stimulated new ways of thinking about class. He narrated the story of how working people used their cultural resources to create class-based political responses to the economic changes that had unsettled and often destroyed their livelihoods".[8] Yet while cognizant that Thompson had made great strides in understanding the texture of working-class lives and the process of class formation more generally, Rose argued that the assumptions behind Thompson's class-struggle model made it difficult, if not impossible, to recover the lives of working-class women, for it unconsciously assumed male working-class experience to be universal. In her words:

> The dominant theoretical portrait of working-class formation represents its class subjects as prototypical and portrays their subjectivities as being constituted by work itself. The class subjects are universal characters – raceless and genderless figures in a unidimensional landscape. Yet the subjects upon which sociologists and historians have based their portrait are actually specific historical actors who cannot be

seen as representative of the working-class as a whole or as prototyp-
ical. These subjects are generally white, male, and skilled workers.[9]

Feminist historians attempted to redress this imbalance, restoring women
to the centre of this history, but in order to do so they had to deconstruct
the class narrative, one that they argued had been constructed as quintessentially male.

Since the 1970s feminist historians have recovered numerous instances
of women's economic and political life ignored by mainstream labour
historians: their lives as factory workers, domestic servants, and laun-
dresses; their negotiation of work and home life; and their role in bread
riots, strikes and suffrage campaigns. Yet however important this might
have been to recovering women's experience, eventually the limits of
such a project became apparent. It made some inroads into labour history, where new scholarship on women workers forced male historians to
take note, although not without resistance. However, in the historical
profession as a whole, women's history was known as a subdiscipline,
ignored by political historians because they continued to see the principal
actors in politics as men. A *History Workshop Journal* editorial in 1985
noted that it was important to recover "the worlds that women have
inhabited' but it could also "lead to a ghettoization of women's history,
and to its presentation in forms which historians working in different
fields find easy to ignore".[10]

Undoubtedly the most important development in feminist historiography in the late 1970s and the 1980s was a shift of intellectual
energy from the study of women to the examination of gender relationships, which, did not, by any means, imply that women were featured less prominently or that the history of women was supplanted by
the history of gender. "By 'gender'", Rose and Laura Frader wrote, "we
mean the cultural meanings associated with perceptions of sexual difference and the ways in which sexual difference forms the basis for
social exclusions and inclusions and constitutes inequalities in power,
authority, rights, and privileges".[11]

In this context an important achievement of feminist scholars and
their allies was to rethink the relationship between public and private
life. In countless ways they demonstrated that both were gendered, the
public sphere being signified as masculine and the private as feminine.
This perspective had important consequences for understanding the
past and present and for critiquing conventional modes of understanding. First, it suggested that the public worlds of work and politics were
not gender free. Second, it argued that historians and sociologists who

ignored the gendered dimension of public life, in fact, implicitly and explicitly helped naturalize the ideological process that had signified male experience as being universal. Rose was by no means alone in recognizing the importance of these developments. Yet few writers have been more adept in exploring their significance. Drawing from debates and discussions on the gendering of the public/private spheres, she explained the consequences of these ideas for labour history and discussed their importance for her own historical work.

For Rose, the binary opposition between public and private did not originate during the nineteenth century, but it was then that it developed in important and influential ways. Her analysis wove together an account of this development and an exploration of its consequences for historical understanding. On the one hand, she explored the liberal political theory responsible for producing influential notions of public and private and the spread of these ideologies to social and cultural life, first in the middle class and later among working-class people. On the other hand, she criticized mainstream labour historians, who, she believed, unconsciously reproduced these ideological constructions in their work and hence did not do justice to the historical relationship between class and gender.

Rose argues that shifts in political theory that first developed as part of the liberal theory of the Enlightenment were critical to the gendering of public and private. Here Rose cites the feminist political theorist Carol Pateman, who argues that liberal theory is based on the notion that the public sphere was governed by universal norms – interests, rights, equality, and property – which were in fact masculine. In Pateman's words: "The civil body politic is fashioned after the image of the male 'individual' who is constituted through the separation of civil society from women".[12] Similarly, Rose observes (once again following Pateman) that liberal political theory relegates women to a realm beyond the pale of the social. In this context she cites the political philosopher John Locke, who equated the economy and the public sphere of politics with contract, and the private sphere of the family, where women resided, with nature.

This gendering of the private and public did not only take place in liberal theory. Rose demonstrates that it spread to Marxism as well. While Marx and Engels opposed liberal ideology and saw the private and public worlds under capitalism as impoverished, they nonetheless equated the public sphere with men and the private one with women. Class relations and class struggle in the Marxist tradition were seen as being rooted in industrial production and the public sphere and thus by definition relegated the great majority of women to a supporting role. In Rose's words: "Marx identified the forces and relations of production – located in the social sphere – as fundamental of historical transformation. This meant that social reproduction, while essential for the development and maintenance of capitalism, responded to social change but did not contribute to it.[13]

In making this critique Rose was mindful of the debate among socialist feminists, particularly lively in the 1970s, that sought to create a Marxist analysis that incorporated the private domain of biological and social reproduction, what might be regarded as providing last-ditch counseling for what Heidi Hartmann described as "the unhappy marriage of Marxism and feminism", a necessary but stressful union in which capitalism and patriarchy were distinct but interacting systems of oppression.[14] However, such efforts were doomed to fail. As Rose observed: "Yet even in these discussions conducted at the level of abstract theory, the 'motor of history' remained in the public sphere. While domestic labour was seen to be functional for capitalism, productive relations and the politics generated as a consequence of them remained the stuff of historical transformation".[15] In effect, dual system theory attempted to bridge the gap between gender and class analysis without reducing the former to the latter. In doing so it preserved the public/private dichotomy that made it possible for the male working class to stand in for the class as a whole – to be the "quintessential worker" in Rose's words.

For Rose, assumptions about gender in liberal and Marxist political theory were closely related to changes in broader societal understandings of private and public, notably the spread of the doctrine of separate spheres, which became an underlying principle shaping middle-class life. "Increasingly in the nineteenth century", Rose wrote, "women and men were seen as having essentially different natures. Because of their different natures, men were believed to be best equipped to deal with the worldly matters of commerce and politics; women were believed especially suited to providing moral sustenance as well as physical and emotional nurturance to family members".[16] While observing that such divisions are part of English and American nineteenth-century history may not be new, an innovation of the new feminist scholarship was to see them as potentially empowering, a "world of love and ritual", as the title of an article by Caroll Smith-Rosenberg suggested.[17] As Nancy Hewitt observed, American feminists saw separate spheres as oppressive and restrictive, but they also believed that "the counterpart of subordination in or exclusion from male-dominated domains was inclusion in an all-female enclave".[18]

A large body of feminist historical scholarship has contributed to understanding the dynamics of nineteenth-century separate spheres. Yet, as Rose observed, despite the importance of such work, a substantial part of it never questioned the binary opposition that produced the idea of separate spheres in the first place. In her view "instead of taking these findings as indicative of the natural proclivities of women, or as stemming directly from family relationships, we need to ask why there were these distinctive cultures, how they were formed, and what accounts for the connection between women's family lives and their politics".[19] Arguably the key text that challenged assumptions regarding separate spheres was Leonore Davidoff and Catherine Hall's *Family Fortunes: Men and Women of the English Middle Class, 1780–1850* (1987). Based on detailed case studies drawn from the urban setting of Birmingham and from rural Suffolk and Essex, the book was one of the most influential works of social/cultural history in the last twenty years. It charted the emergence of a distinctive middle-class consciousness, linking the increasing economic dependence of middle-class women on their husbands and their intensified marginalization in public affairs to the creation of clearly delineated realms appropriate to men and women. This process was facilitated by the ideological vision of evangelical Christianity, for which the masculine, grubby and public world of capitalism was to be offset by the feminine, spiritually grounded domain of home and family. If Davidoff and Hall believed that the remapping of gender via the ideology of separate spheres powerfully defined English society – both the world of the middle class and beyond – they did not regard it as total. In the introduction to the 2002 edition, they explained that their original intention "was always to move beyond the public/private divide". In their words: "We fleshed out these arguments, demonstrating in numerous instances the crossing of the boundaries, both in their imagined and material forms: the energetic women who claimed the right to vote in church meetings or speak in public".[20] Davidoff and Hall, in effect, overcame the dichotomy of dual system theory, asserting that class and gender were deeply intertwined. They argued "that the men and women of the provincial middle class adopted distinctively different class identities, that the language of class formation was gendered".[21]

Like many feminist historians, Rose regarded *Family Fortunes* as a major achievement. In her words: "Davidoff and Hall expose the artificiality of the ideology of separate spheres by showing the many ways that home and family were central to middle-class male identity as well to their enterprises". Rose was not a historian of the middle classes, but her efforts at reworking labour history might be regarded as representing an analogous project to theirs. "While these developments in bourgeois society", she wrote, "shaped the assumptions of the emerging disciplines that concerned themselves with the social world generally, there were related developments in the working class that were of special consequence for what was to count as labor history". Here Rose was referring to the fact that working-class men had been able to define the working-class public sphere and that working-class people more generally produced, under the influence of the middle classes, their own often different version of separate spheres. She was also suggesting that labour historians had failed to question the assumptions that went into this gendering process that privileged men's over women's activities. "Instead of understanding their particularity and exclusivity, historians took them as *models* for labour activism, resistance, and class identity. In other words, they provided the template for conceptualizing working-class formation. The consequence was to privilege certain male subjects and their actions as worthy of study and to ignore what fell outside the mould."[22]

Rose argued that labour historians should treat the language of separate spheres as a cultural construction, that despite appearing to be fixed and immutable it was, in fact, fluid. "I want to suggest here", she writes, "that public and private might better be understood relationally as a multidimensional matrix rather than a unidimensional opposition. Public and private are not fixed categories or spheres of existence. Rather, they are defined in relation to one another and often are matters of contest."[23] This approach, in her view, opened up more complex ways of seeing the relationship between home and family, on the one hand, and work and politics, on the other, for it suggested that they were intertwined rather than separate. In effect, Rose not only challenged the assumptions of conventional labour history, but also advocated a discursive and cultural alternative to it.

The linguistic turn

Rose's advocacy of a cultural alternative was part of a broader movement among feminists scholars committed to exploring the ideological construction of gender, but it was also informed by, and a response to, an intensifying crisis in social and labour history. Indeed, by the 1980s and 1990s, class theory and analysis – and social approaches more generally – were subject to serious attack, most importantly by left-wing scholars, once their leading advocates. Emblematic of this change was a collection of essays by a group of mostly American historians of French labour history: *Rethinking Labor History: Essays on Discourse and Class Analysis*

(1993). In the book's introduction its editor, Lenard Berlanstein, wrote that "the new labor history has entered the 1990s uncertain about the authority of earlier achievements and divided about basic methods and concepts". He spoke of "a widespread sense among an expanding circle of scholars that the shades have fallen from their eyes and that labor history will not be the same and should not be the same".[24] The broader context of this crisis was the emergence of identity politics and new social movements, including feminism, which were transforming the political terrain. These identity shifts resonated with the emergence of postmodernism, whose opposition to universal narratives and essentialist thought; insistence on pluralism and difference in the social, political and cultural fields; and tendency to think in terms of fragmented subjects clashed with the totalizing ambitions of the original social-history project.

A critical challenge to the social-history model came from the poststructuralist-inflected thinking of the emerging "new cultural history". Cultural historians stressed the role that language played in constructing the reality that it described. They regarded experience and consciousness as being linguistically ordered. Rather than individual and group interests being rooted in an objective structure, they were, in fact, produced through language and culture. Such perspectives entered British historical studies with the publication of Gareth Stedman Jones' "Rethinking Chartism" – one of the essays in his *The Languages of Class: Studies in English Working Class History, 1832–1982* (1983). Stedman Jones rejected the dominant social interpretation of the Chartist movement – the first nationwide working-class movement that advocated universal manhood suffrage and reform of the electoral system. Rather than view Chartism as the collective consciousness of class experience, Stedman Jones regarded it as an outgrowth of an older tradition of political radicalism whose discursive structure set limits to and pressures on working-class political action. Stedman Jones's understanding of the Chartists, and the early labour movement, more generally, was replete with political and theoretical implications. His contention that Chartism could be framed as part of a much older radical tradition challenged the Thompsonian idea that it was the fruit of "the making of the English working class". Just as important, Stedman Jones' argument rejected the foundation of Thompson's class-struggle model, which, while emphasizing popular cultural traditions, nonetheless privileged relationships of production.

Among feminist historians, Joan Scott's poststructuralist and feminist critique of Stedman Jones helped frame subsequent debates about the relationship between class and gender. Scott found Stedman Jones' rereading of Chartism to be theoretically innovative, while not fully pursuing the logic of his own argument. Despite claiming to deploy a nonreferential theory of language, he never fully explored one of its central insights, the contention that meaning was produced through discursive systems of difference founded on binary oppositions. She argued that Chartism shouldn't be reduced to "a formal political struggle or a particular strategy offered by an organized group." It should be analyzed as a "process through which class was conceived".[25] Scott understood gender in similar terms. She defined it as a constitutive dimension of social relationships, based on perceptions of sexual difference, and a primary means of signifying power relationships. For her, these perceptions were inscribed in symbolic representations based on normative concepts, helped define numerous social and cultural practices, and played a critical role in the construction of subjectivity and identity.

Scott's contention that gender relationships were rooted in language and discourse was simultaneously influential and contentious inside and outside of feminist circles. Discussion of her work polarized her defenders and detractors, the terrain being defined partially by Scott herself, as a consequence of her polemical responses to the critiques of first Christine Stansell and later Laura Lee Downs.[26] A contingent of historians, however, affirmed Scott's notion of gender, yet expressed reservations regarding the implications of a full-blown discursive interpretation, notably its minimizing of agency and experience in political practice. Agency and experience had not only been critical to Thompson's class-struggle model: they were also pivotal to the feminist politics of much of women's history as well. Catherine Hall, for instance, a supporter of cultural and linguistic approaches, believed that Scott had reached conclusions that she herself had reached through a different route. Hall nonetheless had reservations: "The deconstructionist death of the subject, even a de-centred version, can lead to a loss of any notion of agency. The poststructuralist critique of the old humanist illusion of autonomous individuals acting in the world, together with an insistent emphasis on the categories which allow the construction of identities can, when driven to the limits, result in a curious loss of feeling in historical writing."[27]

Rose enthusiastically embraced the linguistic understanding of gender and deployed it as part of her critique of conventional labour history. Yet at the same time she insisted that discourse was a material force and that the language of gender was embedded in structured processes of inequality. As she stated it:

Language is a set of social symbols that create distinctions. These symbols can vary in meaning and use, but in order for them to communicate meaning they must be understood. Similarly, gender is a process of making distinctions in ways that are widely recognized and understood. The language of gender is expressed in a variety of social practices that positioned people differently in relations of power. In nineteenth-century England, these positions were linked to differential access to political and economic resources.[28]

Indeed, Rose argued that historians who adopted the linguistic approaches didn't necessarily take on board the insights feminist historians offered on the gendering of the historical process. She suggested that Patrick Joyce, a labour historian who championed postmodernism, "makes an effort to include women in his analysis by indicating women's presence" but "generally his strategy is to link women and families".[29] In effect, he reinforced the ideology of separate spheres rather than deconstructing it.

Significantly, Rose's embrace of the linguistic turn didn't preclude jettisoning her cultural Marxist roots, made clear by her acknowledgment of her debt to the literary scholar and cultural theorist Raymond Williams, a writer who, while often cited as a "founding father" of cultural studies, was a brunt of criticism when the field took a poststructuralist and postcolonial direction.[30] Rose affirmed Williams' contention that "ideologies or particular systems of meaning never fully capture the lived experience of people, even if they become accepted as to be seen as common sense". This constitutes a defence of "experience" that went against the grain of poststructuralist thought.[31] In short, while some historians embraced the linguistic turn and burned their bridges with their Marxist past, Rose was not one of them. She sought to go beyond the existing polarities found in historiographical debates: she combined discursive with social and cultural Marxist perspectives.

Limited Livelihoods

Rose's efforts to deploy social and cultural approaches in the writing of labour history were part of a broader movement among American and British feminist historians who wanted to rewrite the British working-class narrative established by Thompson's generation, while retaining their respect for its achievement. This "gendering of the British working class" highlighted the gender conflicts within working-class life and analyzed their implications for class consciousness and struggle.[32] Theodore Koditschek, the author of a pivotal essay defining this trend in historiography, cites Deborah Valenze's analysis of the early phase of the Industrial Revolution in *The First Industrial Woman* (1995), Anna

Clark's reframing of the territory marked out by Thompson in *The Struggle for the Breeches: Gender and the Making of the British Working Class* (1995), Rose's exploration of working-class life in the second half of the nineteenth century in *Limited Livelihoods*, and Ellen Ross' revisiting of some of the terrain first explored by Stedman Jones in her *Love and Toil: Motherhood in Outcast London*, 1870–1918 (1993) as central texts to this process of gendering working-class life.[33] "In the aftermath of these books", writes Koditschek, "we may with reasonable certainty anticipate that the entire field of British working-class history will never again be the same. Labour historians of every school and stripe will have to take as their starting point the fundamental conclusion that these books so painstakingly and so compellingly reach, that the dynamics of class formation and transformation must always be examined in gendered terms".[34]

Limited Livelihoods focuses on the interconnection between class and gender and the consequences of this relationship for political action in the northern textile industries. Rose's general conclusion is as follows: "Gender was implicit in the struggle between workers and employers in the nineteenth century, and it was central to some arenas of that struggle. A consequence was that workers' solidarity could easily be diffused by gender politics. In addition, the connection between masculinity and working-class respectability promoted a working class divided along occupational lines."[35]

Rose treats the second half of the nineteenth century as an intermediary phase. When it began working-class families still commonly depended on the wages of women and children. By the time that it ended, the ideal of men as the sole breadwinner and women presiding over the home had become dominant, even though the wages of women were often necessary for working-class families to make ends meet. Rose attributes this shift to the spreading influence of a middle-class discourse of separate spheres and the growing importance of "respectability" in working-class life. To achieve respectability, a group of working-class men demanded a "family wage" to support their wives and conduct themselves at work and in public life in "manly" or honourable ways. However, while the discourse of the family wage had the effect of limiting the possibilities for married women in the public sphere, its material consequences were more complex: "Where women earned wages", Rose observed, "was less important in their lives than was the necessity for them to combine other aspects of their domestic lives with a variety of makeshift strategies to make ends meet".[36] Women were often forced to accept industrial homework, which became a way of cutting labour costs for manufacturers and was indispensable for families making ends meet in difficult times. For Rose, the linguistic and nonlinguistic dimensions of social life deeply intertwined.

Rose demonstrates the complexity and scope of the class/gender relationship in the working-class experience. In the Kidderminster carpet industry, "major industrial disputes erupted ... when various manufactures attempted to change the labor process in carpet weaving by introducing new technology, altering machines already in use, or manufacturing a new product, and then hiring women rather than men to do the work".[37] Men fought a rearguard battle to preserve their jobs and wages, but, for the most part, maintained segregation by sex in the workplace. In contrast, female power-loom weavers in Lancashire established themselves in the trade prior to the men. Male and female weavers worked together; they were often of a similar age and marital status; they received relatively equal rates of pay; and they belonged to the same unions. For Rose, their lives revealed the limitations of viewing the working-class experience through the lens of separate spheres: work and political activism, on the one hand, and home and family, on the other, could be deeply intermingled. Most important, given that the class situation of female and male weavers seemed comparable, the fact that men and women experienced it so differently underscored its gendered nature.

Although male and female weavers had relatively equal rates of pay, a closer examination reveals that men had privileges denied to women. Rose argues that men were able to work on more looms at once than their female counterparts, which meant they would make more when paid by a piece rate. While men were allowed to tune their own looms, women had to wait for others to do it for them. And men, unlike women, were able to work during their lunch hours and overtime. Similarly, women and men might belong to the same unions; they both participated in strikes; and union leaders campaigned for equal rates of pay for both sexes. However, when push came to shove, the union leadership signified strikes in gendered terms, with men at their centre and women accorded a secondary role. Or as Rose states it: "Although strike leaders recognized that females and males were present at public meetings and demonstrations, men were the subjects of their discourse and women were usually mentioned only in contexts that stressed the desirability of their absence as workers. Public rhetoric that made men central and women peripheral to the workplace portrayed working women as outside working-class politics." Rose further argues that among the weavers the interests of men were equated with that of the working class as a whole. Working-class interests were ultimately signified in terms of masculine values. As a result, union leaders at one level might strive to be inclusive, but ultimately they proved unable to produce an all-encompassing version of class politics: In Rose's words: "Unexamined ideas about gender difference and a masculinized construction of work stymied working men in soliciting women's active involvement in union organization. Ideas about what it meant to be woman and what it meant to be man blinded working-class leaders to different ways of articulating the interests of women and men."[38]

Rose treats the intertwined relationship between private and public – family, work, and politics – in working-class life in her analysis of the Factory Acts of 1874, legislation limiting the hours that women and children in the textile industries could work but in practice led to reduced hours for the working class as a whole. Rose's analysis focuses on the debates leading up to the passage of the bill: she highlights the debate's relationship to discourses of separate spheres and their consequences, in the form of state regulation, for gender and family relationships. While the original intent of the reform movement was to include all workers, it soon became clear that it could only be framed in terms of women and children. To do otherwise would explode the myth that the state remained aloof from economic affairs. It was one thing to regulate the hours of women and children who were regarded as dependents; to do so for men as well interfered with the free negotiation of contract.

As the debate ensued, Rose argues, it coalesced around the status of married women workers, whose dependence on their wages to supplement their husbands' income, and thus keep their families afloat, was deemed a threat to the health of their children and a negation of their "natural" roles as mothers. In her view, "the public concern with motherhood was linked to eugenicist concerns with the quality of the race".[39] Moreover, rather than holding the state and community responsible for child health and welfare, reformers of various stripes admonished working-class men for being bad husbands. It was the responsibility of the men to achieve sufficient earnings so that their wives didn't have to earn wages and thus see to their domestic duties. Rose doesn't dispute that reformers were genuinely concerned about improving the quality of working-class life, but she insists on justifying reform in terms of separate spheres, they created a problem rather than solved one that existed. One solution put forth to solving these imagined problems involved forcing women who had just had children to stay away from their jobs for a prescribed period of time; another was to make sure that the wages of men went directly to their wives. While neither of these proposals made it into the legislation, Rose argues that the discourses produced by the debate and the laws that were enacted had important consequences for working-class life, including forcing women into various forms of sweated labour, which at the time fell outside government purview.

Rose's analysis of the factory laws demonstrated that gender discourses were a crucial dimension of public policy and contributed to the materialization of separate spheres in working-class life. More generally, her overall argument was discursive, framed through the perspective of the new cultural history. "The debates about this legislation" she wrote, "and about the law itself were cultural productions which contributed to the formulation of the social problem of the 'working mother', promulgated an interpretation of who caused the problem, and reinforced a particular view of who was responsible for social reproduction". Yet if she privileged the role that cultural production played in public policy and state action, Rose retained a cultural Marxist emphasis, evoking E. P. Thompson, for whom the legal system was integral to facilitating the workings of productive relations. Rather than viewing the state as autonomous, a position often taken by those at odds with the emphasis of the Marxist tradition, Rose saw it as deeply embedded in economic relationships. In short, she might have made the linguistic turn, but she regarded it as combinable with social and cultural Marxist approaches – not as an alternative to or a negation of them.

Conclusion

Since the 1980s Thompsonian social history has been subject to widespread debate. Its portrayal of British historical development and its theoretical assumptions have been called into question. Historical accounts challenging this view tended to stress the constitutive role of cultural and political developments and rethought class relationships and class struggle. In some cases class has been rejected as meaningful altogether; in others it has been viewed in relationship to other forms of identification – notably race, ethnicity, gender, and nation.

British feminist historians must count as major contributors to creating alternatives to the class struggle model deployed by social historians. They began in the 1970s by illuminating the lives of women who were "hidden from history" (the title of an influential book by Sheila Rowbotham), extending the class-oriented model of history from below to include the family and the household.[40] Subsequently, they came to investigate the process of class formation itself – seeing class and gender as inextricably linked. Among these historians, Sonya Rose has played a critical role. She might distance herself from E. P. Thompson's male-centered account of class formation. However, she followed his efforts to situate the culture, language and ideologies of historical actors within their material context, without reducing them to mere representations of objective interests. She was attentive to Joan Scott's discursive under-standing of the classed and gendered subject but was reluctant to jettison the categories of agency and experience or follow her exclusive focus on discourse.

Since *Limited Livelihoods* and the various essays discussed in this chapter, Rose's work has undergone considerable changes. After a decade of writing on the nineteenth-century working class, she subsequently focused on the domestic front in Britain during World War II, a move ini-tially triggered by her discovery of a diary written by her father, a flight surgeon in the US Air Force.[41] In this project Rose's principal concern has been the multiple and conflicting constructions of citizenship and national identity in wartime and the ways in which dominant representa-tions of belonging marginalized alternative versions. Rose was still inter-ested in the relationship between gender and class, and "masculinity" continued to play a prominent role in her thinking. But she also focused on the relationship between race, empire and nation, a shift reflecting her immersion in the historiography of the "imperial turn" and postcolonial theory. Rose's recent work stands at considerable remove from the dis-cussions of class and gender in which she was involved for so long. Yet she remains committed to combining cultural and social approaches. "We need a multistand and more flexible approach to symbolizing", she wrote, "one that begins with the idea that cultural practices and patterned social practices are indelibly interwoven".[42]

In recent years a growing chorus of historians have expressed frus-tration with the polarizing debates of the 1990s and have advocated com-bining cultural and social perspectives. William Sewell Jr., for instance, called for adopting "a conception of the social in which every sphere of life – from production, to art, to family life, to the state – is constituted by both discursive and extradiscursive logics that are always tightly inter-twined in social practice".[43] Rose was even more to the point. Regarding the future of class theory, she wrote: "I think the way forward in scholar-ship on class is to creatively combine critical Marxian historical analysis, postmodern sensibilities, and keen attention to issues of race, gender, and ethnicities to produce various forms of resistance and contestation and discourse. Hopefully the result would be an amalgam that would syner-gistically produce new historical insights."[44] Whether such an amalgam emerges or not only time will tell. If it does, numerous scholars will have been responsible. But certainly Sonya Rose will have played a prominent role in making it possible.

Notes

1 I originally presented this essay as a paper at the annual meeting of the Pacific Coast Conference of British Studies in Spring 2007 at the University of Puget Sound in Tacoma, Washington. I thank the commentator, George Behlmer, the panelists, and the audience for their feedback.

2 See Dennis Dworkin, *Cultural Marxism in Postwar Britain: History, the New Left, and the Origins of Cultural Studies* (Durham, NC, 1997).

3 Dennis Dworkin, *Class Struggles* (London, 2007).

4 For a discussion of Davidoff's background and work, see *Ibid.*, 143–4.

5 See Introduction to *Limited Livelihoods: Gender and Class in Nineteenth-Century England* (Berkeley, CA: 1992); "Gender and Labor History: The Nineteenth-Century Legacy", *International Review of Social History* 38, Supplement (1993): 145–62; "Class Formation and the Quintessential Worker", in *Reworking Class*, ed. John R. Hall (Ithaca, NY: 1997), 133–66; and "Resuscitating Class", *Social Science History* 22 (September 1998); 19–27. See also Laura L. Frader and Sonya O. Rose, "Introduction: Gender and the Reconstruction of European Working-Class History", in *Gender and Class in Modern Europe*, eds. Laura L. Frader and Sonya O. Rose (Ithaca, NY, 1996), 1–33.

6 Rose, *Limited Livelihoods*, 2.

7 E. P. Thompson, *The Making of the English Working Class* (Harmondsworth, 1968), 10.

8 Rose, *Limited Livelihoods*, 2.

9 Rose, "Class Formation and the Quintessential Worker", 138.

10 *History Workshop Journal*, "Editorial: Women's History and Men's History", *History Workshop Journal* 19 (1985): 1–2.

11 Frader and Rose, "Introduction", 20.

12 Cited in Rose, "Class Formation and the Quintessential Worker", 140.

13 *Ibid.*

14 Heidi Hartmann, "The Unhappy Marriage of Marxism and Feminism: Towards a More Progressive Union", in *Women and Revolution: A Discussion of the Unhappy Marriage of Marxism and Feminism*, ed. Lydia Sargent (Boston, MA, 1981), 1–41.

15 Rose, "Class Formation and the Quintessential Worker", 141.

16 *Ibid.*, 141–2.

17 Caroll Smith-Rosenberg, "The Female World of Love and Ritual: Relations between Women in Nineteenth-Century America", *Signs* 1 (1975): 1–29.

18 Nancy Hewitt, "Beyond the Search for Sisterhood: American Women's History in the 1980s", *Social History* 10 (1985): 299.

19 Rose, "Gender and Labor History", 158–9.

20 Leonore Davidoff and Catherine Hall, *Family Fortunes: Men and Women of the English Middle Class, 1780–1850* (Chicago, 2002), xvi.

21 *Ibid.*, 450.

22 Rose, "Gender and Labor History", 152, 153, 155–6.

23 Rose, "Resuscitating Class", 22.

24   Lenard R. Berlanstein, "Introduction", *Rethinking Labor History: Essays on Discourse and Class Analysis*, ed. Lenard R. Berlanstein (Urbana, IL, 1993), 8.

25   Joan Scott, "On Language, Gender, and Working Class History", *International Labor and Working-Class History* 31(1987): 7.

26   See Scott, "On Language, Gender, and Working Class History"; Christine Stansell, "A Response to Joan Scott", *International Labor and Working-Class History* 31 (1987): 24–9; and Joan Scott, "A Reply to Criticism", *International Labor and Working-Class History* 32 (1987): 39–45. For the exchange between Downs and Scott see *Comparative Studies in Society and History* 35 (1993): Laura Lee Downs, "If 'Woman' Is Just an Empty Category, Then Why Am I Afraid to Walk Alone at Night? Identity Politics Meets the Postmodern Subject", 414–37; Joan Scott, "The Tip of the Volcano", 438–43; and Laura Lee Downs, "Reply to Joan Scott", 444–51.

27   Catherine Hall, "Politics, Post-Structuralism and Feminist History", *Gender and History* 3 (1991): 210.

28   Rose, *Limited Livelihoods*, 16.

29   Rose, "Gender and Labor History", 160. The text that Rose is discussing here is Patrick Joyce, *Visions of the People: Industrial England and the Question of Class, 1848–1914* (Cambridge, 1991).

30   See, for instance, Dennis Dworkin and Leslie G. Roman, (eds), *Views Beyond the Border Country: Raymond Williams and Cultural Politics* (London, 1993).

31   Rose, *Limited Livelihoods*, 13.

32   Theodore Koditschek, "The Gendering of the British Working Class", *Gender and History* 9 (1997): 333–63.

33   Ross's title is a variation on Gareth Stedman Jones' classic study *Outcast London: A Study in the Relationship Between Classes in Victorian Society* (Oxford, 1971).

34   Koditschek, "The Gendering of the British Working Class", 350. Certainly not all labour historians took the gendering of the working class to heart. In Neville Kirk, *Change, Continuity and Class: Labour in British Society, 1850–1920* (London, 1998), a book which covers much of the same timeframe as *Limited Livelihoods,* written by an ardent defender of E. P. Thompson, Rose's work is barely acknowledged.

35   Rose, *Limited Livelihoods*, 153.

36   *Ibid.*, 100.

37   *Ibid.*, 102.

38   *Ibid.*, 175, 183.

39   *Ibid.*, 64.

40   Sheila Rowbotham, *Hidden from History: 300 Years of Women's Oppression and the Fight Against It* (London, 1973).

41   Sonya Rose, *Which People's War?: National Identity and Citizenship in Britain, 1939–1945* (Oxford, 2003), v.

42   Sonya Rose, "Cultural Analysis and Moral Discourses: Episodes, Continuities, and Transformation", in *Beyond the Cultural Turn: New Directions in the Study of Society and Culture*, eds. Victoria E. Bonnell and Lynn Hunt (Berkeley, CA, 1999), 228.

43   William H. Sewell Jr., "Whatever Happened to the 'Social' in Social History?" in *Schools of Thought: Twenty-Five Years of Interpretative Social Science*, (ed.) Joan Wallach Scott and Deborah Keates (Princeton, NJ, 2001), 222.

44   Sonya O. Rose, "Resuscitating Class", 20.

3
In Search of Free Labour: Trinidad and the Abolition of the British Slave Trade

James Epstein

In 1797 Britain seized the island of Trinidad from Spain; in 1802 the island was formally ceded to Britain at the Peace of Amiens. To both the government and anti-slavery leaders the question of how the colony was to be developed under British rule proved critical, particularly with the prospect of the abolition of the British slave trade. The island's plantation economy was a relatively recent development, dating from Spain's reversal in 1784 of its policy of excluding foreign settlement and linked predominantly to the movement of slave owners from French islands. From this point until 1802, the importation of slaves into the colony rapidly increased, spurred by the French and Haitian revolutions and intense warfare in the Caribbean.[1] In the event, the British government decided to halt this trend, ceasing to grant land and thus preventing the realization of the island's full potential as a slave-based plantation economy. In turn, however, this decision raised the question of what sort of labour system and what groups of workers should stand in place of slavery: how was colonialism in the Caribbean to be imagined without slaves? The capacity to envisage a labour regime to replace that of slavery was a pre-condition for the abolition of the British slave trade and of slavery in the Caribbean.[2] This chapter explores the various (failed) schemes to settle free workers in Trinidad during the first decade of the nineteenth century and debate over free labour in the British Caribbean. These proposals, and the thinking underpinning them, are best viewed within the context of both metropolitan and colonial forms and practices that defined the continuum between "free" and "unfree" labour.[3]

Trinidad held a special place in debates over the abolition of the British slave trade, representing an experimental space for re-imagining colonization in the West Indies. In a defining speech following the peace treaty of 1802, George Canning, one of William Pitt's young disciples, expressed his deep concern that grants of unclaimed land in Trinidad were to be made by the crown. He reminded the House of Commons of its former pledge – resolved in 1792 and reconfirmed in 1797 – to enforce the "gradual" abolition of the slave trade; he warned that Trinidad's transformation into a major sugar colony could initiate a new phase in the Atlantic slave trade.[4] He calculated the staggering scale of human misery were Trinidad's vast, fertile lands to be cleared and made ready for cultivation to the same level as Jamaica: one million new slaves, or nearly double that of the entire slave population of the British West Indies, would be poured "into the forests and morasses of Trinidad, to perish yearly, and yearly to be supplied by fresh importations". Canning appealed to the Commons to view Trinidad "in a different light"; unencumbered by the vested interests of British planters, it offered the chance "for the establishment of a guiltless, bloodless colony". His speech was framed by the determination of Providence: "This day is a day of tests; I trust we shall all abide the trial." It was also framed by events in Saint Domingue, which summoned slavery's awesome danger. As the leading abolitionist James Stephen wrote in his *Crisis of the Sugar Colonies*, published to coincide with Canning's initiative: "To found a new slave Colony ... seems to me scarcely less irrational, than it would be to build a town near the crater of Vesuvius."[5]

Instead of employing African slaves, Canning proposed an "experiment"; the lure of quick profits should be eschewed in favour of establishing a colony whose future was secured by free settlers. Rather than making large grants or sales to "great capitalists", they should look "among the class of men who will be induced to become residents in the island", requiring grants of land that would enable them to sustain themselves and their families "in a state of moderate independence". They wanted men capable of serving in the militia and possessing a vested stake in order. Such men might be found among soldiers serving in the West Indies, free persons of colour and creoles from other islands, "peons" from the Spain main, native Indians (small in number to be sure), and others.

Canning had forced the government's hand. In his response to Canning, Henry Addington, as chancellor of the exchequer, announced that instead of selling crown lands in Trinidad, the government, in fact, had decided to appoint a commission to survey the island and report its findings in order to formulate future policy, promising that whatever grants might take place, "none would have the effect of discouraging the population of whites or creoles".[6]

In accordance with this policy, Lord Hobart, secretary for war and the colonies and the cabinet's only firm abolitionist, instructed the newly appointed commission to investigate the best mode of developing Trinidad's land. He stressed the "advantages which might be expected to accrue from the introduction of an European Yeomanry", and noted the need to check speculations in land by keeping new settlers "in the Class of Yeomen, Tradesmen, Artificers or Mechanics" and leaving "open to them such encouragement as may be requisite for giving a stimulus to their industry". Given that such a class of settlers would arrive unable to provide for their own immediate accommodation and support, Hobart sought direction about constructing small houses and supplying provisions and implements needed until they could sustain themselves by their own industry. Along with this new breed of yeoman farmer, he instructed the commissioners to consider the desirability of introducing implements designed to lighten field labour, and strongly recommended "the superior advantages of the steam engine wherever it can be used".[7] "Improvement" and the settlement of free labour became the by-words for future colonization.

As was often the case, policy formulated in London translated poorly into colonial settings. First, the commission which superseded the office of governor proved an utter disaster.[8] While the former governor, General Thomas Picton, was retained as second commissioner, Colonel William Fullarton was appointed as first commissioner, with Admiral Samuel Hood as third commissioner. Fullarton was connected to Hobart through the minister's brother-in-law, John Sullivan, who served as Hobart's undersecretary, and through previous service in India. Member of Parliament for Ayrshire, product of the Scottish enlightenment and author of books on agricultural improvement and military reform in India, Fullarton was sent out to Trinidad with a mandate for innovation and improvement.[9] In light of his efforts to bring order and military security to Trinidad, Picton felt betrayed; he believed that the first commissioner had been discharged in order to bring him down. Almost immediately the two men fell out over issues of personal style, policy and modes of colonial authority. The commission lasted less than a year, ending in personal recrimination, legal charges back in London and chaos in Trinidad. More to the point, Picton was out of step with government policies. A staunch ally of the island's large-scale planters, he favoured Trinidad's full development as a sugar colony. Indeed, his own speculations in land and slaves amounted to a small fortune. Before the appointment of the commission, Hobart had solicited Picton's views on how best to colonize the island without the further importation of slaves, including "the possibility of establishing a Colony of White Inhabitants of the labouring class for the purpose of bringing the hilly and most healthy parts of the Country into early cultivation". Having dutifully addressed various possibilities – European settlers for the dry plains, Spanish peons for clearing land, free persons from other islands, meritorious soldiers from West Indian regiments – Picton reiterated his fundamental position. "Upon the whole as a sugar colony", he doubted whether it would be possible "to advance it to any higher degree of splendour without the assistance of Africans from the Coast". He concluded by denouncing "the representations of pretended philanthropists" as to the condition of slaves which was "in point of comfort and care, at least equal to a great majority of the European peasantry".[10]

The question of free labour was inextricably linked to government concerns about security and the desire to redress the dangerous imbalance between slaves and free white inhabitants.[11] Despite shared anxieties about the infectious spirit of slave insurrection, Picton reflected general opposition among Trinidad's planter elite to proposals aimed at curtailing the growth of slavery and transforming the island into anything but a sugar colony. However, unlike earlier British West Indian colonies, Trinidad (together with what became known as British Guiana) came under direct crown rule, allowing metropolitan government greater freedom for innovation than in islands with their own legislative assemblies. Exchanges between the governor and the colonial office revealed the gap between metropolitan direction and local doubts about the feasibility or desirability of free-labour schemes. The most obvious options were seen as highly improbable in practice. Attracting an increased number of free persons of colour from other islands was a non-starter for Trinidad, where they outnumbered whites and were generally understood to be contaminated by French revolutionary ideas. In light of their role in the Haitian revolution, the loyalty of free persons of colour remained suspect. The prospect of settling retired black soldiers from West Indian regiments was also viewed with suspicion. As for Spanish "peons", they were generally employed as jobbers used in felling woods and clearing land for cultivation. According to Picton, they were "incapable of any regular continued labour. Nothing but want can stimulate them to exertion and their activity never fails to disappear with the cause". Few native inhabitants of Trinidad had survived Spanish colonization; moreover, Picton reported that those that had, together with any Indians that might be induced to move from elsewhere, were utterly useless as workers.

The point is not merely to record the prejudices of Picton or Trinidad's ruling elite, but to illustrate the disjunction between metropolitan and colonial perspectives on the problem of labour and settlement in the Caribbean. If government officials, domestic politicians and abolitionists condemned planters' intransigence to social change, planters and governors believed, in turn, that their own judgement reflected the realities of colonial experience. Both parties made assumptions about various groups' innate capacities for productive labour in the Caribbean. While there was general agreement that Europeans were unfit for field labour and the cultivation of sugar – coffee, cocoa and cotton were regarded as more suitable for white labour – Picton argued against all plans for "a colony of White settlers", observing that such schemes had proved unsuccessful in other islands. As he explained, a European required three years of seasoning, and due to fatigue and exposure to agricultural pursuits over this period, will be exposed to severe fevers requiring expensive medical treatment. With the best of medical care, one-third of Europeans would perish in the first year, leaving their families as a burden on the community. A European attempting to support a family by his own agricultural labour "must lead a life of extraordinary fatigue and privation", driving him ultimately to rum and ruin. Moreover, given that "dislike of Labour" was what usually induced the European to leave his country, was it likely, he asked, "that he will become more inclined to it in a Country unfavourable to the production of enterprising Energies in a European?" Picton condemned humanitarian improvers for misleading the country with their delusory and potentially costly schemes; slave labour was essential to sustaining production in the West Indies.[12]

British fears of life in the Caribbean were long standing, exacerbated during the 1790s by the extraordinarily high death rates of European soldiers from disease.[13] Unsurprisingly, attempts to settle a white yeomanry in Trinidad did not prosper. In fact, a group of settlers accompanied Fullarton to Trinidad, to which were added a hundred retired German troops and ninety settlers from Surinam. Plans were also afoot, dictated by the "absolute necessity" to counterbalance the island's French and Spanish population, to attract British subjects disappointed in their hopes of settling in America.[14] However, the principal proposal envisaged establishing a colony of five hundred Scottish Highland families on the island, a scheme elaborated during January 1803 is in correspondence involving Father Alexander MacDonnell, Charles Yorke, secretary at war, and Addington MacDonnell, Roman Catholic priest of Glengarry and chaplain to the First Glengarry Fencibles which he had helped to organize, proposed a state-sponsored plan for redirecting soldiers of disbanded Highland regiments from settlement in Canada to

Trinidad. He emphasized the Highlanders' loyalty and sacrifice to the cause of war against revolutionary France, noting "those barren and thinly inhabited Mountains furnished ...16 Battalions of the line".[15] Inverness, from where much of the present emigration flowed, raised three regiments of the line, seven fencibles and forty-three volunteer corps: "And these are the men who are now compelled to quit their native Soil, & seek for themselves, & their hapless families that scanty subsistence in the Wilds of America which their Country denies them". MacDonnell asked the government to extend "liberal encouragement" in terms of providing transport, dwellings, tools, loans to hire labour to clear land, two chapels and two schools, together with paying the salaries of a surgeon and mate "who are Masters of the Gaelic Language" to remain with the settlers, a Catholic chaplain and an assistant who spoke both Gaelic and Spanish, in order to help settle disputes, and schoolmasters to be placed under the control of the clergy. Land was to be granted forever free of tithes and heritable to settlers in amounts based on military rank, ranging from 100 acres for the common soldier to 300 acres for a field officer.[16]

Trinidad was now proposed as an alternative to the Scottish lowlands or Canada as a site of settlement and improvement for these warriors. The traditional Highland clan system was founded on the activities of war and agriculture, constituting a social group based on strong ties of loyalty to the clan's chief. For over half a century, since the Jacobite rising of 1745, schemes to civilize the Scottish Highlands had abounded. The establishment of villages, construction of bridges and roads, encouragement of new kinds of manufacture and employment and attempts to improve agriculture had produced relatively small results despite large state and private expenditure.[17] The Highlands remained wild and remote, and its inhabitants continued to live in what most commentators described as semi-feudal dependence, poverty and idleness. The Commissioners of Forfeited Estates had apparently failed in their 1771 charge to "Reclaim the Inhabitants of these Estates from their long habits of Sloth and inactivity and reconcile them to the love of Labour, Industry and Good order".[18] Whether the Highlands were overpopulated or its inhabitants merely underemployed – in short, whether emigration to America was desirable – remained a matter for debate.[19] Similarly, opinion differed as to whether Highland culture and the Gaelic language could be reconciled with economic and cultural improvement in new environments. In 1805, the earl of Selkirk, one of the chief proponents of colonization of British North America, noted with regret that Highlanders were losing their "genuine manners"; he hoped "a portion of the antient spirit might be preserved among the Highlanders of the New World – that the emigrants might be brought together in some part of our own colonies".[20] Romantic ideas about Highland life continued to colour the attitudes of writers sympathetic to the Highlanders' plight.

Yet given prevailing convictions about the Highlander's lack of "habits of regular and steady industry", expressions of optimism about their adaptive capacities in the Caribbean – much less viewing them as vehicles for gradually eradicating the need for slave labour – appeared overly sanguine.[21] "If this mode of Colonization should be generally adopted in the Island [of Trinidad]", wrote Charles Turner, an officer of the Queen's Regiment and a Highland native, "I question much whether it would not entirely do away the necessity of employing Slaves as the population would soon encrease [sic] by holding out encouragement to Marriages, & a rapid extension of Cultivation must follow, to support it, & I have no doubt but with those people, a mode of farming might be adopted somewhat similar to that used in England".[22] In his *Travels in Trinidad*, P. F. McCallum detailed the three months he spent on the island in 1803. McCallum, an admirer of Fullarton's and fellow Scot, reiterated the case for settling "a White Population ... to consist of Scotch Highlanders – a hardy race, that will vegetate in any climate, and less intemperate than others" in the Caribbean. After all, Highlanders had settled successfully in the Carolinas. He agreed that colonial strength was dependent on the number of whites, but they must be small planters. McCallum translated a Scottish version of "agrarian patriotism" and the cult of the virtuous yeoman farmer to Trinidad, and set it against the moral corruption of planters as well as the unsuitability of Africans as free labourers.[23] While in his native land, the Highland labourer "enjoys a sort of legitimate freedom", according to McCallum, this did nothing to better his condition, as the dependence of the labourer on uncertain conditions meant that even the "most active industry can barely provide for his family from day to day". In contrast, in Trinidad "the labourer's wants would be reduced to a mere trifle, and with little industry, he might experience all the comforts of a decent competency".[24] Here was the sort of fanciful rhetoric that Picton denounced. The need for improvement, along with the dangers and hardships of West Indian life and labour, were ultimately resolved in terms of the island's easy abundance.

At the same time that Addington was considering MacDonnell's plan to bring Highlanders to Trinidad, Sullivan received Patrick Colquhoun's extremely detailed proposal for transporting prostitutes from the metropolis. Sullivan and Hobart had requested a report from Colquhoun who was a stipendiary magistrate at Worship Street police office and well-known author of treatises on metropolitan crime, police and indigence. As with all his works, in his "Preliminary Observations" Colquhoun produced a list, enumerating the causes of prostitution in London and speculating on which categories of such women might be induced to abandon their shameful lives for a new start in Trinidad.[25] Thus he deemed female children of parents "who have been broken down by misfortunes", peculiarly susceptible to seduction and ultimately going "upon the Town". Although such girls were frequently well educated, "through long habits of vice, become exceedingly depraved and [are] not likely to be reclaimed". In contrast, out-of-work servants differed from younger unfortunates, as many of them were reluctant converts to vice, particularly those from the country, and because of their former lives were able to make comparisons between "the comforts arising from a life of Innocence and Industry" as opposed to the "evils and miseries attached to Prostitution". Colquhoun calculated the effect that the reproaches of friends and relatives might have on various categories of prostitutes, inclining them to rescue themselves from public infamy by going to Trinidad. The Magdalen hospital, lock hospitals and workhouses of the metropolis offered potential recruits, women who otherwise had nowhere else to turn on their release but to the street.

No women over thirty years old, or who had been on the town from an early age, or "who did not manifest certain marks of contrition", or did not consider emigration an opportunity of bettering themselves and "restoring them to society", should be recruited for Trinidad. For qualified recruits the government would pay for their passage, lend each woman £4 for apparel, and guarantee suitable employment until they either married or hired themselves into service. They would be "free settlers", free to choose their employment and their own partners. They were, however, to understand that they would face "severe punishment" for cohabiting outside of marriage or returning to prostitution. Any infraction or "irregularity" before leaving England would be punished by instant dismissal and the necessaries provided would be reclaimed. "Acts of misbehaviour such as Intoxication or Instances of Lewdness" with seamen during the voyage "will subject the offender to the ignominy of being placed on the *degraded List*", and thus exclusion from the society of "well behaved women, and employed after arrival as servants to the well behaved, to perform such labor as shall be a meaner and more laborious kind". After arrival, "free settlers" found guilty of drunkenness, lewdness, or common prostitution forfeited all claims to protection and support, and "shall be subject to imprisonment and hard Labour in the House of Correction". Colquhoun thought there would be no problem meeting an annual target of four to five hundred women for humanitarian resettlement in the West Indies.[26] Colquhoun's suggestions reflected a broader metropolitan discourse within which older philanthropic perspectives were amalgamated with more scientific views of political economists, aimed at promoting national moral regeneration and countering the rising tide of social and political disorder. The disciplinary and moral logic associated with domestic reform was thus projected onto a site of colonial disorder in which the prostitute might be rehabilitated.[27]

In the event, neither the scheme to settle Catholic Scottish Highlanders nor to reclaim metropolitan prostitutes in Trinidad came to anything. MacDonnell rejected Addington's offer of free passage to Trinidad for his people, along with eighty acres of land and cash to purchase four slaves for each family, on the grounds that the climate was too unhealthy.[28] No action appears to have been taken on Colquhoun's plan. However, as exercises in experimental thinking, these sundry ideas shed light on how West Indian colonization free from slavery might be imagined. Such planning confirmed the British government's willingness to engage in ambitious projects of social engineering at the peripheries of empire, where social reconstruction involved marginalized groups, long-standing targets of domestic reform efforts.[29] In effect, a set of social and geographical margins were to be reconfigured. Colonial solutions were offered for domestic social problems, just as Britain's social casualties were thought to supply the needs of colonial development. While retired Scottish soldiers had been previously recruited for colonization in British North America, state-assisted resettlement in the West Indies undertaken to provide an alternative to slavery was truly innovative. If the establishment of a "white yeomanry" in Trinidad did not necessarily preclude, but often assumed, continued dependence on some measure of slave labour, it offered a model for future development, a step on the way to ending the slave trade and slavery altogether.

The problems associated with these speculative ventures were also plainly in evidence. As a local military officer informed Sullivan, regarding settling whites in Trinidad: "Nature does not admit their labour in the heat of a vertical sun and feeling at once a superiority as free men over slaves, a pride arises that has been frequently observed to prevent humble industry because it was the same nature as the negro's labour".[30] Most crucially, loomed the question of what beyond necessity would motivate Europeans to engage in productive labour in the West Indies. Given the potential pool of recruits, how were habits inimical to industriousness to be overcome? Here, Colquhoun's reasoning revealed the difficulties in evaluating the springs of human motivation, and the not too delicate balance to be struck between inducement to self-reform and coercion. Prostitutes would be "free settlers", becoming proper wives presumably for European men, but an elaborate set of punishments guaranteed their good behaviour; the line between misfortune and criminality was thin. The "freedom" of retired Highland soldiers, many of whom had been compelled to join their regiments, was also at best severely limited.[31] Moreover, the very idea of reclaiming one's moral virtue in the West Indies would have struck contemporaries as richly ironic, if not downright preposterous. The Caribbean was known as the site of moral loss, as a breeding ground for idleness, sexual license, drunkenness and dissipation. Yet in this social and moral climate, plagued by the institution of concubinage, former prostitutes – those previously regarded as "the antithesis of the productive mother and wife", destructive to national welfare and social harmony[32] – were to be reclaimed as wives and mothers, fostering moral order on the edge of empire.

Hopes of establishing a white yeomanry in Trinidad went unrealized. However, among various proposals forwarded to Hobart in 1802 was an alternative suggestion for creating a bulwark against African slaves. After running through various categories of white settlers – "industrious [Scottish] Protestants", ex-soldiers, convicts looking to reduce their terms of transportation through good conduct – the author acknowledged that, in fact, improvement "could not be much advanced by the individual labour of Europeans or their unmixed descendants". Instead of relying on Europeans, he proposed turning to the Chinese, "whose disposition to migrate is known, whose Industry and Ingenuity are proverbial".[33] This final suggestion was based on a longer document, "Hints for the Cultivation of Trinidad", written by Captain William Layman of the Royal Navy. Layman's proposal set in motion plans that culminated in late 1806 with the arrival of Trinidad's first Chinese workers – their arrival coinciding with the abolition of the British slave trade.[34] The formal proposals that laid the intellectual groundwork for establishing Chinese settlers as a "middle" group within Trinidad society reveal much about experiments in free labour, the construction of racial hierarchies and about how a discourse of colonial development was conceived across a series of linked imperial sites.[35] They also speak to the deep fear engendered by the Haitian revolution. As stated in a colonial office memorandum relating to Chinese immigration, events in Saint Domingue "arouse apprehensions similar to those at the time of the French Revolution". Every effort should be made to guard Britain's West Indian possessions, "and to prevent the spirit of Insurrection arising amongst Negroes".[36] The threat of slave insurrection, linked to the abolition of the slave trade, thus formed the backdrop to free labour schemes.

In addition to Layman, Joseph Foster Barham, among the few West Indian planters sympathetic to abolition, and Robert Townsend Farquhar, Lieutenant Governor of Prince of Wales Island (Penang, Malaysia), also drew up plans to introduce Asian free labour into the West Indies. But Layman's was the most carefully developed plan, which he subsequently published in fuller form.[37] His work starts by enquiring whether it was in the interests of planters themselves to cultivate their estates "by the industrious hands of freemen". Invoking Adam Smith's authority, Layman claims, "the experience of all ages and nations" demonstrates the inferiority of work done by slaves, as nothing can be expected from someone motivated solely by the dread of punishment, and being "deprived of every mental exertion, he becomes indolent in body and debased in mind". "The want of invention, ingenuity, or exertion" in the West Indies, adds Layman, was thus only to be expected. Since those who were familiar with no other system would not be convinced by theoretical reasoning alone, the unprofitable character of the present labour regime had to be demonstrated "by example". To this end, Layman compiled a set of elaborate, hypothetical calculations, detailing the comparative capital costs of a sugar plantation employing Chinese workers as opposed to slaves, thereby proving free labour to be the more profitable system.[38] Interestingly, Layman relied entirely on interest-driven reasoning. However, certain abolitionists, including James Stephen, believed just the opposite, that slavery was indeed profitable; they were, therefore, wary of free labour projects, fearing that their failure might undermine abolitionist efforts.[39] Such reservations clearly were not shared by the proponents of bringing Chinese labourers to cultivate West Indian plantations. In 1806, Barham proposed taking a Jamaican plantation in actual cultivation and substituting Chinese workers on long term contracts for slaves: "the results will immediately become apparent". Not only would "all motive, as well as all pretence", for continuing the slave trade immediately cease, but the Chinese would both "form a check on the Negroe [sic] population" and serve as "examples of domestic life & voluntary industry" by which "the moral & civil character of the Negroes cannot fail to be thereby improved".[40]

Crucial to all plans, whether set in Trinidad or Jamaica, was the estimate made of Chinese character, particularly in contrast to that of Africans. Not only must settlers be inured to the tropical climate, according to Layman it was essential that they possessed the necessary "industrious habits"

which Africans and native inhabitants so obviously lacked. He cited a
Privy Council report claming that in the West Indies no free black was
ever known to hire himself, or had been employed in agriculture of
any kind: "The men are averse to labour the ground, even for themselves; and when they do it, it is only to supply their immediate
wants". At the same time, he believed that freedom was a universal
human desire; for this reason, the horrors of Saint Domingue threatened all the Caribbean. The Chinese, on the other hand, were "habit-
ually industrious, sober, peaceful, and frugal, and eminently skilled in
the culture and preparation of every article of tropical produce". Due
to government encouragement, China was the world's "most fertile
and best cultivated" country.[41] The Chinese were quintessentially a
people driven by the prospect of gain; in this, they differed not only
from Africans, but also from Scottish Highlanders who were viewed as
trapped in a pre-commercial stage of civilization.

Layman drew on his own experience in the West and East Indies, as
well as the writings of those who had traveled to East Asia. In their broad-
est terms, assessments of the Chinese depended on forms of colonial
knowledge about the Far East derived from Captain James Cook's voyages
and Lord Macartney's failed mission in 1793 to open China to British
trade.[42] According to Cook, there was "nothing which a Chinese will not
do for pay".[43] Farquhar similarly maintained: "The leading opinion of a
Chinaman consists in the belief that gain is positive good, loss positive
evil, unembarrassed by those prejudices which influence the minds of
weak and scrupulous people".[44] Economic man might be unscrupulous
but in the West Indies this became a virtue. Unlike European settlers, the
Chinese would work for wages on a contract basis, and thus might
directly substitute themselves for slaves. The prospect of becoming small
landholders, after having fulfilled their labour contracts with planters,
should be held out to provide "an excitement to industry, economy, and
good conduct". In short, Layman presented the Chinese as the key to the
gradual abolition of slavery, the improvement of the African creoles and
the persuasion of the planter of the superiority of free labour.

> The Chinese husbandman, indeed, seems fitted by Providence to be
> the humble means of qualifying the hitherto ignorant and oppressed
> African for the enjoyment of rational liberty, by setting him a practical
> example of the blessings to be derived from the application of free
> and honest industry, and by leading the West Indian planter, by that
> strongest of human motives, *self interest*, to a full conviction of the
> policy of granting to his slave, at some future period, when thus fitted

for the inestimable boon, that liberty for which God and nature designed him.[45]

Importantly, not only could the Chinese be motivated beyond the horizon of economic necessity, under the right conditions, they could be induced to embark on a long voyage to an unknown land of hard work and possibility. In late 1802, Sir George Thomas Staunton, having recently returned from Canton where he served the East India Company, wrote a long letter to the colonial office, reiterating the Chinese empire's strong dislike of foreigners and explaining the difficulty of recruiting Chinese for emigration.[46] However, while mainland China might remain closed to foreign intervention and direct recruitment, a large Chinese diaspora had spread through trade-networks across the Malay and Indonesian archipelagos, including Batavia (Jakarta), Java, Malacca and British-held Prince of Wales Island. By late 1802, Hobart had initiated secret plans to bring Chinese husbandmen to Trinidad, plans requiring the cooperation of the East India Company and the Governor General of India, and cautious handling so as not to incur the Chinese Emperor's displeasure. The British government commissioned Kenneth MacQueen, an acknowledged expert on China with extensive recruiting experience in the Far East, for the task.[47] With the formation of the "all talents" ministry in February 1806, and improved prospects for the slave trade's abolition, the Trinidad experiment gained urgency. After considerable delay and with Farquhar's help, MacQueen managed to recruit 143 Chinese at Prince of Wales Island, and to add another 53 at Calcutta from where they set sail for Trinidad. In October 1806, 192 Chinese arrived at Port of Spain to start their new lives.[48]

The scheme to introduce Chinese workers into Trinidad was driven from the metropolis. As with other such schemes for recruiting free labour to the West Indies, fantasy played a serious role. In Trinidad, officials scrambled to accommodate the new settlers. Soon after their arrival, the governor, General Thomas Hislop, issued a proclamation, explaining that the British government had found it desirable to introduce "a free race of cultivators, who from habit and feelings, will keep themselves distinct from the Negroes; and who, from interest, will be inseparably attached to the European proprietors".[49] Certain influential inhabitants welcomed the experiment. Archibald Gloster, Trinidad's attorney general and a large-scale planter, wrote to the London merchant Joseph Marryat, crediting Hobart for his "wisdom and forethought", as in his opinion, "nothing will serve so much to secure these colonies, as a liberal introduction of these people". He noted that but for their dress, "you would conclude them to be Mulattoes, or Mestees". Their intermediate position, between planters and slaves, but "attached" to European owners, was expressed in intersecting racial and social terms. Gloster maintained that substituting Chinese for "negro labour is out of the question" as the Chinese were unaccustomed to "*the common business of a plantation* ... nor can we force them by the same methods". He envisaged the Chinese settlers aiding planters, attending their mills, working as "mechanics", gardening and providing provisions for slaves.[50] Certainly the discourse promoting the introduction of East Asian labour into the West Indies emphasized the essential difference between independent Chinese and enslaved African workers. Layman's grand experiment envisaged Chinese free labourers replacing African slaves. However, as Gloster understood, in the West Indies to do the work of slaves, planting and cutting cane, was to share a tainted equivalence with them. The notion of introducing a "free race of cultivators" who might substitute their labour for that of slaves was inherently contradictory given prevailing social and racial hierarchies and modes of production.

The scheme's failure need not detain us; many of the Chinese returned on the same vessel that had brought them.[51] However, it did not take long for the colonial office and the island's oligarchy to again solicit ideas for attracting free labour, turning over many of the same options as before. But as the planter and council member, William H. Burnley concluded, "from Asia alone" would they find suitable settlers.[52] Indeed, Trinidad had glimpsed a fragment of its future, and it lay to the east. The vision of establishing a white yeomanry faded, as that of Asian migration came more distinctly into view. Former slaves proved resistant to wage labour, confirming earlier views of their imperviousness to capitalist incentives. Yet rather than resolving the question of free labour, indentured migration from India and China that followed the abolition of slavery (1834) further destabilized the meaning of free labour. The history of West Indian colonization doubled back on itself by reintroducing a category of labour that slavery had superseded. Accompanying claims of a labour shortage and unprofitably high wages, planters defended "free immigration" and indentured Asian workers as "free" agents.[53] The stark opposition between slave and free worker which abolitionists had embraced as a necessary fiction proved unsustainable in the post-Emancipation world.

Notes

* Thanks to Catherine Molineux for her helpful comments on this chapter.
 1 Bridget Brereton, *A History of Modern Trinidad, 1783–1962* (Port of Spain and London, 1981), 22–7, 45. In the five years between 1797 and 1802,

the number of slaves nearly doubled, from around 10,000 to just under 20,000.

2 On this question more generally, see Seymour Drescher, *The Mighty Experiment: Free Labor versus Slavery in British Emancipation* (Oxford and New York, 2002); Christopher L. Brown, "Empire without Slaves: British Concepts of Emancipation in the Age of the American Revolution", *William and Mary Quarterly* 3rd series, 61, no. 2 (1999): 273–306, and *Moral Capital: Foundations of British Abolitionism* (Chapel Hill, NC, 2006), chap. 4.

3 See Douglas Hay and Paul Craven, eds., *Masters, Servants, and Magistrates in Britain and the Empire, 1562–1955* (Chapel Hill, NC, 2004), particularly the editors' "Introduction", 1–58; Robert J. Steinfeld, *Coercion, Contract, and Free Labor in the Nineteenth Century* (Cambridge, 2001). For the myriad ways in which gender as a cultural process structured British working-class lives and labour, see Sonya. O. Rose, *Limited Livelihoods: Gender and Class in Nineteenth-Century England* (Berkeley, CA, 1992).

4 *Parliamentary History of England* 36 (London, 1820), cols. 854–76 (27 May 1802), and his earlier notice, cols. 442–5.

5 James Stephen, *The Crisis of the Sugar Colonies ...to which are subjoined Sketches of a Plan for Settling the Vacant Lands of Trinidada* (London, 1802), 157. For the concerns of abolitionists about government plans for Trinidad and St. Vincent and behind the scenes lobbying, see Robert I. Wilberforce and Samuel Wilberforce, *The Life of William Wilberforce*, 5 vols (London, 1838), 3: 30, 35–7.

6 *Parliamentary History* 36, cols. 876–81; George Pellew, *The Life and Correspondence of the Rt. Hon. Henry Addington, First Viscount Sidmouth*, 3 vols. (London, 1847), 2: 67–8; Patrick C. Lipscomb, "Party Politics, 1801–1802: George Canning and the Trinidad Question", *Historical Journal* 12, no. 3 (1969): 442–66; James Millette, *Society and Politics in Colonial Trinidad* (Port of Spain and London, 1981) 78–87, for the full background to this debate; also Claudis Kelvin Fergus, *British Imperial Trusteeship: The Dynamics of Reconstruction of British West Indian Society, with Special Reference to Trinidad, 1783–1838* (PhD diss., University of the West Indies, 1995), chap. 4.

7 Public Records Office, National Archives, Colonial Office (hereafter PRO, CO) 295/3, Hobart to the Commissioners for Trinidad, 16 October 1802, fols. 2–10.

8 See Millette, *Society and Politics*, pt. 2.

9 See Michael Fry's entry *in Oxford Dictionary of National Biography* (Oxford, 2004), 21: 134–6.

10 PRO, CO 295/2, Hobart to Picton, 18 February 1802, fols. 40–5; Picton to Hobart, 12 April 1802; also see his earlier assessment, PRO, War Office 1/94, Picton to Hobart, 28 June 1801, fol. 248.

11 Concerns about stability, slave resistance and the need for white settlement had a long history. See Catherine Molineux, *The Peripheries Within: Race, Slavery, and Empire in Early Modern England* (PhD. diss., Johns Hopkins University, 2005), 113, 139–40, 153–7.

12 PRO, CO 295/10, Picton's report of February 1804, fols. 28–35. Picton did hold out the prospect of small-scale European cultivators employing five or six slaves to complement large planters.

13   Karen Ordahl Kupperman, "Fear of Hot Climates in Anglo-American Colonial Experience", *William and Mary Quarterly* 3rd series, 41 (1984): 213–40; Michael Duffy, *Soldiers, Sugar, and Seapower: The British Expeditions to the West Indies and the War against Revolutionary France* (Oxford, 1987), chap. 14; David Patrick Geggus, "The Cost of Pitt's Caribbean Campaigns, 1793–1798", *Historical Journal* 26, no. 3 (1983): 699–706.

14   PRO, CO 295/4, Commissioners to Hobart, 3 March 1803, fols. 47–50; Fullarton to Hobart, 3 March, fol. 62, refers to "the increase of such a White Population", as the most urgent object.

15   On the flow and conditions of recruitment from the Highlands, see Andrew Mackillop, '*More Fruitful than the Soil': Army, Empire and the Scottish Highlands, 1715–1815* (East Lothian, 2000); T. M. Devine, *Scotland's Empire* (London, 2004), chap. 13.

16   PRO, CO 295/6, Yorke to Addington, 28 January 1803, MacDonnell to Yorke, 14 and 29 January 1803, MacDonnell to Addington, 1 January 1803, "Proposals for Establishing a Colony of Highlanders in the Island of Trinidad", fols. 26–39.

17   See A. J. Youngson, *After the Forty-Five: The Economic Impact on the Scottish Highlands* (Edinburgh, 1973).

18   Scottish Records Office, Forfeited Estates E730/32, quoted in Youngson, *After the Forty-Five*, 36.

19   See, for example, Thomas Telford, *A Survey and Report on the Coasts and Central Highlands of Scotland: Made by Command of the Right Honourable Commissioners* (London 1803), 15–17.

20   Sarl of Selkirk, *Observations on the Present State of the Highlands of Scotland, with a view of the causes and probable consequences of emigration* (London, 1805), 3.

21   *Ibid.*, 49. Selkirk commented, "The independence and irregularity to which he is accustomed, approach to that of a savage".

22   PRO, CO 295/6, "A Plan to Government by Mr. Turner for Promoting the Colonization of the Island of Trinidad", fols. 188–91.

23   For Scottish "agrarian patriotism", see C. A. Bayly, *Imperial Meridian: The British Empire and the World, 1780–1830* (London, 1989), 85–6.

24   Pierre F. M'Callum, *Travels in Trinidad during the months of February, March, and April 1803* (Liverpool, 1805), 28, 82–5.

25   See Patrick Colquhoun, *A Treatise on the Police of the Metropolis* (London, 1794) and *The State of Indigence, and the Situation of the Causal Poor in the Metropolis, Explained* (London, 1799). Two decades later, Colquhoun was to propose employing the "redundant population" of Britain in southern Africa.

26   PRO CO 295/6, Colquhoun to Sullivan, 12 February 1803, fols. 44–50.

27   See Donna T. Andrew, *Philanthropy and Police: London Charity in the Eighteenth Century* (Princeton, NJ, 1989), chap. 6; also see Miles Ogborn, *Spaces of Modernity: London's Geographies, 1680–1780* (New York, 1998).

28   J. M. Bumsted, *The People's Clearance: Highland Emigration to British North America* (Edinburgh, 1982), 111. MacDonnell went on to settle with his clansmen in Glengarry County, Canada, and became the first Roman Catholic bishop of Upper Canada.

29   See Joanna Innes, "The Domestic Face of the Military-Fiscal State: Government and Society in Eighteenth Century Britain", in *An Imperial State at*

War: Britain from 1689 to 1815, ed. Lawrence Stone (London, 1994), 96–127. In 1767, along with a scheme to settle five hundred Scottish highlanders in Florida, Sir Alexander Grant had proposed to the government bringing "reformed penitents" from the Magdalene House of which he was vice president to east Florida. Bernard Bailyn, *Voyagers to the West: A Passage in the Peopling of America on the Eve of Revolution* (New York, 1986), 463–64.

30　PRO, CO 295/9, J. P. Kingston to Sullivan, 26 January 1804, fols. 333–40. Kingston, who held the rank of lieutenant colonel and commandant of the Trinidad Rifle corps of militia, cited failed French experiments at Cayenne and Martinique and noted that at Barbados whites had never been induced to labour.

31　While economic need and landlord coercion were critical to recruitment, see Andrew Mackillop, "For King, Country, and Regiment? Motive and Identity within Highland Soldiering, 1746–1815", in *Fighting for Identity: Scottish Military Experience c. 1550–1900*, ed. Steve Murdoch and A. Mackillop (Leiden, 2002), 185–211, stressing the contractual aspects of Highland recruitment and service.

32　Andrew, *Philanthropy and Police*, 188.

33　PRO CO 295/3, Hobart to Commissioners, 16 October 1802, enclosure, "Suggestions with Respect to the Population and Settlement of Land in Trinidad", fols. 13–20; CO 296/4, enclosure #20, fols. 69–73. It is unclear who composed this memorandum.

34　PRO, Board of Trade [BT], 16 July 1802, and Layman's "Supplement to Hints for the Cultivation of Trinidad", 28 August 1802 (the volume carries no folio enumerations). Also found in CO 296/4, enclosures #22 and #27; also see CO 295/2, George Wilson to Vansittart, 22 July 1802, fol. 203, with enclosures of Layman's proposal. For fuller discussion, see B. W. Higman, "The Chinese in Trinidad, 1806–1838", *Caribbean Studies* 12, no. 2 (1972): 21–44.

35　Cf. Alan Lester, *Imperial Networks: Creating Identities in Nineteenth Century South Africa and Britain* (London, 2001), 5–7.

36　PRO, CO 295/6, "Memorandum relating to the introduction of Chinese Settlers into the West Indies", 7 April 1803, fol. 156, apparently from Hobart and Sullivan to Chairman and Deputy of Board of Directors of the East India Company.

37　Layman, *Outline of a Plan for Better Cultivation, Security, & Defence of the British West Indies Being the Original Suggestion for Providing an effective substitute for the African Slave Trade* (London, 1807).

38　Layman, *Outline of a Plan*, 10–15. For Adam Smith's contribution to free labour ideology, see Drescher, *Mighty Experiment*, chap. 2.

39　Layman, *Outline*, 108–9.

40　PRO, BT 6/70, 28 August 1806, and also Barham's "Proposal to Government for the Purpose of Introducing Natives of the East as free labourers to Jamaica", 8 January 1807. Layman was also deeply involved in this scheme. See Windham (Secretary of War) to Grenville, 28 November 1806, pressing for immediate action on "so important and promising an experiment", in *Report of the Manuscripts of J. B. Fortescue, Esq., Preserved at Dropmore* (Historical Manuscripts Commission, 1910), vol. 8, 481–2; British Library, Add. Ms. 37, 885 (Windham papers), Fawkener to Sir George Shee, 28 Jan. 1807, fols. 242–5; Add. Ms. 37, 886, Barham to Windham, 14 Feb. 1807, fols. 48–50.

41   Layman, *Outline of a Plan*, 21–4, 81.

42   In addition to Cook himself, Layman cited works by Captain James King, John Barrow, Carl Peter Thunberg, and others. For Macartney's embassy, see J. L. Cranmer-Byng, "China, 1792–94", in *Macartney of Lisanoure, 1737–1806: Essays in Biography*, ed. Peter Roebuck (Belfast, 1983), 216–44; Victor Kiernan, *The Lords of Human Kind: European Attitudes to the Outside World in the Imperial Age* (Harmondsworth, 1972), 152–5, and 165–71, for later estimates of Chinese character; Vincent T. Harlow, *The Founding of the Second British Empire, 1763–1793*, 2 vols. (London, 1964), 2: 544–94, for the full background to Pitt and Dundas' commercial designs in East Asia.

43   Layman is quoting from James Cook, *A Compendious History of Captain Cook's First and Second Voyages* (London, 1784), 141.

44   Robert Townsend Farquhar, *Suggestions Arising from the Abolition of the African Slave Trade, for supplying the demands of the West India Colonies* (London, 1807), 47; also his "Observations", PRO, BT 6/70.

45   Layman, *Outline of a Plan*, 82.

46   PRO, CO 295/3, Staunton to John Roberts, 18 December 1802. fols. 200–4. At age twelve, Staunton accompanied his father as page to Macartney's embassy to China, and was the only member to actually learn Chinese. See George Thomas Staunton, *Memoirs of the Chief Incidents of the Public Life of Sir George Thomas Staunton, Bart* (London, 1856).

47   PRO, CO 295/6, MacQueen to Sullivan, April 1803, fols. 148–9; Hobart to MacQueen, 21 April 1803, fols. 152–5. In addition to a monthly salary, MacQueen was given 5 per cent on the sale price of a consignment of articles to be sold in the West Indies.

48   PRO, CO 295/14, Hislop to Windham, 7 October 1806, fol. 165, and 26 October 1806, 169–71; BT 6/70, MacQueen to Windham, 17 October 1806.

49   PRO, CO 295/14, fols. 194–6, and *Barbados Mercury*, 4 November 1806, copy in CO 295/14, and also see extracts of the minutes of Trinidad's Council, fols. 175–83. In the first instance, most of the immigrants wished to be hired as wage-labourers.

50   PRO, CO 295/17, Gloster to Marryat, 3 April 1807, fols. 154–5.

51   PRO, CO 295/16, Minutes of Trinidad Council, 20 July 1807, fols. 147–8; Hislop to Castlereagh, 23 July 1807, fol. 154; Higman, "Chinese in Trinidad", 30–5. Layman maintained that this botched scheme in no way invalidated his own proposal. For a similar evaluation, see [John Sanderson], *Emancipation in Disguise, or, The True Crisis of the Colonies* (London, 1807), 132–6.

52   PRO, CO 295/37, fols. 97–106, for Burnley's proposal, one of several from council members in 1814–15. Cf. William Hardin Burnley, *Observations on the Present Conditions of the Island of Trinidad, and the Actual State of the Experiment of Negro Emancipation* (London, 1842).

53   Madhavi Kale, *Fragments of Empire: Capital, Slavery, and Indian Indentured Labor in the British Caribbean* (Philadelphia, 1998); Walton Look Lai, *Indentured Labor, Caribbean Sugar: Chinese and Indian Migrants to the British West Indies, 1838–1918* (Baltimore and London, 1993); K. O. Laurence, *A Question of Labour: Indentured Immigration into Trinidad and British Guiana, 1875–1917* (Kingston, 1994).

4
Race and the Regulation of Prostitution: Comparing Public Health in the U.S. and Greater Britain

Philippa Levine

I

Writing in 1900 on the pros and cons of legalizing prostitution, New York physician Sigmund Lustgarten declared that the laws of the United States were derived to a large extent from those of England. His praise for the principles of American law were lofty. "It breathes forth that spirit of individual rights, personal liberty and freedom, that reverence for the sanctity of the private home and life within it, that has ever been the pride of Englishmen and Americans".[1] Lustgarten's context for this Anglo-American association was a vigorous rejection of the regulation of prostitution as a measure "foreign to the spirit" of the American people and their laws.[2]

Yet despite this rhetoric, in the U.S. as well as in Britain and its colonies, experiments in the regulation of prostitution were common in the nineteenth century. Britain and America came late to regulation; much of continental Europe had long organized prostitution via police regulation and regular medical checks. The British Contagious Diseases (CD) acts of the 1860s imposed registration on women engaged in prostitution in military areas in Britain, while colonial ordinances set up similar and often more stringent rules within Britain's empire. In the U.S. the regulation of prostitution was more localized, as befitted a federated system. Various cities and states at least considered the possibility of introducing a system of reglementation.[3] One of the earliest to do so was the city of St. Louis where a "Social Evil Ordinance" became law in the summer of 1870.[4]

In the light of English and American enthusiasm for claiming, if not always pursuing governmental non-intervention in the commercial sphere, these instances of the regulation of commercial sexual activity raise interesting questions. In particular, the long-standing rhetoric which differentiated European decadence from Anglo-Saxon righteousness paralleled a rhetoric which saw *laissez-faire* and individual liberty as similarly characteristic of a superior Anglo-American background.[5] Here were two countries assiduously constructing themselves in opposition to what they derided as the decadent sexuality of continental Europe, yet in the arena of public health seeking solutions for controlling prostitution increasingly similar to those favoured in Europe.

We are faced with some curious contradictions which yoke these otherwise disparate experiments in social legislation together. How and why in these two countries – dominated at least by lip service to an ethos of *laissez-faire* in labour as in trade, and by an alleged commitment to the liberty of the subject – could there be so comfortable "an interventionist social agenda" for prostitution?[6] And why invoke the economic principles of non-intervention in a debate which, some would argue, is about moral conditions rather than economic ones?

This latter point is worth pursuing, for it reframes the grounds on which we might read nineteenth-century prostitution and attitudes towards it. While public discussion of prostitution, and the many diatribes which condemned it at this time, focused on the idea of a moral compass gone awry, there was a parallel rumbling which saw the sex trade as *economically* disruptive.[7] Selling sex powerfully disrupted ideas about women's economic role, for in the period before its criminalization women in the sex trade routinely worked for themselves (or to feed a family) rather than for a male entrepreneur; a considerable body of work has demonstrated how criminalization allowed organized crime to add prostitution to its burgeoning business empire.[8] Prostitution blurred the boundaries of public and private, because an act deemed private became available in that most public of spaces, the marketplace. And, of course, in its distance from the mainstream economy, prostitution (like other informal economic activities) complicated the principles of economic freedom, and most particularly the free market.

This essay seeks to pursue these questions in a triangulated comparative framework, contrasting St. Louis, Britain, and Britain's colonies. To separate domestic Britain from its empire in this period of high colonialism would misrepresent not only the reach of British law and policy, but the ways in which an evolving nineteenth-century British national identity increasingly looked to the empire for its compass.[9] Clearly a comparison which pits national policy against that aimed at a single city is fraught with danger. But the differences are less distant than they seem on first consideration. The British acts, although the product of national statutory law, were highly localized and operable only in "scheduled" military districts. Though aimed at soldiers and sailors, their effect on the local civil populations was considerable. They affected local hospital provision, the informal economy, and often the formal one too, the visibility and levels of policing in the town's working-class neighbourhoods, and, of course, the public freedom of working-class women.[10] The St. Louis ordinance had remarkably similar characteristics, influencing the changing geography of the town and demarcating the respectable from the unrespectable in critical ways. And while the ordinance was directed to a civilian population, much of the impetus for prostitution legislation in the U.S. can be traced to the military concerns of the previous decade. Other American cities certainly implemented forms of regulation, but St. Louis was alone in formalizing its policy through statute.[11] Despite the formal political differences enshrined in national and local governance, these two sets of regulations shared much in their impact on the population, in their assumption about the location of prostitution, and in the need for its subjugation to formalized control.

II

In the late 1860s, as the U.S. emerged from civil strife and Britain from the medical mismanagement exposed during the Crimean War, anxiety over military efficiency was key to the shaping of health policy. It was not only battle fatalities which stirred alarm; anxiety over the impact of venereal disease on soldiers palpably increased in this period. A concomitant interest in urban public health more generally ensured that prostitution, increasingly identified as an inevitable feature of city living, came to be seen in medical circles as a prime conduit of venereal infection.[12] The reglementation efforts of this period duly emphasized the consequences of unchecked venereal disease transmitted from prostitute to client.

The curious melding of coolly detached public health provision and a strident language of morality in the legislation demonstrates the particular vulnerability of a group marginalized both by gender and by engagement in commercial sexual activity. Ava Baron has pointed to the use made by the legal system's recognition of sexual difference as a means to enact and legitimate subordination. Her analysis suggests why, even in countries where there was hostility to state intervention, regulating prostitution was acceptable, attempted most visibly on the bodies of poor and often non-white women.[13] State intervention on health grounds was first instituted on "the bodies of those who were least able to protest".[14]

In Britain, the domestic CD act of 1864, modified twice before the decade was out, required women suspected of prostitution in designated military and naval districts to submit to internal vaginal examination. If infected, they were compulsorily hospitalized and recorded as prostitutes, which meant submitting to regular examinations. The penalty for refusing examination or registration was imprisonment with hard labour. At around the same time, and in some cases even earlier, Britain introduced similar, though often more far-reaching, legislation in many of its colonies – in Asia, the Malay Archipelago, many African possessions, and most of its Caribbean and European territories.

Across the Atlantic, the experiment in St. Louis was not the first such attempt in America, though Ian Tyrrell argues that it was certainly the most notorious.[15] Rising venereal disease rates during the war years of the 1860s, coupled with the long-standing assumption of a link between venereal transmission and commercial sex, had catalyzed some cities close to military encampments to license women prostitutes.[16] These, however, were temporary expedients actuated by the extraordinary conditions of battle. The St. Louis ordinance of 1870 was a peace-time measure, intentionally aimed at a civilian population. Later efforts at regulation often looked to its experience. Indeed, its failure lent public officials elsewhere the skills necessary to implement effective regulatory practices whilst apparently maintaining a distance from *de jure* and planned licensing.[17]

By the time of the ordinance regulating prostitution, St. Louis was by no means a frontier town short on women and over-populated by men. Jeffrey Adler has traced the mid-century development of the city from a center of crusading Yankee zeal and commercialism to a conservative mid-west town, less vital economically than Chicago and more inward-looking.[18] Eric Foner, assessing its border status, sees the state of Missouri emerging from the Civil War "a free state but a profoundly divided society".[19] That divide, in St. Louis, was as much social, racial and judicial as it was political. It was in this environment before 1870 that prostitution was largely tolerated,[20] though mob attacks on brothels were not wholly unknown.[21] Brothels, in particular, enjoyed a degree of impunity, a privilege carried over in many respects into the 1870 legislation.

The Social Evil ordinance came about by a revision to the city charter approved by the State Legislature in March 1870. This Revising Act widened the legislative powers of the city council with regard to contagion and hospital control, permitting the city to "regulate or suppress bawdy or disorderly houses, houses of ill-fame or assignation".[22] Ordinance 7330 took speedy advantage of that enabling clause. Passed by a convincing majority of the city council, it went into effect four months later in July 1870. Though the ordinance included the power to suppress prostitution, its principal purpose was to bring prostitution under a mix of medical and police control. William Eliot, a prominent anti-ordinance campaigner, was acutely aware of that power base. He wrote rather stingingly of it to his son Thomas: "the Doctors & Police officers, & all the average men who like fish & do not like to wet their feet, are against us".[23]

In common with the domestic British acts, the St. Louis measure provided for medical inspection and hospitalization of contagious women. Unlike its British counterpart – indeed, resembling far more the colonial regulations enacted under British rule – women in St. Louis were registered because they *practised* prostitution, not because they were *suspected* of so doing. In Britain, the legalizing of brothels was self-consciously avoided as distasteful to public sensibilities (though their prosecution was not a police priority much before the late 1880s) while control of the brothel lay at the heart both of the Missouri experiment and British colonial legislation.[24] With such detailed and close control of the physical whereabouts of women, the logical corollary – absent in the British acts – was a ban on public solicitation. In Britain solicitation remained legal, unless it caused annoyance to persons solicited or to passers-by who would testify to that effect. In British colonial territories, where the liberty of the subject was less critical politically, the outright ban on street-walking and solicitation, though spectacularly unsuccessful, was nonetheless as integral to the control of prostitution as it was in the Missouri legislation.

From its inception, the St. Louis legislation forbade women to conduct any part of their business on the streets. In keeping with this marked practice of housing sexual activity behind closed doors, the inspection of women in St. Louis was conducted in-house. Board of Health-appointed physicians visited the brothels at least weekly. In the military and naval towns of England, on the other hand, controversy continually raged over the siting and suitability of the rooms where the regulated women were examined. Opponents of the acts offered lurid descriptions of knowing, jeering crowds gathering on examination days, with paying customers waiting for the women to emerge with their guarantees of sanitary safety.

In British colonial settings, by contrast, an effective apartheid spatially divided indigenous women prostitutes from white foreigners. The small number of white women who practised prostitution in colonial cities were often entitled to appoint a private doctor of their own choosing to conduct the examinations, while indigenous women under the control of civil and military authorities were summonsed on a regular basis to local venereal hospitals for inspection. Moreover, registration and surveillance were mostly limited to women with a European clientele, and especially those servicing the burgeoning militia necessitated by colonial growth and new forms of imperial rule. The ordinances thus routinely instituted two classes of prostitute: a first class comprised of those consorting with Europeans, and a second class reserved for local men and to whom medical and military authorities paid scant attention. Women of the first class were not only subject to regular inspection and possible hospitalization, but were often directed to live in designated areas.

A further dimension to this careful spatial divide may be found in the distinction between the "professional" and the "amateur" prostitute. Commentator F. R. Sturgis argued that what distinguished the amateur was her "going abroad to seek her prey".[25] In the colonies, British medical officers complained frequently about "clandestine" prostitutes, women who evaded registration and the brothel, instead soliciting in public. Registration as a "professional" indicated not the autonomy commonly associated with professionalism but rather domestication through containment in the less visible structure of the brothel. Such women earned the privilege of medical treatment and of freedom from arrest. In St. Louis it was native-born white women who could most easily find work behind the closed doors of the brothel and employment in the better-paid of these houses. This hierarchy, which distinguished the brothel inhabitant from the lowly streetwalker, further deepened the racial divisions which structured the sexual marketplace, and serves to broaden George Mosse's contention that racism be understood, at least in part, as a "visually-centered ideology".[26] The distinction between visible and invisible modes of prostitution critically bears the marks of racial difference, and effected a marked influence on who was most likely to fall foul of the law.[27]

III

The St. Louis ordinance came into effect just at the moment when organized opposition to the British CD acts was emerging as a powerful force in national politics. The most striking feature of the British anti-regulation movement was its domination by women, who seized upon the opportunity to challenge male prerogative and the double standard on a public platform. The freedom accorded the male customer became a critical focus for resistance in St. Louis as well as in Britain and its colonies. Witness the report in the *St. Louis Democrat* that when the police raided the "Wash Home" brothel in the summer of 1873, the women working there were arrested, while "a large and distinguished party of gentlemen... [were] left to wend their several ways home alone".[28]

In St. Louis, the male-led protest spearheaded by James McGinnis and Unitarian minister and educational reformer William Greenleaf Eliot (grandfather of the poet, T. S. Eliot) has tended to obscure the mass women's opposition organized by Anna Dickinson and suffrage and temperance activist Rebecca Naylor Hazard. In the late 1860s, a lively and vigorous suffrage movement had begun to attract support among affluent white women in St. Louis.[29] At women's meetings, men spoke by invitation, as was the case when the Reverend Mr. Felton was invited to address a women's meeting on how the new ordinance was leading "men of higher social position and standing" to desert their moral leadership for the brothels.[30] One hundred and fifty women listened to his speech, adopted a memorial condemning the legislation, and appointed a committee of women to present the memorial to the city council. City politicians took these women's meetings seriously; state Representative O'Neil and city Mayor Brown both attended a women's meeting called to discuss the ordinance in April 1873.[31] William Eliot went so far as to argue that the registration of the prostitute's clients would make the St. Louis law acceptable because equal, a remarkable position to adopt in the 1870s when sharp distinctions between active male and passive female sexuality dictated a double standard.[32]

On both sides of the Atlantic, women campaigners framed their stand in specifically Christian terms, castigating their respective political systems for turning their backs on the moral weight enfranchised women would carry. In St. Louis, Mrs. Mary Falley urged her listeners to see how in the courts "in the forming of which women have been given no outward expression, or any voice in framing their codes... there we find one of our sex dragged to be sentenced for a crime which she cannot commit alone".[33] In Britain, campaigners wielded the acts as a weapon in the fight for the suffrage, displaying their political muscle to great effect in a campaign mounted against parliamentary contender Sir Henry Storks, who had introduced a system to regulate prostitution during his gubernatorial tenure in Malta.

Reporting on a women's anti-ordinance meeting, the *St. Louis Times* described those attending as "good motherly looking ladies, a few serious and sober minded young wives and modest maidens".[34] This description of the respectable and activist women served, of course, to highlight their stark contrast to the women on whom the ordinance bore. Indeed, the reporter for the *Times* noted with a "practised eye ... several representatives of the unfortunate class ... dressed in subdued tints ... listen[ing] quietly" to the proceedings.[35] A transparently polarizing device, this served to separate those offended by "immoral" legislation from those whose livelihoods were affected by it. In Britain, the press and politicians alike made much of the involvement of "respectable" women in antiregulation campaigning, warning that proximity to the issue would degrade and make them unfit wives and mothers.

Those most concretely affected by the legislation were also vocal, although distinctively moreso in St. Louis than in Britain. Despite the assertion made by the City Health Officer that "these women ... even during the agitation of the question of the repeal of the law ... yielded willing obedience to it",[36] some women identified with prostitution were willing to throw down the public and legal gauntlet. Moreover, they did so independently of "respectable" agitators. In August 1873 William Eliot filed charges for violating not the city ordinance but Missouri state law prohibiting the keeping of a bawdy house against Kate Clark and Lizzie Saville, two of the city's most conspicuous brothel keepers and amongst the undisputed queens of their trade.[37] Eliot's plan was to demonstrate the profound inconsistency between the state's continued denial of the legality of prostitution and the legalization extant in the city. When the two women were found guilty of violating state law, they audaciously filed an appeal with the Missouri Supreme Court, even threatening to sue the city for return of fees in the likely event that the ordinance was overturned. The initial judgment in the Court of Criminal Corrections was hastily set aside by the Supreme Court in December 1873. Not surprisingly, a rash of cases followed the December decision, to the horror of Eliot and his campaigners for whom an appeal to state prohibition of prostitution had badly misfired, not least because of the willingness of established brothel keepers to fight back with formal legal weapons.[38]

In stark contrast, the scheduled districts of Britain seldom yielded women of Clark or Saville's confidence or, indeed, apparent wealth. In part, this was because large brothels were a less prominent feature of sexual commerce in Britain's garrison towns where the trade was drawn primarily from the working-class military rank-and-file. Street-walking, as we have noted, was the dominant form of sexual commerce recognized by the CD acts, and it was thus poor women who were mostly affected in Britain. Although they would, on occasion, risk a court challenge to their registration, it was invariably under the guidance and financial wing of the Ladies' National Association for the Repeal of the CD Acts, the best known of the anti-regulation organizations working for domestic repeal, and dominated by middle-class women. However much was made of the class basis of the acts, middle-class women's protests were those most often heard.

Colonial resistance, needless to say, took as many different forms as there were colonies, though two methods dominated. Petitions to the local authority requesting exemption from registration were common practice among Indian women.[39] These met with varying degrees of success, but they suggest an attention to formal detail similar to that proffered by Saville and Clark. More common, however, was the kind of informal activity to which so many of Britain's registered women also had recourse. Women evaded registration, failed to attend exams, absented themselves without permission from hospitals, and generally went about their business in quiet defiance of the law.

If such forms of resistance are, as Robin Kelley suggests, "elusive", they nonetheless hit their mark, for colonial and domestic administrators alike never ceased to complain about what they dubbed women's recalcitrance.[40] Women effectively rendered the system unworkable, a fact not lost on endlessly frustrated officials.

IV

Clark and Saville were white native-born women, managers as much as workers.[41] The available evidence suggests, not surprisingly, that those women willing to challenge publicly the legislating of moral behaviour in St. Louis were exclusively native and white.[42] They were neither from St. Louis's small black community (less than 5 per cent of the population) nor from amongst the city's recent immigrants.

Of the 766 women registered as prostitutes in 1873, some 12 per cent (92) were African-American, and though the numbers are small, their presence as working prostitutes was disproportionate to the overall black population of the city.[43] Their high representation in this occupation, coupled with their utter absence from newspaper reports of challenges to the ordinance, suggests that theirs was a voice consistently silenced. St. Louis was by no means the only American city where women of colour were disproportionate in the indices of underprivilege, working in prostitution and vulnerable to arrest.[44] In nineteenth-century St. Paul, blacks and immigrants both figured prominently among arrestees.[45] In mid-century Boston, as in other east coast cities, immigrant Irish women figured predominantly among women convicted of prostitution.[46] In Austin, Texas, the best-known red-light district was increasingly Hispanic Guy Town. Late nineteenth-century charge sheets for Austin show that though most prostitute women were white, black women in the trade were far more prone to arrest. Between 1880 and 1918, 26 per cent of those arrested for prostitution were white and a massive 72 per cent were black.[47] How far these disparities relate to the higher visibility of a street prostitution peopled by immigrants and black women I have been unable to quantify, but contemporary observations would suggest that the raced availability of work in the trade ensured the higher arrest rate of non-white and non-native women. Certainly in St. Louis, black women outnumbered black men, and their access to paid work outside the low-paying domestic sphere would have been limited.[48]

This pattern of racially-selective punitive action had a significant impact on city geography. Just as Austin's effective zone of prostitution was centered on a poverty-ridden Mexican neighbourhood, so the St. Louis ordinance effected an informal zoning of the city. James Wunsch has argued that when prostitution was driven out by energetic police action, former vice districts were likely to become black rental zones in which whites did not and would not live, and that in such areas prostitution rapidly re-established itself as a segregated black activity, doubtless with prices scaled lower to reflect the black economy. Wunsch argues specifically that, "the black neighborhood itself came to define the limits of prostitution".[49] The division of St. Louis into three operating districts for ease of administration created a political geography defined, reinforced and arguably invented by sexual commerce.

Just as the British CD acts acknowledged the relationship between the military and prostitution by limiting regulation to military towns, the St. Louis ordinance similarly accepted a set of sexualized boundaries governing who lived where and the prices they paid for accommodation, both commercial and residential. It protected white middle-class neighbourhoods – where permission to operate a licensed bawdy-house was automatically denied – and consolidated the association between vice, poverty and race. Such racial segregation was not limited to the city districts in which prostitution was permitted. The Social Evil Hospital, built with the medical and registration fees levied on registered women, separated inmates by race. While whites were housed in the hospital, African-American women were confined to the carriage house, practices reminiscent of the segregation of white and indigenous women in hospitals in the British empire.[50] The spatial dimensions of segregation were also apparent in colonial brothels. Men of colour attempting to use white brothels were liable to assault by white customers. Social purity activist John Cowen vividly described scenes of violence when Europeans discovered local men in the brothels they thought of as theirs: "nowhere is race hatred more bitter than in the brothel quarters".[51]

Such racially motivated policing effected a distinctive intervention in the free market economy, all but ensuring that white prostitutes would be more successful. They could live outside increasingly colour-ghettoized areas, avoid regular, or at least frequent arrest, and command a higher price for their services. Though presumably there was some white client base for the black prostitutes of St. Louis, no evidence of this has survived. James Wunsch's assessment that "the ordinance protected middle-class brothels" is nuanced by attention to how race meshed with class in this instance.[52]

Foreign birth operated in ways not dissimilar to race. Immigrant women worked largely in the poorer brothels of St. Louis.[53] Three hundred and eighty-eight of the 2,052 women registered as prostitutes between 1870 and the spring of 1872 were foreign-born, the German and the Irish comprising the two largest groups, as the city's overall demographics might suggest.[54] Although the figure was larger than that of registered black women (286), it was substantially lower than the number of registered native-born white women. In stark contrast, foreign women working in colonial British brothels were often able to turn their exotic foreign-ness to advantage. Playing on their whiteness, they were able to command higher prices for their services, and while their numbers were always tiny, their shrewd manipulation of their racial advantage always worried British colonial officials, fearful that such women tarnished whiteness and Britishness.

A good number of European women who peopled the brothels of India and Singapore were East European Jews, and, by the late nineteenth century, the alleged profiteering in prostitution by Eastern European Jews had become a widespread myth. One of St. Louis's better-known male under-world characters, who apparently peddled underwear to women working in the city's brothels, was known to everyone as "Jew John". The tempting and simplistic association of Jews and easy money is more important than whether John was, in fact, actually Jewish.

Anti-Semitism was only one of the varieties of anti-immigrant sentiment which linked unrespectable sex and foreignness. In their jocular guide book to St. Louis, published shortly after the repeal of the Social

Evil ordinance, J. A. Dacus and J. W. Buel caricatured the courtroom appearance of a young German prostitute.

> The marshal calls out "Mina Schlessel". A *deutsches madchen*, who, but for the unmistakable expression of a corrupted nature, would be regarded as a comely girl, takes her place by the side of the prosecutor.
> "You are charged with being a street-walker – plying your vocation on the public street. Are you guilty or not guilty?"
> "What say you, Mina? Do you speak English?"
> "Ya," she says. "Ich Englisch sprech".
> "Well, are you guilty of the charge?"
> "Vell. Ich dells you de trut. Vat you calls geelty? Ich var yust talking a leedle mit a shentlemans von der politzman komt und sagt, "Sie, geht mit mir". Das ist alle".[55]

In both Britain and St. Louis, prostitution operated as a racially definable category with an association between white nativity and respectability as a normative guideline. New York neurologist George Beard drew a sharp distinction between white and black libido, claiming that "if you would find a virgin among them [African-Americans], it is said you must go to the cradle".[56]

Moreover, venereal disease, so closely associated in the public mind with sexual looseness, became a convenient metaphor for savagery or primitiveness powerfully underscoring the connection between race and extravagant forms of sexual behaviour. In a health memorandum issued to British troops in India, the commander-in-chief warned that "the common women as well as the regular prostitutes in India are almost all more or less infected with disease".[57] In America, a fear of black autonomy dominated in this postwar era. Black prostitutes may have been more susceptible to control than their white counterparts, but the black customer remained unrecognized. It was the irresponsibility of wealthy white men evading the consequences of their actions while women were penalized that captured the occasional headline about the client base of prostitution. The assumption that black men desired white women above all else tacitly fed the growing rape myth so potent by the turn of the century. White men paid; black men stole; immigrant men (such as Jew John) profited.

In Britain, discussions of the dockside brothels in port cities acknowledged a black customer base in ways which reinforced narrow notions of a white national identity. Liverpool, for example, had a significant black minority population by the nineteenth century, related largely to its maritime trade. Physician Frederick Lowndes declared that the women who worked in "Blackman's Alley" were chiefly Irish immigrants.[58] His observations may well be accurate, given the constraints working against upward mobility in the trade for immigrant women. The validity of his claim notwithstanding, in ascribing the black trade – the cheapest and lowest trade – to Irish women, Lowndes also upheld a sense of English prestige.

Discourses about race and national characteristics seem to me as central in assessing the role and significance of this sort of legislation as they do in understanding Victorian typologies of sexuality *per se*. They also illuminate the relationship of such legislation to other forms of public health policy and practices of the same period. In St. Louis, racial considerations worked on three levels: a punitive stand against an indigenous African-American population, a fear of the habits of new groups of immigrants, and a populist and nativist antipathy to the importation of European customs.[59] Opponents and regulationists alike were alert to the alleged dangers not only of venereal disease but of the business of prostitution itself, and both the disease and this means of acquiring it were, as we have seen, frequently represented as decadent grafts. William Barrett, St. Louis's Health Officer at the time of the ordinance, likened street-walkers to "the wild dogs of the East [who] infest all unregulated cities", and in the same report spoke of "dissolute Paris".[60] He thus distanced himself simultaneously from the idea of an indigenous American prostitution and from explicit approval of French regulation. Indeed, though Barrett castigated England for "sights of libertinage and vice beyond the most dissolute cities of the continent", it was still to England as a non-European entity that Barrett looked for moral support.[61] After all, the passage implies, something is dangerously askew when England compares unfavourably with the definitionally dissolute.

> If England would clean her own Augean stable, would look to her colonies, her maritime stations around the globe, she would do much for health and morals. England and America dishonor liberty by the infamous license given to the propagation of disease.[62]

Foreignness was detrimental to the spirit of America, more particularly that associated with declining civilizations giving way to the vigorous growth of new powers. Ironically, the distaste invoked by the architects of the ordinance for the spectacle of an infested Europe was shared by their opponents. Chicago Surgeon Edmund Andrews, one of Eliot's most ardent supporters, deplored any hint of European influence. "The American public sentiment is as different from [the French] as the north wind is from the breath of a cess-pool".[63] Lieutenant-Governor Johnson, perhaps the ordinance's fiercest critic in the Legislature, concurred, castigating "the false and capricious philosophy of a Continental and Parisian society".[64] And N. F. Cooke, a physician who characterized prostitution as "Satan in Society," was adamant: "That an old European custom which has long ago demonstrated its entire inadequacy to the end proposed should be revived in this nation of 'rational progress' is, we confess, an enigma".[65]

Both the practice of sex, and the immigrant or African-American woman, was a purveyor, an infester. The immigrant woman or the woman of colour – the latter not singled out legislatively but clearly a differentiated target of attack – was a dubious moral category. Her alleged reluctance to conform to Anglo-American moral principles connoted a measure of racial recalcitrance. One military medical officer in India even wondered whether it was worth registering "a few women called prostitutes, out of a multitude of unchaste women".[66] As Gail Bederman has argued, sexual restraint in nineteenth-century America was the proving ground of a properly manly and definitively white civilization.[67] Both the unchaste woman and the unrestrained man threatened to unhinge the racial and the sexual boundaries constructed around proper behaviour. And in Britain, the prostitute woman found herself likely to be compared, and not favourably, with the "savages" whose conquest was Britain's manifestation of its virtues: "in the nineteenth century... race becomes the organizing grammar of an imperial order in which modernity, the civilizing mission and the 'measure of man' were framed".[68]

These racial configurations of early health policy, and their clear links to a legislation based on moral precepts, illuminate the complex ways in which contested arenas, such as those associated with the control of prostitution, depend as much on their opposition to mythological monsters created out of foreignness and racial difference as they do on the concerns of the medical, the urban or the governmental. These were all powerful lobbies at this juncture, and indubitably implicated in the fashioning of such monsters.

V

[R]ightly or wrongly, the proposed appropriation of money would, in the eyes of very large numbers of persons, be to the last degree odious and immoral... They would see the prostitute kept in hospital at their expense for weeks or months, not necessarily from the exigencies of severe illness of her own, but essentially that she might be made safe for the local concubinage-market... does the detriment which venereal infections cause to the public health reach those limits at which principles generally preferable ought to be exceptionally abandoned by the State?[69]

These lengthy musings of Sir John Simon, Medical Officer to the English Privy Council, on the politics of intervention suggests that those involved in the fledgling public health system juggled notions of the state as enforcer, as provider and as benefactor. If the state was to expend money or political capital, then what should it expect? A more tractable class of women? A healthier or more morally upright populace? A realignment of sex roles and a restoration of feminine dependence on male bounty? Prostitution swept off the streets? A racial cleansing?

These were the questions which plagued legislators and policy-makers sensitive to public disapproval. The St. Louis system tried to solve the moral dilemma with a fee-based system; brothel-keepers and workers paid fees for inspection and registration, allowing legislators and city officials to claim that the taxes of the law-abiding were not spent on the dissolute, and that the wages of sin were, in effect, being spent on its own policing. When brothel-keepers Clark and Saville raised the question of fees illegally demanded of them, the entire legitimacy of the system began to unravel. In Britain and its colonies, fees were always contentious. No fees were levied in Britain where politicians knew they would face violent criticism, but they were less squeamish in the colonies where fees were applied, albeit unevenly. One feature of the system carefully obscured for public consumption was the gratuitous treatment of hospitalized women in the colonies; women received a small daily sum for dieting as well as free treatment and board. In Britain also, treatment was free.[70] But the very question of a fee-based model, whether implemented vigorously or with cold feet, returns us to the ways in which economic questions were always central to debates in prostitution, even if muted in an era of religious and social conformity. Extracting fees from the women involved in prostitution effected a form of taxation, a recognition of the success that sex workers could have in that most manly and Victorian of pursuits, the turning of a profit. St. Louis and the colonies embraced fees for both economic and moral reasons: in this way the taxpayer and the ratepayer could not be said to be underwriting sin, but regulation

could be sustained. It was a neat resolution to a moral and an economic dilemma. Britain's rejection of the principle was palpably not
taken as a matter of principle, given the use of fees in the colonies.

In an era when citizenship, rights and the broad parameters of independence were so frequently declared as ideals to be practically fulfilled
by wise governance, the laws regulating prostitution found interesting,
if not always consistent, justification. While personal autonomy remained
central to legal principles, the submission of women to police and medical surveillance was couched frequently in terms of the benefits accruing
to them as well as to the greater good. [71] Effectively, regulation of prostitution with its protective overtones (albeit translatable rapidly into punitive action) was a form of special needs legislation which restored the
dependence associated with femininity to women active in the market
place on male turf, and simultaneously kept racial issues central in the
discursive terrains of sexual order and disciplinary practice.

Both the Social Evil ordinance and the CD acts constitute examples of
white fraternal discourse at a self-conscious point of "modernization" in
these two societies, St. Louis emerging as a major mid-west city after the
Civil War, and Britain poised for what it saw as long-term imperial and
industrial predominance. That in the one case we are dealing with the
actions of a city government entrenched in localism, and in the other
with an increasingly elaborate central administration complicated by
colonial governance, merely suggests that what Michel Foucault has
dubbed "governmentality" is not monopolized by the "big states" of the
modern world, but has resonance in variously-placed and sized structures
of policy-making and power anxious to regulate and sanitize troublesome
populations.[72]

In both instances, the gendered inequalities so visibly written into
venereal disease legislation masked the racial concerns which were crucial
to the successful maintenance of a system which had no intention of
destroying the institution of prostitution but sought rather to dom-
esticate it literally and symbolically. It was thus that both Britain and
St. Louis could claim ideological commitment to policies of a *laissez-
faire* nature while embarking upon palpably coercive courses of control,
aimed indubitably at women, and also in material ways at the women
least well placed to offer active resistance. Women of colour, immigrant women and women living under the yoke of colonialism bore the
double burdens of gender and racial inequality. While women engaged
in commercial sex invariably faced both social disapproval and legal
obstacles, those belonging to these specific groups experienced most
drastically disadvantage, surveillance and, of course, poverty. Race and

foreign-ness powerfully determined policies intended to govern female sexuality and sexual commerce in the late nineteenth century.

Notes

1 S. Lustgarten, M.D. "The Question of Legal Control of Prostitution in America", *Medical Record* 57 (13 Jan. 1900), 57.

2 Lustgarten, 58.

3 Neil L. Shumsky, "Tacit Acceptance. Respectable Americans and Segregated Prostitution, 1870–1910", *Journal of Social History* 19 (1986), 669.

4 John Burnham, "Medical Inspection of Prostitutes in America in the Nineteenth Century: The St. Louis Experiment and Its Sequel', *Bulletin of the History of Medicine* 45 (1971), 203–18, and "The Social Evil Ordinance – A Social Experiment in Nineteenth Century St. Louis", *Bulletin of the Missouri Historical Society* 17 (1971), 203–17.

5 For further discussion of Anglo-Americanism in an imperial context, see Paul A. Kramer, 'Empires, Exceptions, and Anglo-Saxons: Race and Rule between the British and United States Empires, 1880–1910,' *Journal of American History* 88, no. 4 (2002): 1315–53, and Kramer and John Plotz, 'Pairing Empires: Britain and the United States, 1857–1947', *Journal of Colonialism and Colonial History* 2, no.1 (2001).

6 Charles E. Rosenberg, "Disease and Social Order in America: Perceptions and Expectations", in *AIDS. The Burdens of History*, eds. Elizabeth Fee and Daniel M. Fox (Berkeley, 1988), 22.

7 A theme discussed by Sonya O. Rose in her essay "Cultural Analysis and Moral Discourses: Episodes, Continuities and Transformations", in *Beyond the Cultural Turn*, eds. Victoria E. Bonnel and Lynn Hunt (Berkeley, 1999), 217–40.

8 See especially Ruth Rosen, *The Lost Sisterhood: Prostitution in America, 1900–1918* (Baltimore, 1982).

9 Antoinette Burton, "Who Needs the Nation? Interrogating 'British History'", *Journal of Historical Sociology* 10 (1997), 227–48.

10 Judith Walkowitz, *Prostitution and Victorian Society* (Cambridge, 1980) spells out these ramifications in rich detail.

11 Sharon E. Wood, *The Freedom of the Streets. Work, Citizenship, and Sexuality in a Gilded Age City* (Chapel Hill, 2005), 163.

12 Eric H. Monkkonen sees prostitution explicitly as "an indicator and aspect of urbanization". *The Dangerous Class. Crime and Poverty in Columbus, Ohio, 1860–1885* (Cambridge, MA, 1975), 59.

13 Ava Baron, "Feminist Legal Strategies. The Powers of Difference", in *Analyzing Gender. A Handbook of Social Science Research*, eds. Beth B. Hess and Myra Marx Ferree (Newbury Park, CA, 1987), esp. 490.

14 Dorothy Porter and Roy Porter, "The Enforcement of Health: the British Debate", in *AIDS. The Burdens of History*, 106.

15 Ian Tyrrell, *Woman's World. Woman's Empire. The Woman's Christian Temperance Union in International Perspective, 1880–1930* (Chapel Hill, 1991), 196.

16 James S. Wunsch, "Prostitution and Public Policy: From Regulation to Suppression, 1858–1920", (PhD. diss. University of Chicago, 1976), 37–41; Lawrence R. Murphy, "The Enemy Among Us: Venereal Disease among Union

Soldiers in the Far West, 1861–65", *Civil War History* 31 (1985), 257–69; Anne M. Butler, "Military Myopia: Prostitution on the Frontier", *Prologue*, 13 (1981), 233–50; James B. Jones, Jr. "Municipal Vice. The Management of Prostitution in Tennessee's Urban Experience. Part I: The Experience of Nashville and Memphis, 1854–1917", *Tennessee Historical Quarterly* 1 (1991), 33–41.

17 Barbara Meil Hobson, *Uneasy Virtue. The Politics of Prostitution and the American Reform Tradition* (New York, 1987), 148. For alternative prostitution policies in this period, see Joel Best, *Controlling Vice: Regulating Brothel Prostitution in St. Paul, 1865–1883* (Columbus, 1998); Marion S. Goldman, *Gold Diggers and Silver Miners. Prostitution and Social Life on the Comstock Lode* (Ann Arbor, 1981); David Kaser, "Nashville's Women of Pleasure in 1860", *Tennessee Historical Quarterly* 23 (1964), 379–82; Carol Leonard and Isidor Walliman, "Prostitution and Changing Morality in the Frontier Cattle Towns of Kansas", *Kansas History* 2 (1979), 34–53; David J. Pivar, *Purity Crusade: Sexual Morality and Social Control, 1868–1900* (Westport, Conn., 1973); Al Rose, *Storyville, New Orleans. Being an Authentic, Illustrated Account of the Notorious Red Light District* (University, AL, 1974); Neil L. Shumsky and Larry M. Springer, "San Francisco's Zone of Prostitution 1880–1934", *Journal of Historical Geography* 7 (1981), 71–89; Henry J. Wilson and James P. Gledstone, *Report of a Visit to the United States* (Sheffield, 1876). There is also a vast contemporary debate in regional medical journals such as the *Cincinnati Lancet-Clinic*, the *Maryland Medical Journal*, the *Pacific Medical and Surgical Journal*. Doctors overwhelmingly supported medically-based regulation and looked approvingly to the St. Louis model.

18 Jeffrey S. Adler, *Yankee Merchants and the Making of the Urban West. The Rise and Fall of Antebellum St. Louis* (Cambridge, 1991).

19 Eric Foner, *Reconstruction. America's Unfinished Revolution 1863–77* (New York, 1988), 42. For an alternative reading of a "borderland" condition, see Henry Louis Taylor, Jr., preface to *Race and the City. Work, Community, and Protest in Cincinnati 1820–1970* (Urbana, 1993), xiii.

20 Adler, *Yankee Merchants*, 169.

21 Paul S. Boyer, *Urban Masses and Moral Order in America, 1820–1920* (Cambridge, MA, 1978), 83.

22 An Act to Revise the Charter of the City of St. Louis, and to Extend the Limits Thereof. Article III.

23 William Greenleaf Eliot Papers. Washington University Library. Ms. 101/00/ 3/2. Box 11. W. G. Eliot to T. L. Eliot, 14 November 1871.

24 This was the case in St. Louis even before the promulgation of Ordinance 7330. See Jeffrey Adler, "'Streetwalkers, Degraded Outcasts, and Good-for-Nothing Huzzies': Women and the Dangerous Class in Antebellum St. Louis", *Journal of Social History* 25 (1992), 737–55.

25 F. R. Sturgis, *Prostitution: Its Suppression or Control* (New York, 1901), 2.

26 George L. Mosse, *Nationalism and Sexuality. Respectability and Abnormal Sexuality in Modern Europe* (New York, 1985), 134.

27 A theme taken up by Sonya Rose in her study of race and gender in the Second World War, *Which People's War? National Identity and Citizenship in Wartime Britain, 1939–1945* (Oxford, 2003).

28 *St. Louis Democrat*, 17 August 1873, 4.

29 George Lipsitz, *The Sidewalks of St. Louis. Places, People, and Politics in an American City* (Columbia, MO, 1991), 99

30 *S[t]. L[ouis] T[imes]*, 6 April 1873, 5.

31 *SLT.*

32 Eliot Mss. 101/00/3/1/ Box 1, f. 45. Marginal scribbles on newspaper clipping.

33 *SLT*, 9 March 1873, 2.

34 *SLT*, 6 April 1873, 5.

35 *SLT.*

36 *Seventh Annual Report of the Board of Health of St. Louis*, 1874, 28.

37 For an account of the trial, see Duane Sneddeker, "Regulating Vice: Prostitution and the St. Louis Social Evil Ordinance, 1870–1874", *Gateway Heritage* 11 (1990), 33–4.

38 State v Clark 53 Mo. 17 (1873); State v de Bar 59 Mo. 395 (1874).

39 See, for instance, [British Library] O[riental and] I[ndia] O[ffice] C[ollections] P/525, Proceedings of the Government of India, Sanitary Department, P/525 (1873) and Military Collections, L/MIL/7/13855.

40 Robin D. G. Kelley, *Race Rebels. Culture, Politics and the Black Working Class* (New York, 1994), 7.

41 The distinction is a difficult one, for while legal documents – and many historians – assume a distinct separation between the brothelkeeper and those who work in the brothel, that distinction becomes less tenable when the managers are women. Many women who managed brothels were women with personal experience of prostitution; the available evidence suggests that in the case of Clark and Saville, they may well have undertaken dual careers as both managers and prostitutes, a common phenomenon though generally undocumented.

42 Wood found a similar demographic pattern at work in Davenport, Iowa: *Freedom of the Streets*, esp. 14–15.

43 *Tenth Annual Report of the Board of Police Commissioners*, 1871, 29

44 Leonard P. Curry demonstrates the disproportionate conviction rates for blacks, and before 1850 or so, the startlingly high rate of conviction and incarceration of black women: *The Free Black in Urban America 1800–1850. The Shadow of the Dream* (Chicago, 1981), 113–15.

45 Joel Best, "Keeping the Peace in St. Paul: Crime, Vice and Police Work, 1869–74", *Minnesota History* 47 (1981), 245

46 Hobson, *Uneasy Virtue*, 35.

47 David C. Humphrey, "Prostitution and Public Policy in Austin, Texas, 1870–1915", *Southwestern Historical Quarterly* 86 (1983), 498. Humphrey offers no explanation for the low Mexican count among prostitutes which he estimates at 6–7 per cent in this period.

48 Curry, *The Free Black*, 9 et seq.

49 Wunsch, "Prostitution and Public Policy", 158–9. Shumsky argues conversely that the red-light district as ghetto was not ethnically motivated ("Tacit Acceptance", 666), though he acknowledges that the ghetto was "universally restricted to poor or marginal neighborhoods" (672).

50 James S. Wunsch, "The Social Evil Ordinance", *American Heritage* 33 (1982), 51; Philippa Levine, *Prostitution, Race and Politics: Policing Venereal Disease in the British Empire* (New York, 2003). Wood notes that black women in

Davenport, Iowa, remained virtually untouched by the regulation intro-duced there in 1893: *Freedom of the Streets*, 178–9.

51   John Cowen, "Extracts From A Report Upon Public Prostitution in Singapore", *The Shield* 3rd series, 1 (1916), 85.

52   Wunsch, "Prostitution and Public Policy", 46.

53   Wunsch, "Prostitution", 24.

54   German and Irish immigration comprised more than 40 per cent of the city's population by the end of the 1850s: Steven Rowan and James Neal Primm, *Germans for A Free Missouri. Translations from the St. Louis Radical Press, 1857–1862* (Columbia, MO, 1983), 4.

55   J. A. Dacus and J. W. Buel, *A Tour of St. Louis; or the Inside Life of A Great City* (St. Louis, 1878), 394.

56   George Beard, *American Nervousness* (New York, 1881), 188, quoted in Kevin J. Mumford, "'Lost Manhood' Found: Male Sexual Impotence and Victorian Culture in the United States", *Journal of the History of Sexuality* 3, no. 1 (1992), 46.

57   Women's Library, London. Papers of Henry J. Wilson. Lord Kitchener's Memorandum to the Troops, 1905.

58   Frederick W. Lowndes, *The Extension of the Contagious Diseases Act to Liverpool and other Seaports Practically Considered* (Liverpool, 1876), 31.

59   In *Freedom of the* Streets, Wood argues (163–5) that a German immigrant population made Davenport's highly visible regulation acceptable, because they found nothing offensive in a system widely deployed in continental Europe. In St. Louis while it was an Anglophone elite which peopled the opposition to regulation, foreigners were still outsiders. The German presence did little to smooth the path of this controversial legislation.

60   Barrett, *Sixth Annual Report of the Board of Health of St. Louis*, 1873, 44; 34.

61   Barrett, *Sixth Report*, 32. See Stuart Anderson, *Race and Rapprochement. Anglo-Saxonism and Anglo-American Relations 1895–1904* (Rutherford, NJ, 1981) for a discussion of the high-point of this racialized alliance.

62   Barrett, *Sixth Report*, 35.

63   Edmund Andrews, *Prostitution and Its Sanitary Management*, (n.p., 1871), 1.

64   Charles P. Johnson, *The Social Evil. A Speech delivered in the Senate of Missouri*, (Jefferson City, Mo, 1874), 7.

65   [N.F. Cooke] *Satan in Society: By A Physician* (Chicago, 1891).

66   OIOC. L/MIL/7/13810. Surgeon-General of Bengal to Director-General, Army Medical Department, London, 9 June 1884. Letter 9903-A.

67   Gail Bederman, *Manliness and Civilization. A Cultural History of Gender and Race in the United States, 1880–1917* (Chicago, 1995).

68   Ann Stoler, *Race and the Education of Desire. Foucault's History of Sexuality and the Colonial Order of Things* (Durham, NC, 1995), 27.

69   National Archives, London. HO 45/9322/17273. Confidential Memorandum of Sir John Simon, 3 April 1869.

70   The appropriation of monies for funding the free treatment of preventable disease was an early reality in pre-welfare state Britain, and even earlier in its colonies, though paid for largely by the military and not the sanitary wing of government.

71   Ursula Vogel, "Under Permanent Guardianship: Women's Condition under Modern Civil Law", in *The Political Interests of Gender. Developing Theory and*

Research with a Feminist Face eds. Kathleen B. Jones and Anna G. Jonasdottir (London, 1988), 143.

72 In her discussion of prostitution laws in Helena, Montana, Paula Petrik sees the instigation of moral reform campaigning as a sign of the city's transition to maturity. While I remain sceptical that prostitution legislation signals meaningful urbanity, her analysis does demonstrate that small as well as large political entities were centrally concerned with controlling prostitution: "Strange Bedfellows. Prostitution, Politicians, and Moral Reform in Helena, 1885–7", *Montana*, 35 (1985), 13.

5
The Colonial Actress: Empire, Modernity and the Exotic in Twentieth-Century London

Angela Woollacott

Sonya O. Rose has been a major influence on recent modern British history, through her generous mentoring of a sizeable cohort of currently active scholars, her always-constructive commentary on the work of younger scholars in the field, and especially through her own imaginative and meticulous research. In 1992 Rose compelled the attention of the field to the interconstitutive process in which gender ideologies and class structures evolved and shaped the daily lives of working women and men in the nineteenth century.[1] In 2003 she recast the central subject of national identity and citizenship in World War II Britain, using social and cultural history methodology to explore the political processes of inclusion and exclusion at a defining historical moment. In this chapter, I pay tribute to Rose's work by addressing some of its themes in the context of my own recent research on gender, women's lives and the colonialism that stretched between Australia and the British metropole. In *Which People's War?*, her study of World War II, Rose considered the controversial figure of "the good-time girl", the trope representing young women who challenged sexual propriety, were accused of selfish indulgence and, especially, linked to interracial sex with African-American GIs present in Britain.[2] The controversy over the "good-time girl" was a classic instance of debates over the female body, the fusing of issues of sexuality, gender, race and the nation so characteristic of modernity. I take that focus on the female body and female lives as a central theme here. Like Rose, I also consider the imbrication of race and empire in the construction of the British labour force and British culture. Rose shows the central place of the empire in discourses of national identity and reconstruction during the war, as well as the integral role of the dominions and colonies to the war effort, and the recruitment of colonial workers to supply metropolitan demands for labour.[3]

In the historiographical debates surrounding British national identity since the collapse of empire, the formation of a multiethnic Britain, and whether or not the empire has shaped Britain itself, the temporary and permanent migration to Britain of subjects from the white-settler dominions has been largely overlooked. Tens of thousands of Australian women were drawn to England from the late nineteenth century onwards for diverse reasons including travel, adventure, escaping home and local gendered constraints, and seeking education, training and careers. London as imperial metropole has exercised a consistent pull for Australian women, despite the growing significance of alternative destinations such as New York. Some factors have stayed the same in this particular component of modern, global mobility, and yet we can also identify factors of change – factors that speak to the attenuation of imperial ties and colonial rights, even as the legacies of colonialism are the fundamental reason for the continuation of an Australian community in London today. Australians have been a continuing and communal presence in London despite their changing status and legal rights there, and the shifting racial understandings of the white colonial, which were in turn historically contingent upon race relations in the Australian colonies or states. The presence of white colonials in the metropole has been one vector through which imperial race relations, and the great diversity within the category "colonial", have been realized at the heart of empire.

David Lambert and Alan Lester have suggested recently that one aspect of imperial networks and systems was "imperial careering". The concept of imperial careering, they contend, serves to trace "colonial lives over time and space" and to go beyond "dualisms of centre and periphery, global and local". Identifying the mobility of colonial personnel as determined "careering" decentres both Victorian notions of biography and their usage to shore up empire, and "contributes to an understanding of trans-imperial (and extra-imperial) networks".[4] The collection of biographical studies Lambert and Lester have edited focuses on colonial governors and their wives, military and other officials, missionaries, a nurse and a labour recruiter, using their stories to suggest imperial decentring, networks and connections. While the collection includes an important subaltern story, that of Mary Seacole, it retains a focus on traditional occupations and the elite. I would suggest that the category of imperial networks could be further decentred through studies of more non-elite occupations such as acting. Transnational theatre circuits constitute a subject of both imperial and popular culture history. From the mid-nineteenth century, travelling theatre companies connected Britain with its colonies and other global sites, creating the fabric of a shared imperial culture (through staging the same canonical productions across imperial sites, often with the same cast) and jobs for itinerant thespians. Acting has been overlooked as an imperial career, and entertainment circuits have not been fully appreciated as imperial systems. From the late nineteenth century, acting became increasingly significant as a career for colonial women, partly because of the expansion of the theatre and then the film and television industries, and partly because it gradually became respectable. With theatre one of the imperial economic networks of the high modern period, and its facilitation of colonial as well as metropolitan women's travels, a focus on acting as an imperial career brings women into view.

Colonial actresses

Australian expatriates in Britain who have become media icons, such as Germaine Greer, have been the subject of historical work.[5] But there is less available work on the tens of thousands of Australians who did not become famous, including those who have worked in theatre, film and television – such as the now-unknown Ethel Haydon who in 1898 was hailed as a "charming young Gaiety actress" who, though based in London, "entirely won the heart of Manchester" through her lead role in a pantomime there.[6] Actresses have constituted a continuing subgroup within the broader category of Australian women in England in the twentieth century, drawn to London for all the attractions of the imperial metropole, with the added pull of London's prominence in theatrical productions of all kinds.

The female body was on display in the period of high modernity, at the same time that women increasingly breached the confines of Victorian gender ideology, becoming travellers, workers, political actors and urban spectators. In both Australia and Britain, as Veronica Kelly has pointed out, young women were increasingly becoming "urban workers with just enough discretionary income to wield their consumer power in the expanding marketplace of cultural choice".[7] Theatre, vaudeville and, later, motion pictures comprised much of the public entertainments and new forms of leisure becoming available in the late nineteenth and early twentieth centuries. Young working women and others were consumers of these forms of mass entertainment, helping to shape the fan cultures and rapidly changing ideas of fashion and modernity to which they were integral. The female body – both in its most fundamental sense of the women whose work, lives and travel contributed to globally emerging industries and consumer culture, and in its representational forms – was central.

By 1908 theatrical work had become a sufficiently significant area of employment for women in Australia that, when the magazine *The Lone Hand* commissioned a series of articles on women's industrial work, "The Chorus Girl" was one subject. The "chorus girl" was defined to include "all classes of theatrical aspirants; the girl who 'walks on' in drama; the girl who sings in a musical play; and she who is no more than a pair of ballet legs", and was thought to be essentially "of the same class as the milliner or waitress".[8] Commentators of this period agreed that the "chorus girl" was woefully underpaid, especially given the long hours of unpaid rehearsals, yet they pointed out that the job was considered so desirable that stage managers and other gatekeepers were swamped with applicants. The early twentieth-century popularity of the job was related, one observer considered, to its new respectability, in contrast to the older view that stage work was "something that an average girl, decently brought up, would regard with grave suspicion; her relatives possibly with alarm".[9] Indeed, by the Edwardian period, theatrical work was sufficiently respectable that it had become a touchstone of nationalist pride. One observer was adamant that the Australian chorus girl was far better talented and trained than her English equivalent, while another asserted: "If I had to select an Australian type of girl who is as representative of the country as the Gibson girl is of America, I think I should point to the chorus-girl. And why not? She is bright, *chic*, vivacious, pretty, and lady-like. What more do you want?"[10]

Part of the attraction of the job was travel, despite the fact that the expenses of touring (such as paying for lodgings) meant that women barely survived on their wages and would have little or no savings at the end of a tour, even with travelling allowances. In Australia, the "chorus girl" could "travel and see her native land from end to end, which is an experience worth much to any woman".[11] Touring Australian companies also crossed the Tasman Sea to "Maoriland", which "though most of the girls are eager" to go for the sake of sight-seeing, "is a very bad financial proposition" because of the travel costs.[12]

Travelling theatre companies took Australian women to a range of countries, but perhaps the ultimate destination was the imperial metropole – which itself incorporated the possibility of provincial touring. Like Caribbean-born writer Jean Rhys herself, as well as Anna Morgan the protagonist of her 1934 novel *Voyage in the Dark*, other white colonial women may have fallen relatively easily into the world of travelling theatre companies because they lacked close family and roots in England. Moreover, their separation from family and home may have lessened the risks to moral and social reputation of what some still regarded as the demimonde of the stage door and cheap boarding houses. At a practical level, joining a theatrical troupe may have had the attraction of providing a ready-made network for recently-arrived colonial women. *Voyage in the Dark* is closely based on Rhys's own experience, and her descriptions of touring life are interwoven with a colonial's assessments of England:

> After a while I got used to England and I liked it all right; I got used to everything except the cold and that the towns we went to always looked so exactly alike. You were perpetually moving to another place which was perpetually the same. There was always a little grey street leading to the stage-door of the theatre and another little grey street where your lodgings were, and rows of little houses with chimneys like the funnels of dummy steamers and smoke the same colour as the sky.[13]

Anna Morgan's exile from and homesickness for the Caribbean, her dependence on an uncaring stepmother, and her slide from chorus girl into being the mistress of an affluent businessman, weave together several kinds of precariousness. They include the isolation of a colonial in the metropole, the marginal and spasmodic work pattern of the theatre and the economic vulnerability of a poorly-paid woman who opts for selling sex, albeit to one man. Anna's thoughts constantly return to the Windward Islands, so that impressions of England are interspersed with scenes from home. Descriptions of England centre on their contrast from the Caribbean, such as one of London with: "hundreds thousands of white people white people [sic] rushing along and the dark houses all alike frowning down one after the other all alike all stuck together".[14] Rhys's negative depictions of London, which contrast with happier memories of her colonial home, raise race as an issue alongside metropolitan class divisions, especially the marginality and poverty of some workers. Colonial women could come to London and find low-level work in the theatre, but Rhys makes clear the financial and emotional precariousness such a life could entail.

Veronica Kelly has analysed the economic imperatives and business practices of the Australian theatre impresarios of the period from the 1890s to the 1920s, showing Australia to have been one "local concentration" in a "global production network" shaped in part by the empire. While London was the world capital of theatre in this period (increasingly encroached upon by New York), Kelly contends that Australian audiences' very "coloniality" helped to constitute their tastes and demands as modern cosmopolitans expecting to receive the world's best productions. Australia's role in this global system included a willingness to export local talent in return for "the import of intellectual property".[15] Australian actresses need to be seen, then, as mobile agents within an imperial (global) system of entertainment circuits.

Australian women were a constant part of the London theatre industry from the late nineteenth century, occupying roles from the lowest rungs of the chorus to those of leading ladies, and even theatre management. The *British-Australasian* (which in 1924 became *The British Australian and New Zealander*) chronicled the success of Australian women on the provincial and London stages consistently for decades, from noticing that there were "three Australian girls" in the chorus of a "new sketch at the Palace in Manchester" in 1910; to noting Althea Glasby of Sydney's appearance in "The Merchant of Venice" at the Old Vic in 1922, and reporting Clarice Hardwicke's success in a leading role at Drury Lane in 1925.[16] In 1922 the London-based newspaper also reported on the eventual success of Australian Marie Lohr as a theatrical producer, who after several "short runs" finally produced a hit with "that most delightful comedy, 'The Laughing Lady'".[17] By 1928 Joan Luxton of Melbourne had also become a theatre producer, founding the Children's Theatre in Endell Street which claimed to be "the smallest theatre in London".[18] By the 1930s, along with other organs of the Australian media, the *British Australian and New Zealander* proudly began to record the success of Australian women in films, such as "Miss Judy Kelly, the charming little Australian girl who has come across to star in British International Pictures".[19] The fact that none of these names still carry any recognition underscores the number of Australian women – like other colonial women – who participated in the British theatre, film and television industries, and whose historical invisibility is a reminder that the colonial presence was so interwoven into the metropole as to blend in as part of the whole.

The careers of two Australian actresses of the early twentieth century exemplify the many women who took advantage of imperial connections to establish themselves. Mary Marlowe reveals the early-twentieth century availability of acting as an imperial career to a young woman of British descent and respectable yet impoverished class status. Rose Quong, more than a decade later than Marlowe, shows acting to have been available too to an Australian marginalized by racial hierarchies:

the ways in which she responded to racial barriers within the theatre world, and the need to see the category of colonial Australian women in the metropole as ethnically complicated.

Mary Marlowe

Mary Marlowe was born in Melbourne in 1884, to a family that had lost its affluence but sought to cling to gentility. Her education emphasized music, singing and dancing, and in 1907, against her family's wishes, she joined the Julius Knight travelling repertory-theatre company, adopting a career that fitted her impecunious status and seemed to offer glamour and excitement. The reality was often prosaic, as Marlowe travelled with productions to Sydney, Adelaide, Perth, Broken Hill, Bendigo and Ballarat, toured New Zealand, and stayed in cheap boarding houses, learning about the harsher side of life from older members of the company.[20]

In 1910, with two of her similarly-ambitious actress friends, she left Australia and headed for the great imperial stage in England. After initial work in the provinces, Marlowe finally landed a contract with a London production. In 1912 she returned to Australia to pursue her acting career, only to head back to England and then in 1913 to tour with a production in Canada. In 1914 she tried the New York stage and toured the southern United States. In 1916 she returned to London, where she became a VAD nurse for the rest of the war, and launched her career as a novelist with *Kangaroos in King's Land*, a fictionalized account of her experiences in the metropole. Finally in 1920 Marlowe returned permanently to Sydney, where her long and prominent career included no further acting but journalism, other novels and radio broadcasting.

Marlowe's story exemplifies the pull of the northern hemisphere for an ambitious Australian actress in the late nineteenth and early twentieth centuries. It also speaks to the diversity of that pull: New York was indubitably a magnet, and Australian actresses and singers also worked the imperial entertainment circuit that took them to Canada, India, South Africa and elsewhere. But it was London, above all, which represented the locus of possibility and success. Like others before and after her, Marlowe was drawn specifically to London by her desires for a career, travel and excitement. Her reaction to London, recorded in her autobiography, was thus: "Inscrutable London! Indifferent London! Adorable London!...I hated it. I loved it. I worship the memory of it".[21] Working on the London stage represented the acme of colonial theatrical achievement, in part because it was such an elusive quest. Marlowe's search for work included one incident when an American producer was hiring actors at Drury Lane: "Hundreds waited for him three mornings in succession. So did I. On the third morning he saw me as he was going out to lunch. 'The type I wanted. You would have suited me exactly. Sorry, but I've just this moment engaged a girl for the part. Sorry, girlie'".[22]

Theatrical touring in England, according to Marlowe, was even more of an education about grim social realities than in Australia:

In England it was "diggings", and they were mainly situated in the slums. On tour nobody knew us. Nobody wanted to. We were merely the troupe that had come into town.... As I moved from town to town, the lives of these people were woven into a pattern such as I could never find in any other way. Their homes, their aspirations, their desperate predicaments were open for me to investigate. I lived now among the people who struggled for a bare existence in factories and breweries and little shops; in coal pits and mills, in shipyards.... I was part of their daily life and I was – God be thanked – their rent.[23]

While aware of English class differences, like other Australians in London, Marlowe was acutely aware of her vexed status as a colonial. Touring Stratford-on-Avon with her upper-class English cousins, Marlowe couldn't resist the opportunity of an empty theatre to try her own voice by projecting a line from Shakespeare. Her female cousin "looked at [her] with an expression which conveyed 'These incorrigible Australians!'"[24] More significantly, her first real break came when a theatre impresario, during an employment-seeking interview, goaded her:

I spent my days in theatrical agents' offices chasing the elusive job. It was a brutal business. Eventually I was sent to the Strand Theatre to be looked over by Stanley Cook. The little man was running a farce there and sending a couple of companies on tour in the autumn. He called me a "colonial". That enraged me. We had a heated argument and I was too busy being annoyed to realize he had started the argument to see if I would light up well. That terrible shyness was always a wall between me and managers, but Cook had broken through.[25]

Her impassioned response to the demeaning epithet "colonial" was so animated that he became convinced of her talent and gave her a six-month contract.

Australians' reactions to English condescension toward them as colonials were one constituent of white colonial identity. This factor of life for Australian women in London changed over the course of the twentieth century but perhaps only subtly. Certainly, complaints by Australian women about being treated as colonials recurred across the twentieth century; even before 1900 it was a theme in the accounts of visitors and longer-term residents. Australians have resisted and resented their categorization as colonials, and refuted particular insults they have perceived to be levelled at them. Both the insults and the resentment, it seems, have been a continuing thread. Australians' resistance to the term "colonials" has perhaps been connected to an unwillingness to acknowledge or examine their own complicity in colonialism within Australia.

Rose Quong

Susan A. Glenn has argued that the burgeoning theatrical world of the late nineteenth century provided an important cultural breeding ground for feminism. By the end of the century, she suggests, theatre supported significant numbers of independent women, who earned salaries robust enough to maintain themselves. While this may not have been true for all the women in the chorus lines, it was the case for successful leading actresses. Material independence enabled social and sexual freedoms. Further, Glenn suggests that the roles provided by the dramatization of anxieties surrounding feminism and New Women lent actresses cultural authority to be transgressive. Both in their theatrical roles and in their own lives, successful actresses created themselves as spectacles, and thus enacted new modern definitions of femininity that lent weight to feminism.[26] Actresses adapted available roles, Glenn argues, even taking roles that emerged from misogynist strands in contemporary culture, and using them as vehicles for their own trademark performances.

Orientalism was a pervasive strand of both high and popular culture at the *fin de siècle* and in the early twentieth century. Susan Glenn and Judith Walkowitz have both studied the theatrical rage for Salome in this period, and its meanings in terms of gender, race and the exotic. Glenn traces the figure of Salome in American popular entertainment forms, arguing that it lost at least some of the misogynist and anti-Semitic overtones it had inherited from the 1892 Oscar Wilde play, and became a staple of vaudeville that intertwined issues of female sexuality and Orientalism.[27] Walkowitz has studied the popularization of Salome by North American music-hall dancer Maud Allan in London from 1908 to 1918, analyzing its contemporary meanings in terms of eroticism and the exotic, cosmopolitanism, gender transgression and reactions to feminism.[28] The enormous popularity of representations of Salome were part of the *fin de siècle* and early-twentieth century fascination with Orientalism, a fascination that would continue in the interwar period and to which Australian actress and lecturer Rose Quong catered in her development of professional Chineseness. As a colonial actress trading upon a racially-mixed identity, Quong followed in the metropolitan footsteps of Pauline Johnson, the Mohawk and English writer and actress who performed in London at the turn of the twentieth century.[29]

Quong, an Australian actor, lecturer and writer, was born and brought up in Melbourne but left in 1924, at the age of 44, with an ambition to make it on the London stage. Rose Maude Quong or Rose Lanu Quong (as she variously gave her full name) was born in East Melbourne in August 1879, the first of four children born to Chun Quong and Annie Moy Quong. Quong's career, which would span Britain, the United States and even China itself, was the result of her marketing of her mixed cultural heritage. She became a skilled purveyor of cultural mixing and cultural difference, casting herself as an essentially qualified interpreter of Chinese culture to the Western world. When Quong arrived in London, she brought with her a successful reputation from repertory theatre in Melbourne, as an actress well versed in Shakespeare and the theatrical canon of the day. Shakespeare was her lifelong first love as a poet and playwright, but her desire to perform on the metropolitan stage as a Shakespearean actress ran up against racial stereotyping. Partly from her own choice and interest, and partly through the repeated suggestions and encouragement of Australian and English friends, Quong carved out instead a niche for herself as a lecturer on Chinese culture and philosophy, an "Oriental" actress and a reciter of Chinese poetry. Her successes – such as acting alongside Laurence Olivier, reciting on BBC radio, appearing on a BBC television programme as early as 1935, publishing two books with a major American publisher, and being cast as herself in a 1971 film – testify to her talent, hard work, energy and determination. But her professional achievements need to be juxtaposed with Quong's separation from her home and family, the marginality of her material standard of living, and the cultural stereotyping that precluded a career in Shakespeare and pushed her instead towards her own careful appropriation of Orientalism.

Quong's explanation of her decision to leave for London might have been given by any number of ambitious Australians, and reveals an archetypal British colonial sensibility, and conception of London, its attractions and possibilities. "I was crazy on Shakespeare and Dickens. I wanted to go to London. I wanted to meet Ellen Terry and Melba. I needed a new experience, change".[30] There is no hint in this capsule explanation for her major life decision to leave the country of her birth, to which she would never return, of any frustration with anti-Chinese discrimination in Australia, or of her desire to develop her own Chineseness. Rather, this articulation suggests a desire to claim and develop her Britishness. Not only were Quong's articulated reasons for going to London typical of the thousands of Australian women making the pilgrimage "home" in this period, her life in London was similar in many ways to those of her British-descended compatriots there.[31]

In fact, compared to some other Australian women in London around the same time, she was better integrated into the Australian community. In her first years there she lived in boarding houses in Earl's Court, mixed often with Australian friends (some of whom she had known in Australia but some not), attended Australian social and community functions, and engaged in all the usual activities of the colonial tourist. Her busy social life revolved around her Australian friends, particularly close women friends with whom she spent much time, some of whom lived either in the same boarding house or another close by. Some diary entries suggest the explicit sharing of an Australian identity. She was invited repeatedly to gatherings of Australian artists at the home of the very successful concert singer Ada Crossley. On at least one such occasion the men in the group sang, then Rose performed scenes from "Macbeth". And she attended significant Australian community events such as an Australia Day church service, followed by a concert by Australian musicians and singers.[32]

Despite determined perseverance at contacting theatre directors, critics and agents, and some initial successes, it became clear that she was not going to make it as a Shakespearean or general actress. Her friends and advisers urged her towards a specialized niche career, that of exotic or Oriental reciter, actress and performer. And at the same time, her own genuine interest in Chinese culture and philosophy, and her desire to develop that dimension of her identity led her towards professional Chineseness. In December 1924 and January 1925 she received a sudden flurry of press interest, facilitated by an acting teacher with whom she studied, and was interviewed by *The Daily Express*, *The Daily Graphic*, *The Glasgow Morning Post*, *The Sketch* and *The British Australian and New Zealander*. In the midst of all this and her auditions, she had publicity photos taken by a professional photographer, for some of which she chose to wear a "Chinese gown". Her quest for the right Chinese outfit to perform in was protracted, partly because some she found did not seem appropriate, and having one made was expensive. In her first years in London she often borrowed items of clothing and props that she thought would produce the right background; her descriptions of these clothes and props sometimes read like a pastiche of "Oriental" objects.[33]

Arguably Quong's greatest success came in March and April 1929 when she starred with Laurence Olivier and the well-known Chinese-American actress Anna May Wong in "The Circle of Chalk", a play by the German dramatist Klabund, based on Chinese legend, first translated into English in 1929, and which would later be adapted by Bertolt Brecht. The 1929 production at the New Theatre, which consisted of 48 performances, was probably the pinnacle of her career. The play certainly helped establish her name in London, and her favourable reviews were celebrated in Australia. The Sydney-based magazine *The Home* reported that her "striking success" was "acclaimed alike by critics and public". Moreover, the magazine asserted, Quong had outshone Anna May Wong; she had "scoop[ed] most of the praise from the critics" and indeed "is credited with having popularized the Chinese literary cult in London". The "Melbourne Repertory Society", the review concluded, "may well be proud of the [most?] famous member it has so far produced".[34]

Quong carefully eschewed the erotic, but in focusing instead on the exotic and Oriental, she also built a career based on her own body. In Quong's case, her body was the signifier of her Chinese authenticity, the essentialist foundation for her carefully constructed performative, diasporic Chinese identity. Quong's modernity centred on her use of ethnicity, but also her claims to cultural and intellectual authority (through lecturing on Chinese culture and translating Chinese literature), a kind of authority not previously much available to women. Quong presents a complicated instance of the gendered politics of Orientalism. Orientalist representations have typically feminized Asians; Asian women especially have been seen as exotic, sensual and submissive.[35] Quong cast herself as exotic but not erotic, and in asserting her status as an intellectual cultural authority, in fact presented quite an androgynous figure.[36]

Conclusion

Tony Ballantyne and Antoinette Burton have suggested that a focus on the body is "a way to dramatize how, why, and under what conditions women and gender can be made visible in world history" because although women have been less visible as historical actors, their bodies "have been a subject of concern, scrutiny, anxiety, and surveillance in a variety of times and places across the world".[37] In this chapter, I have placed women's lives and bodies at the centre of imperial networks, especially connections between Australia and Britain. Mary Marlowe and Rose Quong were part of the sizeable phenomenon of Australian actresses and singers drawn by structures of colonialism to the metropolitan northern hemisphere, and the London stage in particular. Most of the thousands of Australian actresses, singers and musicians drawn to London in the last decades of the nineteenth and first decades of the twentieth centuries failed to achieve lasting fame, and have been historically invisible. Reconstructing this phenomenon allows us to recognize the period's vast musical and theatrical industries, the structural role of colonialism, and the gendered dynamics in which women sought careers, success, travel and adventure, even as they negotiated issues of respectability. With the privileges they claimed as "white" people (in many of which Quong shared due to reasons of class) freshly reinforced in their consciousness from the imperial racial structures they observed on their voyages to England, and their status as colonials reinforced on arrival, Australian women's theatrical and musical careers were shaped by such self-conceptions. Whether they embraced their colonialness and Australianness, or sought to elide it by, for example, voice training to lose their accents, or both, it was an issue which all had to confront. This episode of women's cultural work reveals the economic significance of the imperial entertainment industry, and the ways in which factors of gender, race and colonialism shaped Australian women's self-conceptions as colonials.

Yet ethnicity complicated the category of "white colonial" through the mixing of ethnic identities. Rose Quong's merging of Chinese, Australian and British identities seems complex in retrospect, but it was a juggling act facilitated by the very prominence of ethnic stereotypes in the high modern period of the late nineteenth and early twentieth centuries, not least in popular culture. Mass entertainment forms, such as music hall and vaudeville, relied on ethnic stereotypes for much of their production, and humour of the period was often openly racist. Cultural forms were labelled in racist ways. The journalist who conducted the "industrial survey" of chorus girls in Australia in 1908 commented that some had to sing in accompaniment to "a colored comedian's 'barbaric yawp'" and that they were made to learn "a continually-increasing repertory of coon ditties, and such degenerate music".[38] If racist stereotypes pervaded both high and popular culture in the period, so too did notions of ethnic blurring. Renee Sentilles has suggested that what we now recognize as celebrity status emerged in America in the middle decades of the nineteenth century as a product of the penny press, and has grown in cultural significance ever since. Celebrities, Sentilles argues, were created through performance, and as such were able to mix and shift their identities including in racial or ethnic terms. Her own study of the Civil War era actress Adah Isaacs Menken traces the ways in which Menken variously cast herself as white, Jewish and African American, and thus is a remarkable mirror of American culture of the 1850s–60s.[39] As Joanna de Groot has recently observed, in the British context, by the late nineteenth century the racial stereotyping that pervaded popular songs and pantomime performances was directly linked to the widespread use of racist images in advertising and visual culture. Together they constituted a set of images which not only reduced and demeaned colonized people, but "played a role in shaping British perceptions of their 'imperial' selves" at home in the metropole.[40]

A few of the Australian women in London in the earlier part of the century were of continental European descent, although usually they did not emphasize this. More recently, in 2001 a Maltese-Australian woman Simone Ancilleri posted a submission on the Australian website "WogLife". Ancilleri's submission was headed "A wog in London", and in it she complains of the difficulties she experienced there as a hybrid or hyphenated Australian. Growing up in Western Sydney, she says, she was "just a wog" and her Australian friends accepted the fact she looked Maltese but had a broad Australian accent, and she had friends "from all different backgrounds". When she went to London she had hoped that she would meet "people of all different nationalities with perhaps an Aussie here or there and not the other way around". Instead she found that her "backpacker's house" was "little Australia", and that her housemates introduced her to their friends thus: "This is Simone and she is from Malta". Her indignant reaction was: "What! I was born in Australia and lived there for 23 years of my life [so] I felt that I deserved to be called an 'Australian'". For Ancilleri, while going to London on a working holiday for a couple of years was "the ultimate Australian cliché", her time there only confused her in terms of ethnic and national identities. She complained: "I can't go to the Australian pub and drink VB or XXXX and holler 'Aussie, Aussie, Aussie, Oi, Oi, Oi!' without feeling like a complete fool".[41] Thus while Australian women in London were not wholly of British descent even early in the century, the question of ethnicity versus Australianness is perhaps now more open for discussion.

Australian women arriving in London at very different moments in the twentieth century reacted in strikingly similar ways, evoking at once the familiarity and the imperial nostalgia of metropolitan arrival. In 1901, Australian journalist and novelist Louise Mack reacted this way: "Oh London, London! how did I ever live without you? .... I no longer say to myself, '*You're in London.*' I accept it at last, and surrender to the spell of the City of Mists".[42] Actress Ruth Cracknell's first reactions on her arrival in 1953 were only a little less romantic: "Arriving in London it was as if every reference point was familiar. A monopoly board come to life, all the reading of the preceding twenty or so years making virtually every street and square and garden familiar, but so much more vivid now that one was a part".[43] Romance and fantasy also colour the description, in a recent memoir by television comedian Noeline Brown, of her arrival in March 1965: "As soon as I recovered from my shocking jetlag I started exploring the city. I walked everywhere and loved every minute of it. I was actually Overseas. The little girl who used to hang around the docks and dream about travel was actually doing it".[44]

But some things did change, most importantly from 1962 onwards the rights of Australians to stay and work in the UK. At the turn of the twentieth century a sojourn in London represented "going home". By the early twenty-first century only some of that imperial attachment remains, due to the attenuation of legal ties and cultural identification between metropole and colony. There are other noteworthy factors of change. One important one has to do with "race" or ethnicity, the ways in which constructed racial categories and subordination had very real effects on women's (and men's) lives and ability to travel. For the late nineteenth and early twentieth century, there is no evidence of any Indigenous Australian woman in England. This absence of Aboriginal women is in contrast both to the small number of Aboriginal men who went to England in that period, and also to the small number of Canadian Aboriginal or First Nations women who travelled to England in the same years.[45] In the latter part of the twentieth century, significantly, a few Aboriginal women made the trip – something that was more possible after legislative restrictions on Aboriginal mobility were removed under the Whitlam Government. But before that government came to power, earlier in 1972, Aboriginal activist and writer Roberta Sykes travelled to England at the invitation of a group of Australian expatriates who wanted to draw attention to Aborigines' subordination.[46] In recent years, there has been more of an Aboriginal presence in London. Notable events have included the November 2002 visit by Doris Pilkington Garimara, author of the book *Follow the Rabbit Proof Fence* on which the film was based. And in 2005 the first "Sorry Day" event to be held outside Australia occurred at Lincoln's Inn Fields on 25th May.

Making visible the presence of colonial women in the metropole – even or especially women from one of the white settler dominions – highlights the thorough imbrication of the empire "at home". The female body has been central to modernity, through the sexualization and objectification of women, and the ubiquity of women as spectacle in advertising, theatre, film and television. For colonial women, the growth of theatre as an empire-wide industry opened up travel opportunities and access to the metropole, in jobs that were hard to get, short-term and often poorly paid but which many women saw as a better option than their other limited choices. Putting the spotlight on actresses shows the extent to which colonials pervaded the metropolitan labour force and, at the same time, how issues of political economy, culture and imperialism cannot be disentangled.

Notes

1 Sonya O. Rose, *Limited Livelihoods: Gender and Class in Nineteenth-Century England* (Berkeley, 1992).
2 Sonya O. Rose, *Which People's War? National Identity and Citizenship in Wartime Britain, 1939–1945* (Oxford, 2003), Ch. 3 "'Good-Time' Girls and Quintessential Aliens".
3 Rose, *Which People's War?*, Ch. 7 "'The End is Bound to Come': Race, Empire, and Nation". Sonya Rose's work on the empire as part of British history also includes the book she co-edited with Catherine Hall, *At Home with the Empire: Metropolitan Culture and the Imperial World* (Cambridge, 2006).
4 David Lambert and Alan Lester (eds), *Colonial Lives Across the British Empire: Imperial Careering in the Long Nineteenth Century* (Cambridge, 2006).
5 Stephen Alomes, *When London Calls: The Expatriation of Australian Creative Artists to Britain* (Cambridge, 1999).
6 *The British Australasian*, 20 January 1898, 157, and 21 April 1898, 847.
7 Veronica Kelly, "An Australian Idol of Modernist Consumerism: Minnie Tittell Brune and the Gallery Girls", *Theatre Research International* 31, no. 1 (2006), 19.
8 Beatrix Tracy, "Explorations in Industry: The Chorus Girl", *The Lone Hand* 3 (1 May 1908), 12–13.
9 Egbert T. Russell, "The Ladies of the Chorus", *The Lone Hand* 5 (1 July 1909), 284.
10 Russell, "The Ladies of the Chorus", 284; and Florence Young, "The Australian Chorus-Girl", *The Lone Hand* 3 (1 June 1908), 143.
11 Young, "The Australian Chorus-Girl", 145.
12 Russell, "The Ladies of the Chorus", 283.

13   Jean Rhys, *Voyage in the Dark* (New York, 1982), 8.
14   Rhys, *Voyage in the Dark*, 17.
15   Veronica Kelly, "A Complementary Economy? National Markets and International Product in Early Australian Theatre Managements", *New Theatre Quarterly* 21, no. 1 (2005), esp. 78, 86 and 91.
16   *The British Australasian*, 26 May 1910, 19; 12 January 1922, 12; *The British Australian and New Zealander*, 15 October 1925, 14.
17   *The British Australasian*, 7 December 1922, 17.
18   *The British Australian and New Zealander*, 22 March 1928, 7.
19   *The British Australian and New Zealander*, 25 August 1932, 10.
20   Mary Marlowe, *That Fragile Hour: An Autobiography* (North Ryde, NSW, 1990), 26–51.
21   Marlowe, *That Fragile Hour*, 55.
22   Marlowe, *That Fragile Hour*, 80.
23   Marlowe, *That Fragile Hour*, 70–2.
24   Marlowe, *That Fragile Hour*, 59.
25   Marlowe, *That Fragile Hour*, 59.
26   Susan A. Glenn, *Female Spectacle: The Theatrical Roots of Modern Feminism* (Cambridge, MA, 2000), esp. Introduction.
27   Glenn, *Female Spectacle*, chap. 4 "The Americanization of Salome".
28   Judith R. Walkowitz, "The 'Vision of Salome': Cosmopolitanism and Erotic Dancing in Central London, 1908–1918", *American Historical Review* 108, no. 2 (2003), 337–76.
29   Cecilia Morgan, "'A Wigwam to Westminster': Performing Mohawk Identity in Imperial Britain, 1890s–1900s", *Gender & History* 25, no. 2 (2003), esp. 320–4.
30   Kim Rosston, "From Australia to the West Side: The 93-Year Journey of Actress Rose Quong", *Manhattan Tribune*, 13 May 1972, 9.
31   On this topic, and for details of Australian women's lives in London in this period, see Angela Woollacott, *To Try Her Fortune in London: Australian Women, Colonialism, and Modernity* (New York, 2001).
32   Diary entry for 26 January 1925, Rose Quong Papers, Mss 132, Series II, Box I, Folder 7, Historical Society of Pennsylvania.
33   Diary entry for 27 October 1925, Journal 1924–1925, Rose Quong Papers.
34   "Melbourne Musings", *The Home*, June 1929, 13.
35   On this see, for example, Karen Shimakawa, *National Abjection: The Asian American Body Onstage* (Durham, 2002); Mari Yoshihara, *Embracing the East: White Women and American Orientalism* (New York, 2003); and Karen J. Leong, *The China Mystique: Pearl S. Buck, Anna May Wong, Mayling Soong, and the Transformation of American Orientalism* (Berkeley, 2005).
36   For further detail, see Angela Woollacott, "Rose Quong Becomes Chinese: An Australian in London and New York", *Australian Historical Studies* no. 129 (2007): 16–31.
37   Tony Ballantyne and Antoinette Burton (eds), *Bodies in Contact: Rethinking Colonial Encounters in World History* (Durham, NC, 2005).
38   Tracy, "Explorations in Industry", 14.
39   Renee M. Sentilles, *Performing Menken: Adah Isaacs Menken and the Birth of American Celebrity* (Cambridge, 2003).
40   Joanna de Groot, "Metropolitan Desires and Colonial Connections: Reflections on Consumption and Empire", in *At Home with the Empire*, 189.

41 Simone Ancilleri, "A wog in London", posted 17/4/2001 on the 'Wog Life' website http://www.wog.com.au
42 Louise Mack, *An Australian Girl in London* (London, 1902).
43 Ruth Cracknell, *Ruth Cracknell: A Biased Memoir* (Ringwood, Vic., 1997), 88.
44 Noeline Brown, *Noeline: Longterm Memoir* (Crows Nest, NSW, 2005), 97.
45 See for example, Cecilia Morgan, "Performing for 'Imperial Eyes': Bernice Loft and Ethel Brant Monture, Ontario, 1930s–1960s", in *Contact Zones: Aboriginal and Settler Women in Canada's Colonial Past*, eds. Myra Rutherdale and Katharine Pickles (Vancouver, 2005), and "A Wigwam to Westminster".
46 Roberta B. Sykes, *Black Majority* (Hawthorn, 1989), 157–9.

Part II

Gender, Identity and the Second World War

6
British Feminism in the Second World War

Harold L. Smith

The Second World War introduced destabilizing forces that threatened to undermine gender and class hierarchies. Although the British home front used to be viewed as an example of total war generating social unity, historians now are more aware of the ways in which the war heightened gender and class tensions as the equal citizenship rhetoric aroused expectations inconsistent with gender and class structures.[1] As a result, recent studies have focused on explaining how the wartime pressures for change were contained or diverted into less threatening channels.[2]

One of the war's striking consequences was the revival of the British feminist movement. Feminists remembered the First World War as having enabled women to gain political equality, and when the Second World War began anticipated that women's contributions to the war effort would bring comparable gains, such as economic equality.[3] This expectation was based on the assumption that womanpower would be essential to the war effort, and that the government would recognize this.

Despite women workers' crucial contributions in the First World War, however, the government originally planned to make minimal use of womanpower in the Second World War, and then only in traditional roles. It established the Women's Voluntary Service (WVS) in 1938 to recruit female volunteers to assist in the war effort in ways that reinforced traditional gender roles: to evacuate children from the cities, feed people bombed out of their homes, and establish creches and nurseries. By 1942 over one million women – most middle or upper-class working part-time – were contributing to the war effort as unpaid WVS volunteers.[4]

Feminist groups protested when they became aware that the government's war plans largely ignored women, except as unpaid volunteers.

In January 1939 the Women's Freedom League (WFL) urged the government to make maximum use of the nation's womanpower, and to do so on a gender equality basis: equal opportunities, equal pay and the removal of the marriage bar.[5] During 1939 Ray Strachey, the Women's Employment Federation's (WEF) director, established an Emergency Register at the WEF of professional women with specialist qualifications who could be useful in the war effort.[6] Since the Ministry of Labour was preparing a National Register of persons available for war work, she offered them her Women's Emergency Register, and was furious when they did not accept it. As the ministry's disinterest in educated women workers became evident, women's groups concerned with equal employment opportunities, such as the British Federation of Business and Professional Women (BFBPW), began meeting with the women M.P.s to insist that the government's war policies treat women fairly.[7] When the ministry continued to rebuff their efforts, Strachey organized a deputation of women M.P.s and the leaders of key women's organizations concerned with womanpower. She met with the women M.P.s to secure agreement on the points the deputation would make, drafted their speeches, and collected evidence for the brief that they presented at the meeting.[8]

Lady Astor, Conservative M.P., led the deputation of all the backbench women M.P.s and the leaders of several women's organizations, including Strachey, that met with the Financial Secretary to the Treasury in February 1940.[9] They urged that greater use be made of women's talents, especially those "with professional or other qualifications" in the war effort. They noted that only twenty-one women from a sample group of two hundred with high professional or technical qualifications who had listed their names with the Ministry of Labour's central register were employed in positions appropriate for their level of training and which had direct relevance to the war effort. The deputation expressed serious concern at the tendency of both government departments and private employers to employ women only on junior or routine work, while avoiding appointing women to positions of responsibility. It concluded by urging the government to plan for the maximum use of womanpower, to pledge that women would be "equally represented" on bodies responsible for such planning, and to appoint one or more women to government positions with policymaking responsibility for womanpower.[10]

Although Strachey's briefing of its editor resulted in a favorable *Times* leader the following day, she was "profoundly discouraged" by the government's response to the deputation.[11] Government officials showed no interest in employing educated women except for a few female doctors who were allowed into the RAF, apparently as a result of the February deputation.[12] Six days later the Minister of Labour, Ernest Brown, informed the cabinet that there was "no great demand for women in engineering, except in occupations in which they were ordinarily employed".[13] BFBPW leaders and the women M.P.s continued to press the issue, however, and in April a deputation to the Ministry of Supply secured an agreement that graduates of the Women's Engineering Society's training program would be employed as Woolwich Arsenal supervisors and paid the standard rate for that work.[14]

The Woman Power Committee

The Coalition Government's formation in May facilitated the transformation of this informal women's group in June 1940 into what became one of the most important wartime women's organizations: the Woman Power Committee (WPC). Strachey had urged the women M.P.s to continue meeting following the February deputation, and the relaxation of party discipline under the Coalition Government for the first time enabled them to organize as a continuing cross-party women's pressure group.[15] Chaired by Irene Ward, Conservative M.P., the WPC's original members also included several prominent feminists, including Strachey and Caroline Haslett.[16] It eventually included twenty-one members: ten M.P.s, three trade union women, and eight representatives from key women's organizations such as the BFBPW.

The WPC's efforts to secure Labour Party and Trades Union Congress (TUC) women representatives suggests that class and party feeling remained stronger than gender identity. The Standing Joint Committee of Working Women's Organizations[17] (SJCWWO) was invited to have a representative on the WPC, but declined after Jennie Adamson and Ellen Wilkinson, both Labour M.P.s who had refused to join the WPC, warned them against it.[18] The TUC refused to allow its female leaders to join the WPC until the latter abandoned its claim to represent all women workers. After the WPC announced that it only spoke for non-industrial workers, three TUC women joined the WPC.

The immediate issue dividing the feminists from Labour and trade union women was whether upper-class women would be given preference in positions supervising women factory workers. Wilkinson informed Ernest Bevin, the new Minister of Labour, that she and other Labour women had initially supported the BFBPW's efforts to obtain increased employment opportunities for women, but had changed their position when it began to press for the introduction of educated women into factories as forewomen since this eliminated the only means by which women factory workers could obtain promotion. Wilkinson stressed that she had no objection to the WPC representing professional women's interests, but considered it a "most undesirable precedent" if a group of women M.P.s, most of them Conservatives, "are allowed to interfere, even if it is only in the sense of giving advice, into the conditions of the women in factories".[19]

The WPC wanted Bevin to appoint it to be the Ministry of Labour's womanpower advisory committee, but Wilkinson's warning reinforced his reluctance to do this. Within the Ministry of Labour the WPC was perceived not only as a feminist group, but one that was originally dominated by Ward, a Conservative, which was a further reason why ministry officials wanted to keep their distance from it.[20] After rejecting several of the WPC's proposals – including its scheme to have Women's Engineering Society trainees employed as forewomen in factories – Bevin established a new Women's Consultative Committee instead of authorizing the WPC to fill this role. Although the WPC had two representatives on the new committee, its formation denied the WPC the main function it wanted to perform. Even so, press reports of the WPC's claims to speak for working women had alarmed trade unionists, and created a backlash against it. Union leaders expressed concern to Ministry of Labour officials at the growing influence on the ministry of groups representing the "feminist movement" that resented the trade unions serving as negotiating bodies for women.[21]

The government's 1941 proposal to conscript women provided an opportunity to claim that equal service to the nation should entitle women to equal rewards, but it also threatened fundamental class and gender distinctions. Opponents warned that it would undermine one of the fundamental markers of gender difference while allowing the government to coerce women into working under unfair conditions, including gendered pay. The National Union of Women Teachers claimed that a government commitment to equal pay and equal compensation should be a precondition for accepting women's conscription, but representatives from the leading women's organizations overwhelmingly voted down a similar resolution at a November 1941 conference on the conscription of women.[22]

The WPC reflected women's differences on the issue. Agnes Hardie, Labour M.P., used the gender difference argument that motherhood, rather than war, was women's business in opposing conscription as a matter of principle. Despite her opposition, the majority of the WPC initially supported conscription provided there were guarantees that conscripted women would be treated fairly – i.e. given equal pay, etc. Ward (the WPC's chair), however, argued that the need for conscription had not been proven. Other members noted that some upper-class women were quite distressed about the issue. Eleanor Plumer, Principal of St. Anne's College, Oxford, claimed that young women in university towns were "very agitated" at the possibility of being conscripted.[23] Eleanor Rathbone, one of the strongest proponents of conscripting women, did so partly to prevent upper-class women from being able to avoid national service. She had been informed that well-to-do parents were applying for their daughters' admission to Oxford colleges in greater numbers than before the war, and it was believed that this was being done in order to enable their daughters to avoid national service.[24] Rathbone proposed a resolution that the WPC did not oppose conscription in principle provided that there were safeguards, but the majority voted against it, with Ward casting the decisive vote.[25] Although most of the women M.P.s continued to insist that if women were required to participate equally in the war effort they were entitled to equal treatment (including equal pay), when the National Service (No. 2) Act was passed in December 1941 it did not provide equal pay for the conscripted women.

The Equal Compensation Campaign

During the Second World War the number of British civilians killed by enemy action exceeded that in the armed forces until D-day in 1944. The female proportion of civilian casualties was unusually high: women comprised 48 per cent of the British civilians killed or seriously injured.[26] Given this high female casualty rate, it is not surprising that women's groups were especially outraged by the government's gendered compensation scheme.

Anticipating heavy civilian casualties, in September 1939 the government passed the Personal Injuries (Emergency Provisions) Act providing compensation to workers for war injuries. Although the existing Workman's Compensation law was not sex differentiated, the Personal Injuries Act was. It established gendered compensation rates for employed men and women (women received two-thirds the men's rate), and provided no compensation for non-gainfully employed women (housewives). The BFBPW and the London and National Society for Women's Service (LNSWS) immediately organized protests by women's groups. Led by Jennie Adamson, the women M.P.s demanded that the scheme be revised, and in December 1940 they secured the inclusion of non-gainfully employed persons, but the compensation rates for all categories remained sex differentiated. In January 1941 over forty women's organizations organized a deputation to the Minister of Pensions, Lord Womersley, seeking equal compensation rates. The Lord President's Committee reviewed the government's policy in March and admitted that there was a strong case for equal compensation. The Committee did not change the policy, however, because it considered the women's campaign part of an effort to eliminate sex differentiation in the social services and employment and feared that a concession would encourage equal pay advocates.[27]

Although almost all women's organizations supported equal compensation, the question of who was in charge of the campaign created a split between feminist groups that continued throughout the war. The BFBPW took the initiative in bringing women's groups together to demand reform.[28] When it became clear that continuing pressure would be required in order to change the government's policy, several feminist groups, including the BFBPW, created an Ad Hoc Committee to direct the campaign. Although it was chaired by Rebecca Sieff (the Women's Publicity Planning Association's Chairman) and Dorothy E. Evans, the WPPA's organizer, served as the Committee's organizer, the Committee represented a coalition of women's organizations.[29] These other groups were thus very distressed to discover the WPPA leaders publicly giving the WPPA credit for several mass meetings that the Ad Hoc Committee sponsored during 1941.[30]

The BFBPW and the WPC responded by establishing a new organization, the Equal Compensation Campaign Committee (ECCC), in October 1941 to replace the Ad Hoc Committee.[31] Since this was done in order to remove the WPPA's leaders from control, the ECCC members were not pleased when Sieff made public statements implying that she was the ECCC's chair. They proceeded to make Mavis Tate, Conservative M.P., the ECCC chair, and dismissed Dorothy Evans, who had expected to continue as the campaign's organizer.[32] When Sieff proposed the creation of a publicity committee (which the WPPA would assist), the ECCC rejected it. The WPPA Executive Committee was so angered by the way its leaders had been treated that it considered withdrawing from the ECCC, and Sieff did resign from it a few months later.[33]

The ECCC included representatives from the National Council of Women as well as from leading feminist groups such as the BFBPW, the WPC, and the WFL. Since its members were almost entirely middle and upper-class women drawn from the Conservative and Liberal parties, it invited the SJCWWO to appoint a representative. Although the SJCWWO also sought equal compensation, it declined and privately informed government officials that it did not wish to be associated with the ECCC.[34]

Using the slogan "Bombs Don't Discriminate", the ECCC organized mass protest meetings throughout the country, and obtained over 400,000 signatures on an equal compensation petition. The government's August 1942 decision to compel women to do fire-watching was a turning-point in the struggle since fire-watchers were more likely to be injured. Civil servants privately admitted that this was likely to make the government's gendered compensation policy a "storm-centre" since it would bring home more forcefully than anything else the inconsistency in imposing equal sacrifices on both sexes with unequal compensation.[35]

Although the TUC and both major political parties also endorsed equal compensation, Womersley attempted to block reform by insisting that the demand came mainly from "feminist interests" which lacked widespread support.[36] Bevin's warning that granting equal compensation would raise the equal pay issue, and that "industrial peace might be endangered for the rest of the war" if that happened, strengthened cabinet opposition.[37] But since two hundred M.P.s had signed an equal compensation petition due, in part, to Tate's effective lobbying, the cabinet realized that the government could be defeated if the House of Commons voted on the issue. It therefore established a Select Committee with terms of reference that forbade it from considering equal pay.

While the Select Committee was sitting, the conflict between the feminist groups threatened to sabotage the campaign. Shortly after Sieff resigned from the ECCC in April 1942, the WPPA and the Six Point Group (SPG) – both of which had ex-suffragettes among their leaders – announced that they were sponsoring a rally "to determine militant action".[38] This shocked the other feminist groups since they thought there was a real possibility that the Select Committee would report favorably unless antagonized. The WPC urged the WPPA and SPG to refrain from any public action until after the Select Committee reported.[39] The ECCC members voted unanimously to inform the WPPA that it "must very strongly deplore any suggestion of militant action ..."[40] Following these objections, the rally was postponed (and later cancelled), but the incident helps explain why other feminist groups distrusted the WPPA and the SPG so much that they refused to be associated with them for the rest of the war.

While this was occurring, the Select Committee recommended equal compensation, and in April 1943 the government accepted this policy. Securing equal compensation has rightly been viewed as one of the feminist movement's greatest victories during the Second World War.[41]

The Equal Citizenship Bill Campaign

From its beginning in 1921 the SPG included a number of Labour Party supporters – as well as several prominent ex-suffragettes – and in the following decades portrayed itself as the "Left Wing Feminist Group".[42] But the most important campaign that it initiated during the war brought it into conflict with trade union and Labour Party women, thus illustrating the difficulty equal rights feminists experienced with class-related issues.

During the 1941 debate over conscripting women, the SPG developed the idea of a comprehensive bill that would end all forms of sex discrimination: the Equal Citizenship (Blanket) Bill. Dorothy Evans, the SPG's executive committee's chair, wrote to the Prime Minister suggesting that if the government planned to eliminate gender distinctions in its "manpower" policies by conscripting women, then it should also eliminate sex differentiation in other areas, including pay scales and National Insurance benefits.[43] When Churchill did not reply, the SPG asked Evans to report on the parliamentary acts that provided the legal basis for existing types of sex discrimination. During her investigation she conceived the idea of a single bill – a "blanket" bill – that would make all forms of sex discrimination illegal.

Since the SPG was unable to undertake such a major project, Evans and Emmeline Pethick-Lawrence persuaded the WPPA to sponsor a nation-wide campaign.[44] Realizing that it was unlikely to become law if it was introduced as a private member's bill, the campaign was intended to generate such strong public support that the government would sponsor it. The campaign began in September 1943 with a mass meeting at Central Hall, Westminster, that was considered a great success since the audience, primarily young working women with limited means, contributed over £600 to the campaign.[45] It is significant, however, that the National Council for Equal Citizenship was the only feminist group not connected with the SPG that supported the campaign.[46]

The campaign soon encountered difficulties with both the Labour movement and with other feminist groups. Trade union and Labour Party women opposed the bill because it would eliminate the single-sex protective legislation that working-class women valued.[47] The TUC members on the WPC threatened to withdraw from the WPC if it endorsed the bill.[48] The non-union WPC members were also opposed to any association with the campaign because it was sponsored by the WPPA. Ward refused an invitation to speak at a rally for the bill, noting that the WPPA was "constantly" giving a misleading impression of its own importance and of its relationship with the women M.P.s.[49] Although the LNSWS was one of the leading equality feminist organizations, it refused even to participate in rallies for the bill, partly because it seemed impractical but also because the LNSWS did not trust the WPPA's leaders.[50] Due to the lack of support from other women's groups, the campaign was already faltering when Evans' sudden death in August 1944 effectively ended it.[51]

The campaign to elect more women M.P.s

Encouraged by Dr. Edith Summerskill, Labour M.P., the WPPA established a committee in January 1942 to increase the number of women elected to Parliament. By 1943 this had evolved into an independent organization, Women for Westminster (WFW), financed (as was the WPPA) mainly by Rebecca Sieff.[52] Although it had 44 branches with 3,800 members as of May 1945, several key women's groups did not welcome its efforts.[53]

The women's organizations of both major parties originally were interested in WFW, but by 1943 both had turned against it. With Summerskill's assistance, a Labour for Westminster Committee was established to work with the WFW. But after investigating the group, the SJCWWO concluded that it was harming both the Labour Party and the prospects of Labour women candidates, and recommended that party members be "required" to avoid associating with this committee and WFW.[54] Shortly afterwards the 1942 Labour Party women's conference rejected a resolution asking that special consideration be given to female parliamentary candidates after a delegate objected to considering a resolution that implied "feminism or [that] asked for special treatment for women".[55] When the issue was raised at the 1943 Labour women's conference, Barbara Ayrton Gould explained that Labour Party women didn't want "women as women" in Parliament; they "wanted Labour women".[56] The Conservative Party's Women's Advisory Committee refused to have any official connection with WFW, but at first permitted individual Conservatives to join and report back on its activities. By April 1943, however, it had concluded that WFW was a "left wing" organization, and local party officials were asked to dissuade Conservative women from joining.[57]

Partly because WFW was perceived as a "leftish" group, mainstream women's organizations such as the Women's Group for Public Welfare warned their members not to have anything to do with it.[58] When WFW was unable to produce any candidates in the 1945 general election, it went into decline and eventually merged with the National Women Citizens' Association.

The Beveridge Report and Family Allowances

One of the war's most important effects was to stimulate concern about the declining birth rate which led to numerous proposals intended to make motherhood more appealing. This was one of the factors that led to passage of the 1945 Family Allowances Act. It also shaped the assumptions underlying the Beveridge Report. In it Beveridge stated explicitly that his proposals were intended to make motherhood more attractive to women because mothers have "vital work to do in ensuring the adequate continuance of the British race ..."[59]

While the Beveridge Report offered women some improvements over the prewar system, feminists were extremely critical of it because it reinforced traditional gender roles. Mavis Tate claimed that no more "reactionary measure in regard to married women had ever been brought forward".[60] Following a large women's protest meeting in November 1943 against the Report's proposals for women, Elizabeth Abbott and Katherine Bompas drafted a feminist critique of the Report [*The Woman Citizen and Social Security* (London, 1943)], and the National Council of Women organized a deputation from leading women's organizations to the Minister for Reconstruction (Jowitt) to protest its treating married women as dependents.[61]

Although women's groups agreed that the Beveridge Report was unfair to women, they did not agree on what would be fair. Equal rights feminists insisted that fairness meant being treated as equals, but difference feminists believed that women had to be treated differently in order to become equal.[62] Equality feminists, for example, had opposed the 1940 Old Age and Widows' Pensions Act because it reinforced the sex differentiation principle in the government's insurance scheme by reducing women's pensionable age to sixty while keeping men at sixty-five.[63] The LNSWS agreed to join the deputation to Jowitt only if it was allowed to reiterate its objection to the sex-differentiated pensionable age even though it supported most of the deputation's critique of the Beveridge Report.[64] Government officials were not impressed with the women's case, but agreed not to tell them that they had already decided to revise Beveridge's proposals in a way that should appeal to the women, preferring to let the women think they were responsible for the changes.[65]

The family allowances campaign began as a New Feminist (difference feminist) proposal for state payments to the mother to lessen her financial dependence on her husband, but by 1939 it had become a scheme to alleviate family poverty.[66] Equality feminists did not support family allowances prior to 1939, and the issue continued to divide wartime feminist groups.[67] Eleanor Rathbone continued to be its most prominent advocate, but during the war it was taken up by male reformers for non-feminist reasons: the allowances were portrayed as an anti-inflation measure and as a pro-natalist reform that would help increase the birth rate. The 1945 Family Allowances Act is sometimes considered a feminist success, but Rathbone's biographer concludes that it was primarily a victory for reform-minded backbench M.P.s who did not view it as a feminist issue.[68]

Although feminist groups were divided by the reform itself, the government temporarily united them by proposing to pay the allowance to the father. This ignited a storm of gender conflict. At Rathbone's request, women's organizations rallied to demand that the allowance be paid to the mother as originally proposed.[69] Rathbone warned the government that it risked reviving the "sex antagonism" so prevalent during the suffrage struggle, and pledged that at the forthcoming general election every female voter would know how her M.P. voted on this issue.[70] Surprised by the hornet's nest they had stirred up, the cabinet eventually allowed parliament a free vote on the issue which resulted in the allowance being paid to the mother.

The equal pay campaign

Prewar jobs in industry were sex segregated, but an increasing number of positions in occupations like teaching and the civil service were not. Prior to 1939 feminist groups had campaigned for equal pay in these areas in which equal work was undeniably performed, and the increased wartime employment of women on men's jobs revived the issue.

Feminists had hoped that the government would use its September 1943 national women's conference to announce that equal pay would be granted, and were disappointed when it was not. Several feminist groups, including the WPC and the LNSWS-sponsored Joint Committee on Women in the Civil Service, concluded that an equal pay campaign would be necessary to force the government to introduce that reform. Although the Joint Committee had directed the 1930s campaign, Caroline Haslett asked Tate to bring the women's organizations that had been ECCC members together to create a coordinating committee to direct an equal pay campaign. Representatives from one hundred women's groups with a combined membership of some four million women met in January 1944 and agreed to initiate an equal pay campaign. Tate chaired the Equal Pay Campaign Committee (EPCC) that was established with the immediate goal of obtaining equal pay in the civil service "common classes" (those in which men and women were interchangeable).[71]

Although most feminist and Labour organizations supported equal pay, the EPCC's composition reflected the divisions between the groups urging that reform. The WPPA and the WFL were not invited to have a representative on the EPCC.[72] The SJCWWO declined an invitation to join the EPCC, and as a result almost all of its members were middle and upper-class women and predominantly Conservatives. The Civil Service Equal Pay Committee – drawn from the civil service unions – also declined an invitation to join, justifying its refusal on the ground that the EPCC was composed of "feminist organizations".[73]

The equal pay campaign had barely begun when Thelma Cazalet-Keir, a Conservative M.P. and a WPC member, proposed an equal pay amendment to the 1944 Education Bill. Despite the government's opposition, the amendment passed by a vote of 117 to 116; this was the only parliamentary defeat suffered by Churchill's wartime coalition government. The cabinet prevented the amendment from being incorporated into the bill by threatening to resign if the House of Commons did not reverse itself, but it realized that the issue had such strong parliamentary support that it would come up again.[74]

Shortly afterwards the government halted this promising equal pay campaign by announcing it was establishing a Royal Commission on Equal Pay. Feminists correctly considered this a "sinister" development designed to prevent reform.[75] The government's desire to block reform is indicated by the language used in the memoranda concerning the Commission's creation, and by the cabinet's decision that the Commission's terms of reference should not allow it to make recommendations, but should require it to consider the effect that equal pay would have on women's employment (opponents argued that equal pay would reduce women's employment levels; requiring the Commission to examine this was a means of making equal pay seem undesirable).[76] Recognizing the implications of the government's proposal, the WPC was unanimously opposed to the creation of the Royal Commission. Tate and Pippa [Philippa] Strachey persuaded the WPC to write to the

Chief Whip in the "strongest possible language" in an attempt to stop the government from proceeding with its plan, but the latter was not deterred and the Commission's lengthy investigation ended the possibility of wartime equal pay legislation.[77]

Child care and the marriage bar

When the war began the marriage bar and the lack of child care facilities were among the main obstacles to married women's employment. Local authorities provided only twenty-one day nurseries in 1938. Despite the experience of the First World War, the government originally did not envision the large-scale employment of women, especially married women, and thus during 1940 the number of day nurseries increased slowly. When the WPC expressed concern about the shortage of nurseries to a Ministry of Health official in July 1940, it discovered that the government had no plans for expansion.[78] When the registration of women for war work began, Bevin pledged that child care facilities would be provided for working mothers, but there was little progress until the SJCWWO and the trade union women, backed by the TUC, demanded that his promise be implemented.[79] Expansion proceeded rapidly, however, once the government accepted that the lack of child care facilities was hampering its efforts to bring more married women into war industries. By 1943 local authorities had established 1,450 nurseries with places for 65,000 children. During the war's final years women's organizations, including the National Council of Women, pressed the government not to view the nurseries as merely a wartime service, but as an "essential part of the postwar social services".[80]

While the number of state nurseries increased rapidly during the war, it is misleading to claim that the government's attitude towards day care services changed dramatically. The Ministry of Health, which was responsible for the nurseries, remained convinced that they were undesirable, and accepted them only as a wartime measure. Having women in high positions actually impeded reform on this issue. Both Mary Smieton in the Ministry of Labour and Zoe Puxley, Assistant Secretary in the Ministry of Health, believed that mothers should stay at home with their children, and therefore resisted nursery expansion.[81] Citing surveys indicating a significant increase in respiratory tract infection among children in the nurseries, the Medical Women's Federation provided the most sustained resistance to increasing the number of nurseries.[82] The Ministry of Health named them "nursery centres" to identify them as a temporary wartime expedient "to make it easier to get rid of them after the war", and most were closed when the war ended.[83]

Prior to 1939 feminist groups had attempted to eliminate the marriage bar that was in effect for most women in the public services and in some sectors of private industry. During the war the bar was suspended because of the labour shortages, but whether this would be permanent became an important reconstruction issue. Pressure from women's groups, including the WPC, contributed to the government's decision to accept an amendment to the 1944 Education Bill ending the marriage bar for teachers, although the expectation of a postwar teacher shortage and fears that the marriage bar was encouraging homoerotic feelings among women teachers were also factors.[84]

Encouraged by the removal of the marriage bar for teachers, the WPC initiated a campaign led by Cazalet-Keir to eliminate the bar in the civil service too. When Cazalet-Keir's proposal gained the support of nearly two hundred M.P.s, the WPC helped form an all-party deputation to John Anderson, Chancellor of the Exchequer.[85] Anderson agreed that there was a case for changing the government's policy, and formed a civil service committee to review the issue. But because the largest union represented on the committee, the Union of Post Office Workers, opposed ending the bar, the committee made no recommendation. When the Labour Government considered the issue in 1946, Hugh Dalton, Chancellor of the Exchequer, recommended that the bar be retained with some modification, but the rest of the cabinet overruled him because the bar seemed illogical given the government's efforts to alleviate the labour shortage by increasing the number of married women working.[86]

Postwar employment policy

The Coalition Government encouraged the signing of agreements to restore prewar trade practices in order to obtain the trade unions' agreement to dilution, and the 1942 Restoration of Prewar Practices Act gave these a legal basis. This meant that women employed on what had been considered men's work would be dismissed when the war ended, and the prewar sex segregation of jobs would be restored. Government officials understood that they were committed to restoring the man to "his old preferential position" and worried that this could become a "serious problem" if women workers did not consider it fair. Sir William Jowitt, the minister responsible for reconstruction planning, feared that women would not willingly give up their higher paying wartime jobs for the poorly paid women's work that they would be offered at the war's end, and that gender conflict would result.[87] By 1944, however, ministers were correctly anticipating that the main postwar labour problem would be a shortage of workers rather than a shortage of jobs. Feminists objected to the restoration of the prewar sex segregation of jobs with women employed in lower level positions, but their protests were ineffective.[88]

Birth control and abortion

The war brought about the virtual collapse of the promising family planning movement and delayed the development of state-provided birth control services for another twenty years. The Family Planning Association (FPA) went into a severe decline as its members volunteered for war work, and many clinics were closed. The two main efforts it made to advance the birth control issue during the war were only partially successful. The FPA urged the government to provide contraceptive advice to married women in the armed forces and offered to train the Army medical officers who would provide this advice. The head of the Auxiliary Territorial Service medical services considered this an "earthshaking" proposal, and the War Office shared that perception in rejecting it. Since the military had first claim on wartime rubber supplies, severe shortages for the manufacture of contraceptives soon developed. When the FPA pressed the government to make rubber available for this purpose, parliamentary birth control opponents tried to block the release of rubber for contraceptives by forcing a government spokesman to admit that it was not considered a matter of national importance. The Ministry of Health attempted to ignore the issue, but FPA leaders lobbied the other ministries involved and by the end of 1944 the latter had agreed to release enough rubber to supply doctors with contraceptives for their patients.[89]

Although the wartime proposals for a national health service created an opportunity to include family planning among the services provided, the birth control reformers did not press for this. Some appear to have been disheartened by wartime pronatalism. Lord Horder, the FPA's president, was ideologically opposed to the creation of a national health service, while other influential members preferred to promote voluntary birth control centres rather than the government controlled local authority clinics. Finally, the inclusion of birth control services seemed a hopeless cause to some, since neither of the leading political parties was eager to arouse Catholic opposition to the proposed health service by including contraception.[90]

Several of the socialist feminists active in the birth control campaign were also prominent in the 1930s abortion reform movement. Stella Browne, Janet Chance, Alice Jenkins and Frida Laski were among the early leaders of the Abortion Law Reform Association (ALRA) that played a prominent role in efforts to make abortion legal. Although Browne insisted that abortion was the "key to a new world for women" and should be a woman's right, most socialist feminists considered it politically shrewder to advocate it as a means of reducing maternal mortality (by making it unnecessary to resort to back-street abortions) and improving marriage.[91] Working closely with the Women's Co-operative Guild and the Labour Party Women's Sections, socialist feminists generated enough concern about the contribution of illegal abortions to the high rate of maternal mortality (especially among working-class women) that the government established an Inter-departmental Committee on Abortion in 1937. But the outbreak of the war and the pronatalist climate that it engendered effectively halted the growing public debate over abortion reform. With public opinion focused on ways of encouraging population growth, the ALRA suspended most of its work during the war. When it attempted to reopen the abortion law reform issue in 1944 by sending a letter to twenty-five newspapers and journals, none was willing to publish it.[92]

Conclusion

Although the Second World War provided new impetus for gender equality, this had largely dissipated by the war's end. Many prominent feminist leaders were Conservatives, but they were unable to convert their party to their views. At the 1945 Conservative Party conference the delegates rejected a resolution affirming that it was in the nation's best interests that "opportunities and rewards shall be open equally to both sexes...".[93] The 1945 Labour Party election manifesto focused on the welfare benefits that a Labour Government would provide women as wives and mothers, but did not mention equal pay even though it had previously endorsed that reform.

The war brought several important feminist groups into being, including the WPC and the WPPA, but neither survived the war's end. The 1945 general election nearly doubled the number of women M.P.s, but since the vast majority were Labour – and most of the WPC members lost their seats – the wartime experiment with a cross-party women's parliamentary organization ended. By October 1945 feminists were lamenting that "unhappily" the WPC had become a ghost.[94] When the war ended Rebecca Sieff withdrew from feminist activity, and without her financial support the WPPA became inactive. The Equal Pay Campaign Committee was one of the few wartime feminist initiatives that survived the war's end. It continued the equal pay campaign for public employees until the government conceded that reform in 1955.[95]

While the government's determination to prevent the war from bringing about fundamental changes in gender structures was clearly the decisive factor, the wartime feminist movement was handicapped by its inability – with rare exceptions such as compensation for war injuries and the payment of family allowances to the mother – to build the kind of broad-based women's movement that the National Union of Women's Suffrage Societies (NUWSS) had established by 1914. Part of this was due to the war itself: the LNSWS was surely not alone in finding its ability to participate in campaigns limited as a result of its headquarters being bombed, its members scattered by war work and its income sharply reduced.[96] But feminists also struggled against negative perceptions of feminism. Katherine Bompas, International Women's Alliance secretary, admitted in 1941 that feminism "sounded old fashioned, anti-man or something odd".[97]

The wartime feminist movement was weakened by the larger women's organizations' reluctance to associate themselves with feminism. Prior to the war the mainstream women's groups, such as the National Union of Townswomen's Guilds and the Women's Institutes, had established a clear boundary between their support for women's citizenship rights and feminism.[98] This concern to avoid links with feminist groups continued during the war years. The Townswomen's Guilds leaders repeatedly warned its members against associating with the feminist movement or feminist causes, while the Women's Group for Public Welfare had a "blacklist" of organizations – many of them feminist – that its members were warned to avoid.[99]

The wartime women's movement was also hampered by Labour women's reluctance to ally with feminists. The tension between the Labour Party and the women's movement dates back to 1915 when the NUWSS abruptly terminated its electoral alliance with the Labour Party, leaving a lasting residue of ill-will.[100] By the late 1930s Labour women considered feminism discredited, and were unwilling to join with feminists even when they supported the reform being advocated.[101] At a public meeting in 1941 Rebecca Sieff claimed that several of the women's political organizations were "contemptuous" of feminism.[102] Jennie Lee's wartime observation that informal discussions among feminists usually evolved into complaints about the servant problem illustrates how differences in class perspective divided Labour women from feminists.[103] It has been suggested that Labour women drew upon an "equal but different" ideology during the war in advocating both equal pay and reforms to improve motherhood, but only the latter were reflected in the postwar Labour Government's legislative programme.[104]

Historians of the First World War women's movement have noted the irony in a women's campaign for equal franchise rights resulting in the 1918 "motherhood" franchise.[105] It should not be entirely surprising, therefore, that the Second World War began with a campaign for gender equality, but ended with the creation of a welfare state that especially benefited mothers, thereby enhancing women's status but reinforcing gender differences.

Notes

1 Sonya O. Rose, *Which People's War? National Identity and Citizenship in Wartime Britain, 1939–1945* (Oxford, 2003).

2 James Hinton, *Women, Social Leadership, and the Second World War* (Oxford, 2002).

3 Vera Douie, *The Lesser Half* (London, 1943), 25.

4 Helen Jones, *Women in British Public Life, 1914–50* (London, 2000), 182.

5 Florence Underwood, WFL secretary, to Samuel Hoare, 26 January 1939. National Archives [TNA], HO 45/17957. The WFL was established in 1907 by Women's Social and Political Union members who broke away from the WSPU because they preferred to work within a democratic organization and wished to maintain close links with the Labour Party. The WFL, the Six Point Group, and the London and National Society for Women's Service were prominent advocates of equal rights feminism in the interwar period.

6 On Ray Strachey's role in increasing women's employment opportunities during the First World War see Jo Vellacott, *Pacifists, Patriots and the Vote* (London, 2007), chap. 8. Strachey was the NUWSS's parliamentary secretary during the First World War, and as one of the LNSWS's leaders throughout the interwar period played a key role in the 1930s equal pay campaign. See Harold L. Smith, "British Feminism and the Equal Pay Issue in the 1930s", *Women's History Review* 5 no. 1 (1996): 97–110.

7 "War and Waste", *The Woman Engineer* 5 (December 1939): 14.

8 Ray Strachey to Mary Berenson, February 2 and 25, 1939 and February 2, 1940. Ray Strachey Papers, Lilly Library, Indiana University. Also see Organizing Secretary, WEF, to Lady Astor, 6 December 1939. Women's Library, Marjorie Corbett Ashby Papers, box 494, file 127.

9 Ray Strachey had been Astor's parliamentary secretary from 1931 to 1935, while the BFBPW had developed close ties with the Conservative women M.P.s in the late 1930s. Linda Perriton, "Forgotten Feminists: The Federation of British Business and Professional Women, 1933–1969", *Women's History Review* 16 (2007): 85, 87.

10 [Ray Strachey], "Case Presented by the Women Members of Parliament of All Parties to the Treasury", 14 February 1940. Women's Library, LNSWS Papers. The proposal to appoint a woman minister divided feminist groups. Several equal rights groups – the WFL, the Open Door Council, the National Union of Women Teachers and St. Joan's Social and Political Alliance – refused to support this because it did not specify what the policy should be towards women workers. Open Door Council, *14ᵗʰ Annual Report, 1939–40*, 1.

11 Ray Strachey to Ellen Wilkinson, 17 February 1940. Corbett Ashby Papers, box 494, file 230.

12 Ray Strachey to Dr. Letitia Fairfield, Medical Women's Federation, 27 March 1940. Corbett Ashby Papers, box 494, file 230.

13 See Ernest Brown's manpower memorandum, 20 February 1940. TNA, CAB 65/5, W.C. 47 (40) 1.

14 Caroline Haslett speech, "Women in Wartime Industry", National Archive for Electrical Science and Technology, Caroline Haslett Papers, 33/8.8.

15 Strachey to Wilkinson, 17 February 1940.

16 Haslett was the BFBPW's Chairman. Constance Colwill, a prominent barrister and BFBPW member, was added to the WPC early in 1941 as a result of her skillful presentation of the case for equal compensation to the government's representatives. Ray Strachey's unexpected death in July 1940 deprived the feminist movement of an energetic and experienced leader.

17 The SJCWWO was the Labour Party's women's organization. Previously the SJC of Industrial Women's Organisations, it changed its name to reflect its desire to represent all working women, not just industrial workers. This, of course, brought it into direct conflict with the WPC's aspirations and very likely contributed to the tensions between the two groups. SJCWWO minutes, 10 July 1941. British Library.

18 SJCWWO minutes, 25 July 1940.

19 Ellen Wilkinson to Ernest Bevin, 3 July 1940. TNA, LAB 26/59.

20 F. N. Tribe to Mr. Gee, 6 January 1941. TNA, LAB 26/59. In addition to being a Conservative M.P., Ward was a member of the Conservative Party's Central Women's Advisory Committee during the war and kept them informed about developments.

21 Frederick Leggett, Chief Industrial Commissioner, to the Deputy Secretary [F. N. Tribe], 20 March 1941. TNA, LAB 8/378.

22 Pippa Strachey notes on the 26 November 1941 Conference on the Conscription of Women. Women's Library [WL], LNSWS Papers, box G3.4.

23 WPC minutes, 4 February 1941. British Library of Political and Economic Science.

24 Eleanor Rathbone to Mrs. Wise, WEF, 15 October 1941. WL, Marjorie Corbett Ashby Papers, box 494, file 140.

25 WPC minutes, 28 October 1941.

26 Harold L. Smith, *Britain in the Second World War: A Social History* (Manchester, 1996), 4.

27 Lord President's Committee minutes, 18 March 1941. TNA, CAB 71/2, L. P. (41) 10.

28 Caroline Haslett, "A Message", *International Women's News*, 35 (July 1941), 165.

29   The WPPA was established in December 1939 by a group of women, including Rebecca Sieff and Margery Corbett Ashby, with the Ministry of Information's support. Although it was originally intended to provide publicity about British women's contribution to the war effort, in 1940 it became a feminist organization campaigning for gender reforms.

30   For an example of the WPPA claiming that it was the organization directing the campaign, see "Crescendo in Agitation: The Campaign for Equal Compensation", *International Women's News* 36 (October 1941), 5. Unfortunately, some historians have accepted its inflated claim to have been the main wartime coordinating group for equal rights activity. See Hinton, *Women*, 180.

31   The BFBPW convened the meeting at which the ECCC was established to replace the Ad Hoc Committee.

32   Tate was so angry with Sieff and Evans for exaggerating the WPPA's role in the campaign that when she received a request from them to sign a letter to *The Times* supporting equal compensation, she destroyed it and urged Lady Astor to do the same. See note attached to Dorothy Evans to Viscountess Astor (n.d. but shortly after August 1941). University of Reading, Lady Astor Papers, Ms 1416/1/2/242.

33   WPPA Executive Committee minutes, 13 October and 11 December 1941. WL, WPPA Papers.

34   Harold L. Smith, "The Problem of 'Equal Pay for Equal Work' in Great Britain during World War II", *Journal of Modern History* 53 (December 1981): 662. Also see [illegible] to Sir John Anderson, 15 September 1942. TNA, CAB 123/213.

35   [Francis Hemming?], "Compulsory Fire Guard Duty for Women – Publicity Programme". TNA, HO 186/913.

36   Lord President's Committee minutes, 1 October 1942. TNA, CAB 123/213, L. P. (42) 59.

37   Lord President's Committee minutes, 20 November 1942. TNA, CAB 123/213, L.P. (42) 71.

38   SPG *Annual Report 1942*.

39   WPC minutes, 8 December 1942.

40   Mavis Tate, ECCC, to WPPA Chairman, 25 November, 1942. Caroline Haslett Papers, file 5/3.7.

41   Smith, "The Problem of 'Equal Pay for Equal Work'", 663.

42   *Annual Report of the Six Point Group November 1933–November 1934*. Lady Astor Papers, Ms 1416/1/1/1408.

43   Dorothy Evans to Winston Churchill, 29 November 1941. WL, SPG Executive Papers.

44   The SPG had only 234 members by July 1943, with very limited financial resources. WL, Six Point Group Papers, pamphlet box 396.1 (06).

45   WPPA Executive Committee minutes, 29 September 1943. WL.

46   Dorothy Evans to Marjorie Corbett Ashby, 23 May 1944. WL, Teresa Billington-Greig Papers, box 239.

47   The Labour Party women's attitude towards the bill may also have been influenced by their view of Evans. Although Evans was a socialist, she was deeply disappointed in the Labour Party for what she considered its indifference to women's struggle for equality. Some Labour Party

members criticized Evans for "putting Feminism before Socialism", and Frida Laski acknowledged that the Labour movement did not welcome women like her. SPG, *Dorothy Evans and the Six Point Group* (London, 1945), 62, 64. In October 1943 the Labour Party was preparing to blacklist the Married Women's Association because it had published Evans' article on the Equal Citizenship (Blanket) Bill in its journal. SPG Executive Committee minutes, 12 October 1943. Women's Library, SPG Papers, box 523.

48 WPC minutes, 28 September 1943.

49 WPC minutes, 4 August 1943.

50 LNSWS Executive Committee minutes, 31 May 1944. Women's Library. Evans and Pethick-Lawrence had been suffragettes prior to 1914, while the LNSWS leaders included some, like Pippa Strachey, who as pre-World War I suffragists believed that suffragette methods were harmful to the women's cause. The tensions between the two groups were still hampering efforts to unify the suffrage campaign in the 1920's. See Harold L. Smith, *The British Women's Suffrage Campaign 1866–1928* (London, 2nd ed., 2007), 100.

51 Some of the other feminist groups may also have been reluctant to be associated with Evans because of her membership in organizations they considered controversial. In addition to having been a WSPU member, she was a pacifist who, after long service as the secretary of the Women's International League for Peace and Freedom, was a leader of the British Women's Peace Campaign in May 1940. Alan Bishop and Y. A. Bennett, eds., *Wartime Chronicle: Vera Brittain's Diary 1939–1945* (London, 1989), 40.

52 WFW Executive Committee minutes, 21 October 1944. Women's Library. Sieff was the President of the British branch of the Women's International Zionist Organization, and a very wealthy woman (her husband, Israel, and her brother, Simon Marks, were the directors of Marks and Spencer).

53 Notes for Report to WPPA on WFW, November 1943–May 1945. Women's Library, WPPA Executive Committee Papers.

54 SJCWWO minutes, 8 October 1942.

55 Labour Women's Conference, *Annual Report 1942* (London: Labour Party, 1942), 44. Cited in Martin Pugh, *Women and the Women's Movement in Britain 1914–1959* (London, 1992), 280.

56 *Report of the 22nd National Conference of Labour Women* (London, 1943), 25.

57 [Conservative Party], Central Women's Advisory Committee minutes, 13 April 1943. *Archives of the British Conservative Party 1867–1992* (mfm).

58 WGPW Executive Committee minutes, 1 July 1943. Cited in Hinton, *Women*, 195. The perception of the WFW as a "leftist" group may have stemmed in part from the fact that two of its most prominent leaders, Edith Summerskill and Dorothy Evans, were both Labour Party members.

59 Sir William Beveridge, "Social Insurance and Allied Services", *Parliamentary Papers 1942–43*, VI, Cmd 6404, 53.

60 *Women in Council* 4 (November 1943), 3.

61 Minutes of the Deputation to Sir William Jowitt on the Beveridge Report, 25 February 1944. TNA, PIN 8/48.

62 Jones, *Women*, 203.

63 Harold L. Smith, "Gender and the Welfare State: The 1940 Old Age and Widows' Pensions Act", *History* 80 (1995): 384, 387.

64   Pippa Strachey, LNSWS, to Mrs. Cowan, NCW, 2 February 1944. Women's Library, LNSWS Papers, box G3.4.
65   Unsigned Ministry of Reconstruction memorandum, 10 February 1944. TNA, PIN 8/48.
66   Susan Pedersen, *Family, Dependence, and the Origins of the Welfare State* (Cambridge, 1993), 317–18.
67   LNSWS *Annual Report 1938 to 1943*, 11.
68   Susan Pedersen, *Eleanor Rathbone and the Politics of Conscience* (New Haven, CT, 2004), 367.
69   Pedersen, *Family*, 349.
70   Pedersen, *Eleanor Rathbone*, 366.
71   Smith, "The Problem of 'Equal Pay for Equal Work'", 666–7.
72   The WPPA asked to be kept informed of the EPCC's plans, but the EPCC refused. Tate noted that the WPPA's "ill-advised lobbying" had already harmed the campaign. EPCC notes on WPPA, 16 March 1944. WL, LNSWS Papers, "Correspondence 1940s Regarding Equal Pay". The WFL had tried to run an independent campaign instead of cooperating with the other feminist organizations, and may have been excluded because of this. The WPC also viewed it as an "extremist" feminist organization. WPC minutes, 28 September 1943.
73   A. J. T. Day to L. M. Sweet, 8 February 1944. Civil Service National Whitley Council (Staff Side) Papers, Equal Pay (6) C/1010.
74   Smith, "The Problem of 'Equal Pay for Equal Work'", 669.
75   LNSWS *Report 1943 to 1945*, 13.
76   Wilson Smith memorandum to Sir Alan Barlow, 26 April 1944. TNA, PREM 4 16/14; War Cabinet Minutes, 5 May 1944. CAB 65/42, W.M. (44) 62.
77   Joint Committee on Women in the Civil Service minutes, 16 May 1944. WL, LNSWS Papers, box G3.3.
78   Mrs. M. Roth, "Wartime Day Nurseries", TNA, CAB 102/774.
79   Sarah Boston, *Women Workers and the Trade Unions* (London, 1987), 196–7.
80   Mimeographed list of resolutions passed at the National Council of Women's 1944 Annual Conference. University of Reading, Lady Astor Papers, Ms 1416/1/1/1628.
81   Jones, *Women*, 193.
82   Denise Riley, *War in the Nursery* (London, 1983), 110.
83   TNA, MH 55/695. Cited in Riley, *War*, 119.
84   Harold L. Smith, "The Womanpower Problem in Britain During the Second World War", *Historical Journal* 27, no. 4 (1984): 942.
85   WPC minutes, 6 February 1944 and *Women at Work* 18 (Spring 1945): 9.
86   Smith, "The Womanpower Problem", 943.
87   Sir William Jowitt to S. Cripps, 9 October 1942. TNA, CAB 117/151.
88   Smith, "The Womanpower Problem", 938–9.
89   Audrey Leathard, *The Fight For Family Planning: The Development of Family Planning Services in Britain 1921–74* (London, 1980), 69–72.
90   Leathard, *The Fight For Family Planning*, 74.
91   Stephen Brooke, "'A New World for Women'? Abortion Law Reform in Britain during the 1930s", *American Historical Review* 106, no. 2 (2001): 447–8.
92   Barbara Brookes, *Abortion in England 1900–1967* (London, 1988), 144.

93 National Union of Conservative and Unionist Associations, *Notes on Current Politics*, April 1945, 14.

94 LNSWS memo on the 24 October 1945 conference of 19 women's organizations concerning women's admission to the Foreign Service. WL, LNSWS Papers, box 338.

95 Harold L. Smith, "The Politics of Conservative Reform: The Equal Pay for Equal Work Issue, 1945–1955", *Historical Journal* 35, no 2 (1992): 401–15.

96 Pippa Strachey to G. E. Griffiths, 13 March 1942. WL, LNSWS Papers, box G3.1.

97 Katherine Bompas, "The Rise and Fall of the Women's Movement", *Jus Suffragii*, 19, no. 9 (July 1941). Cited in Leila J. Rupp, *Worlds of Women: The Making of An International Women's Movement* (Princeton, 1997), 134.

98 Caitriona Beaumont, "Citizens not Feminists: the Boundary Negotiated between Citizenship and Feminism by Mainstream Women's Organizations in England, 1928–39", *Women's History Review* 9, no. 2 (2000), 426.

99 Hinton, *Women*, 41, 188, 195.

100 Vellacott, *Pacifists*, chap. 7.

101 Pamela M. Graves, *Labour Women: Women in British Working-Class Politics 1918–1939* (Cambridge, 1994), 198.

102 WPPA First Annual General Meeting minutes, 21 August 1941. WL, WPPA Papers.

103 Jennie Lee, "As I Please", *Tribune* (23 March 1945). Cited in Patricia Hollis, *Jennie Lee: A Life* (Oxford, 1997), 154. Middle-class women, both feminist and non-feminist, considered domestic servants essential in order for them to participate in public life. The war exacerbated the servant shortage and aroused such anguish among middle-class women that the government proposed the establishment of a National Institute of Homeworkers to train women for domestic service. This scheme suggests the wartime government's vision of postwar society included restoring class as well as gender structures despite its equalitarian rhetoric. Judy Giles, "Help for Housewives: Domestic Service and the Reconstruction of Domesticity in Britain, 1940–50", *Women's History Review* 10, no. 2 (2001), 316.

104 Pat Thane, "The Women of the British Labour Party and Feminism, 1906–1945", in *British Feminism in the Twentieth Century*, ed. Harold L. Smith (Aldershot, 1990), 136.

105 Susan R. Grayzel, *Women's Identities at War: Gender, Motherhood, and Politics in Britain and France During the First World War* (Chapel Hill, 1999), 213.

7

"Magazines are essentially about the here and now. And this was wartime": British *Vogue*'s Responses to the Second World War

Becky E. Conekin

There is now an established literature on the role British women's magazines played in extolling the double-edged tenets of female "beauty and duty" in WWII Britain.[1] Sonya O. Rose convincingly argues in her acclaimed book, *Which People's War?*, that "glamour" and what she dubs "sexualized femininity" were "marshalled" at various levels of popular and official discourse "to make acceptable the 'gender-bending' obligations of citizenship for women" during the Second World War in Britain.[2] She provides, among many, the example of Antoine, one "famous man", writing in the spring of 1940 in the popular *Woman's Own* magazine of his "ideal woman". There he told British women that their combination of "age old vanity" and "new courage" meant that they were "ready for anything – even the continuance of your coiffure in an air-raid shelter whilst a battle royal is raging overhead".[3] Other British scholars such as Janice Winship, Lucy Noakes and Jo Spence have examined *Woman's Own* and *Woman* magazines and have found, like Rose, that the ideal female citizen during WWII was expected to make a "vital contribution to the war effort while maintaining her femininity".[4]

Unsurprisingly, British *Vogue* played a part in the construction and perpetuation of such discourses of wartime femininity. Yet, a close look at British *Vogue* does reveal some surprises. The magazine's messages were actually much more complicated and heterogeneous than one might first imagine. Surprises in *Vogue*'s pages include the range of topics that the magazine felt it was *their* duty to cover in wartime, as well as the extraordinary work of their own war correspondent in Europe, Lee Miller. Miller had been a model for American *Vogue* in the late twenties and then a photographer and model for Paris *Vogue* in the early thirties. Her personal life took her to Britain in 1940 and the astute editor of British *Vogue*, Audrey Withers, hired her. Thus, Britain's premier fashion magazine,

Vogue, published some of the most harrowing and distinctive articles on the war in Europe, photographed and written by their former fashion model, Lee Miller. Her reportage in word and image was unique. Often witty and sometimes shocking, it disrupted both the pages of *Vogue* magazine and the expected nature of wartime journalism more generally.[5] As Annalisa Zox-Weaver has argued, and we will see, Lee Miller's articles complicated "the protocol of wartime documentation by challenging the boundaries between candid reportage and aesthetic practice".[6]

Britain declared war on Germany on the 3 September, 1939. And about a fortnight later, British *Vogue* announced on its opening page:

Vogue will be published monthly.

In accordance with the Government's wish that businesses would carry on so far as possible, *Vogue* will continue to be published during the war, but as a monthly magazine. It will incorporate *Vogue Pattern Book*, *Vogue Beauty Book* and *Vogue House and Garden Book*... *Vogue* promises you a practical and useful magazine. It will show you how to make shillings do the work of pounds in dress and personal grooming, household management, cooking and gardening. But, *Vogue* in features and format, will continue to be *Vogue* – charming and civilized, a tonic to the eye and to the spirit – more indispensable than ever.[7]

It then informed readers that "wartime conditions and transport problems make it impossible for magazines to be available ... for the casual reader to pick up wherever she pleases", so they needed to have either a postal subscription or a standing order with their newsagent.[8]

A few pages later there appeared a reproduced First World War cover from May 1918, featuring a nurse. The text proclaimed:

Vogue – Veteran of the LAST WAR, COMBATANT IN THE PRESENT, PROPOSES NOW TO CARRY ON: Our policy is to maintain the standard of civilization. We believe that women's place is *Vogue*'s place. And women's first duty, as we understand it, is to preserve the arts of peace by practicing them, so that in happier times they will not have fallen out of disuse. Moreover, we believe that women have a special value in the public economy, for even in war time they maintain their feminine interests and thus maintain, too, the business activity essential to the home front.[9]

This early optimistic injunction to British women to patriotically consume has seldom been commented upon and is interesting to note. Similarly, in the same issue an article entitled "Here and Now Resolve to Shop Courageously to Look Your Best" told *Vogue*'s readers that it was now the normal time of year to buy their autumn wardrobes.[10] "Shop for it now", it insisted. "Every time you hold back from buying, you throw the national economy a fraction off balance. Multiply that by millions, and it becomes a considerable punch on that very chin which the dress trade is trying to keep up". The piece concluded: "It's our job to spend gallantly, to dress decoratively, to be groomed immaculately – in short, to be a sight for sore eyes".[11]

And there were many other expectations of the British woman in wartime expressed by the *Vogue* writers. Early in the same, initial wartime issue a piece appeared that starts off by explaining that "their Majesties" "are the keepers of our nation's conscience and an epitome of the sober virtues of our race", who set an example of how all British people should behave in wartime.[12] Yet, within a few paragraphs the article had turned to what the *Vogue* reader's obligations were in wartime:

> For those who are attached to the auxiliary reserves of the fighting forces, the way is clear; they are under military discipline and must obey orders. Those who have been trained for civil defence also have their work plain before them. For the many who have no official post, no fixed duties, no inevitable daily job, the best advice is to find something to do that will daily demand their attention, take up their time and tax their resources. Don't pick and choose too much or wait about for something that is really worthy of you .... Do whatever you find near you that urgently wants doing – preferably some useful work outside your own interests and necessities ... For obvious reasons the work you find for yourself had better be as near as possible.[13]

It then instructed readers that "apart from this job of work, see that all the resources you possess are used". This included digging up flower gardens and planting vegetables, learning to cook (now that your cook is off to do vital war work), learning to sew or knit, getting company together to play bridge or darts, and learning or re-learning a musical instrument, to entertain and to drown out the "noise of bombardment".[14] And if readers were country-dwellers, they should keep bees, rabbits, hens or goats. The list did enjoin women to do their beauty exercises and to keep their "hair and complexion in good trim", because "it would be a calamity if war turned us into a nation of frights and slovens".[15] But, it is important to recognize that these were not the top priorities and that they appear about midway down the page.

Vogue's thumb is Up

Vogue's thumb is up for charmers who are chic but not chi-chi: who curl, rather than crop their hair: who cling to their hard-won femininity—won back after years of pseudo boyishness; who realise that beauty should always have a place—that discreet maquillage can be the best war-paint: that evenings off should be a treat to the beholder, too: that khaki can pall—in short, that the battle is to the fair.

Vogue's thumb is Down

Vogue's thumb is down on toughs who carry their functionalism too far—far into the night club, restaurant, or home and hearth. Who think war is also declared on all the elegances and artifices of our beauty-conscious age. Who pad around in hairy sweaters and flannel bags, on duty and off; letting themselves go—and other people down—slackers in slacks.

Figure 7.1 "Thumbs Up, Thumbs Down", British *Vogue*, November, 1939, p. 19 ©. Condé Nast Publications, courtesy of the Lee Miller Archives, England, 2008.

On the other hand, two months later there came an illustrated page, divided into two columns headed: "Vogue's Thumb is Up, Vogue's Thumb is Down" (Figure 7.1).[16] An Elizabeth Arden advertisement appeared on the adjacent page, featuring a colour drawing of a woman in profile, dressed in khaki uniform, with tasteful blusher and red lip-sticked lips. The heading read: "THE MODERN WOMAN – ELIZABETH ARDEN'S MASTERPIECE – Beauty Marches on".[17] The advertisement demanded that it was the "'modern woman's 'duty' 'to face the future calm and unruffled. Beauty – like business – must go on'". It then argued that "the wise woman, in a period of strain and crisis, will keep up her regular night and morning routine of Cleansing, Toning and Nourishing", with Elizabeth Arden's products, of course.[18] Similarly, *Vogue*'s thumb was up "for charmers who are chic but not chi-chi: who curl, rather than crop their hair: who cling to their hard-won feminin-ity – won back after years of pseudo boyishness; who realise that beauty should always have a place – that discreet maquillage can be the best war-paint: that evenings off should be a treat to the beholder, too: that khaki can pall – in short, that the battle is to the fair".[19] A drawing of a well-coiffed woman in an evening gown and elegant jewellery, taking a cigarette from her case, accompanied the text.

In the illustration for "*Vogue*'s Thumb is Down" the woman sports short, cropped hair, a military cardigan and loose, pleated trousers with brogues. She stands a bit slumped, hands mannishly shoved into her pockets, with a cigarette dangling from her lips. The text read: "*Vogue*'s thumb is down on the toughs who carry their functionalism too far – into the night club, the restaurant, or home and hearth. Who think war is also declared on all the elegance and artifice of our beauty-conscious age. Who pad around in hairy sweaters and flannel bags, on duty and off; letting themselves go – and other people down – slackers in slacks".[20] This *Vogue* page echoes the concerns that Rose identified in so many other popular and governmental sources, including the sanctity of the home and all the duties of women to remain feminine, attractive, "elegant" and yet, heterosexually appropriate, with neither "indiscreet maquillage" nor "boyish" cropped hair and sweater – and "slack"-wearing. "Padding around in hairy sweaters" evokes thoughts of unshaven, untidy women who move less than elegantly. One addi-tional reference emerges here as well – that femininity in 1939 was considered by some "hard won" after the previous period of "pseudo boyishness".[21] As such, the distaste for short hair and trousers on war-time British women seems even more acute than it might have been without the inter-war fashions.

However, early in 1940 wartime restrictions became more serious. Sugar, bacon and butter were put "on the ration", with tea, margarine, and cooking fats added a few months later, and eggs and dairy to follow. Clothing and furniture were rationed next and there were restrictions on heating and water, as well. The demands that rationing made on middle-class British women can be traced through *Vogue*'s pages. For instance, in the October 1940 issue: "Into the magazine steps a new figure: a new force in the dress world. His Acts might suggest him no friend to fashion; but *Vogue* (hopefully) detects an ally".[22] This possible ally was the 49 year old, Conservative Sir Kingsley Wood, who had been appointed Chancellor of the Exchequer by Churchill the previous May. *Vogue* informed readers that: "His budget compels them to watch their own", and that his Purchase Tax " will set them practising the sound dress maxims that *Vogue* has always preached". *Vogue* argued that this meant that "If women must buy less, they will buy better. If money is short, they will substitute taste. The Government needs the cash; let's also give them the credit. Ladies take off your (twice-trimmed) hats to Sir Kingsley Wood".[23]

And as part of the "no margin for error" measures suggested by *Vogue,* there was a page on "Beauty Savings: Tax cosmetics, says the Chancellor. Tax our ingenuity, says *Vogue.* Use the little grey cells and make the most of..."[24] This piece's "dos and don'ts" ranged from "Don't collect a fleet of half-used lipsticks in a bottom drawer" and "Don't peel off your nail polish wilfully" to "Do give your skin regular care...Do supplement your work with professional treatments...treatments aren't taxed" and "Don't ever put an inferior preparation on your hair; it may do untold harm and prove a very false economy. Don't forget that there's nothing like a glossy coiffure for keeping up morale".[25] Once again, like the other women's magazines, *Vogue* reminded women that it was their wartime duty to be femininely attractive.[26]

By February, 1944 *Vogue* featured the very real "problems" of the "brutal" 12-hour days in a munitions factory that Miss Lily Ehrefeld endured and the toll it was taking on her hands and complexion.[27] (Figure 7.2) "Miss Ehrenfeld's hands are coated day-long in grease and grime", at times even working "under running water".[28] An assortment of treatments were the answer, including painting her nails "with white iodine to harden them" and using "Cyclax Hand Bleach under an old pair of gloves in bed". Her face would be "disastrously dry" without "excellent care", due to the "hot atmosphere of the factory", "charged with small bits of flying debris and dust". A regime of cleansing and moisturizing, along with "good eye lotion and eye pads to

PROBLEM:

Miss Lily Ehrenfeld works from eight till eight, five days a week, in a munitions factory. The work is tiring and is brutal to her hands, hard on her complexion. But she manages, at work and off duty, to look always pretty and well groomed, and, most important of all, to keep in shining health

HER HANDS. These are her major problem. Miss Ehrenfeld's hands are coated day-long in grease and grime, sometimes have to work under running water. She uses Cyclax Hand Lotion whenever she washes her hands. At night she paints her nails with white iodine to harden them, uses Cyclax Hand Bleach under an old pair of gloves in bed, paints her cuticles with castor oil. She manages her own manicure, keeps her nails well shaped but short.

HER COMPLEXION. The hot atmosphere of the factory is charged with small bits of flying debris and dust, disastrously drying to the skin without excellent care. Miss Ehrenfeld uses Cyclax Day Lotion for foundation during the day. When she gets home she gives her face a thorough cleanse with Cleansing Lotion, followed by soap and water, massages in Cyclax Special O at night, leaves a film of it on. She uses a good eye lotion and eye pads to counteract the glare of the overhead factory lights.

HER FEET. Standing all day is very tiring for the arches and the backs of the legs. Miss Ehrenfeld finds that keeping her feet slightly apart and parallel, not toes turned out, relieves the strain on her arches. She has disciplined herself not to slump over her work, but to counteract fatigue of standing by keeping her body easily upright, tummy held in, weight on the balls of her feet. At home after work she practises the simple strengthening exercise of rolling a bottle with her bare foot, and when her ankles have a tendency to swell she finds it very helpful to bind them with crêpe bandages soaked in cold water, starting at the instep and binding upwards. To relieve tiredness, she sleeps with the foot of her bed slightly raised. Occasionally she visits Cyclax for a special foot treatment of mild electrical and hand-and-oil massage for toning up the muscles of the feet, ankles and calves.

HER HAIR. She visits a first-class hairdresser every now and then for an expert taper cut and hair styling, chooses a short easily managed coiffure which she can brush well without disturbing the set, which she can set herself. She washes her hair weekly with Drene Special Shampoo, has learnt to set it into soft curls.

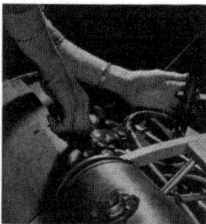

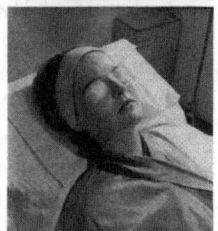

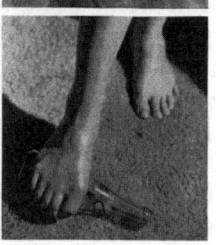

Figure 7.2 "Problem Hands", photographs by Lee Miller, British *Vogue*, February, 1944, p. 34 ©. Condé Nast Publications, courtesy of the Lee Miller Archives, England, 2008.

counteract the glare of the overhead factory lights", were the solution for those problems.[29] Such advice could be read as demanding more than double-duty of women, since many were taking care of homes and children at the end of their workdays, as well. However, as Pat Kirkham has argued, we "should not dismiss" discussions of wartime hair and beauty regimes, as they "formed an important part of women's everyday conversations and culture at the time".[30]

But, there was much more for women to contend with, and *Vogue* felt it its place to help them.[31] For instance, the magazine argued in November 1939 that women needed to organize "an auxiliary source of cooking heat", advising that it was "well to cross this particular bridge before you come to it", and suggesting the purchase of a "small paraffin stove".[32] Similarly, alternative sources of refrigerator power should be investigated, including fitting some types with "oil lamps to supply freezing power". And, in case this sounded a terrible fuss, *Vogue* told readers: "A hot meal may be a life-saver for some exhausted war worker and though good food can be had straight from a tin, to accept a succession of such meals is depressing and wasteful".[33] This theme of being ready to feed visitors at any moment was echoed in a piece in March 1941. "'Come when you can' Cooking", explained that: "'Come when you can', is the way most invitations are, of necessity, phrased nowadays".[34] The article provided numerous recipes that could be prepared quickly beforehand and reheated or slow-cooked and thus served up anytime, with rationing repeatedly addressed.

Throughout the war *Vogue* regularly included features on how to "make good meals" from "simple foods", with "imagination" and spices. "General Economy" "issued his orders" in May 1942 to save thread, hair-pins, "old scraps of soap", "dilute the last drop of nail varnish", "gouge out the last crimson goodness from your lipstick" and "know that a carpet sweeper or a stiff broom is a far better present now than any orchids".[35] In January of that year an article entitled "Get Your Goat" appeared on how keeping a goat could solve your milk shortage problem.[36] "No Nanny" addressed what the middle-class woman should do to manage without one, including what to do about the "marathon" of the children's laundry, now that mothers had to "make do with so few clothes", as well as the scarcity of cots and prams.[37] The article also stressed the importance of not devoting "yourself entirely to your own child", as this was "a waste of woman-power". You should "park" your "child in confidence" at a Nursery School and "go off to your war job".[38]

Vogue also had its own, more elegant, version of "make do and mend", whereby readers were encouraged in one article to stretch their wardrobes and coupons by doing things "the American way" and buying separates.[39] In another piece, they were told how to transform an old black dress by adding "an all-around apron of frothy lace and net", and how to "camouflage" "a languishing afternoon dress" with a "well-draped shawl".[40] Household furnishings could similarly be made "cheer-ful" by edging "gloomy" curtains "with gay braids and tassels and ruches", and taking up needlework to embroider "chair covers, table mats, mirror surrounds – almost anything you fancy".[41] These improve-ments were morale boosters to "give you courage", since now your home *must* be the centre of your life after sunset".[42]

Other articles addressed the realities of bombing and the blackout, including Lesley Blanch's October 1940 piece, "Living the Sheltered Life". Blanch listed the thriving London "subterranean" restaurants, including Hatchetts, where Arthur Young's swing band regularly played and described the assorted amenities available in the London depart-ment stores' bomb shelters – everything from books and magazines to hairdressing and manicures.[43] The next month, more frighteningly, but still in a cheerful register, six of photographer Lee Miller's pictures appeared under the caption "Here is *Vogue* in spite of it all". The text read:

> **Outside** – on several nights, bombs have spattered within twenty yards. This street below our window now holds a new crater, and another length of the arcade has crashed. We were turned out tem-porarily for a time bomb.
> **Inside** – our offices have been strewn with broken glass ... Though five storeys up, our floors have been deep in soil and debris flung through the roof.
> **Beneath** – we work on when our roof-watcher sends us down. Our editorial staff plan, lay-out, write. Our studio photograph in their wine-cellar-basement. Our fashion staff continue to comb the shops. Congestedly, unceremoniously but cheerfully, *Vogue*, like its fellow Londoners, is put to bed in a shelter.[44]

Lee Miller, an American from Poughkeepsie, who had lived abroad most of her adult life, had written to her parents earlier that autumn of the "three solid months of hell at night".[45] Southampton, Coventry and Clydebank in Scotland all suffered bombing, but hardest hit was London. The Blitz lasted from September 1940 to May 1941. Nearly thirty thousand of the civilian deaths from bombing were in London, with an additional almost 90,000 seriously injured.[46] Richard Titmuss, the historian, civil servant and professor of Social Administration at the London School of Economics wrote in 1950 that: "Between the first and last incident, the alert was sounded on 1,224 occasions ... it may be said that Londoners were threatened once every thirty-six hours for over five years, threatened ... going about the ordinary business of their lives".[47]

The "ordinary business" of British women's lives included various forms of war work, reported by *Vogue,* and often photographed by Lee Miller, including Land Girls, WRNS, professional British women in the forces or American Army nurses and Red Cross workers.[48] Miller was a longstanding member of the international *Vogue* family, and when a number of British *Vogue* photographers left to join the war effort late in 1939, Harry Yoxall, *Vogue's* managing editor, obtained a work permit for her and put her on the London staff. From New York, Condé Nast himself cabled that he was delighted that her "INTELLIGENCE FUNDA-MENTAL GOOD TASTE SENSITIVENESS [and] ART VALUES" would be put to use for *Vogue,* once again.[49] By 1939, Lee Miller was an acclaimed photographer who a decade earlier had been Man Ray's model, apprentice and muse.[50] In 1934 *Vanity Fair* had listed Miller alongside Cecil Beaton, amongst others, as one of the "most distinguished living photographers".[51] Her relationship to *Vogue* magazine had commenced long before that, though. Not yet twenty, she was discovered by Condé Nast in Manhattan and appeared as the cover girl for the March 1927 issue of American *Vogue.* From then on leading photographers, Edward Steichen and Arnold Genthe, often photographed her before she moved to Paris and became George Hoyningen-Huene's favourite model for French *Vogue.* By the winter of 1930 she was also photographing for *Vogue* Paris and regularly landing assignments for leading designers, including Patou, Schiaparelli and Chanel. In the summer of 1939 she settled in Hampstead, North London with Roland Penrose, surrealist, collector and a founder of London's Institute of Contemporary Arts.[52]

In October of 1940, the *Picture Post* ran an article on Miller assembling a fashion shoot in which the author, Anne Scott-James, asked the question "Why all this fuss about a photograph when the country is fighting for its life?" She answered her own question, explaining that fashion "maintains Britain's position as the world's greatest exporter of fabrics" and that "fashion pays for planes and supplies".[53] And government officials consulted British *Vogue's* editor, Audrey Withers, before they launched the Utility clothing scheme to save fabric and fastenings for the war effort in September of 1941.[54] Top British designers, such as Hardy Amies, Digby Morton, Victor Steibel and Worth, became involved, and Withers agreed to support and publicize the clothes in the pages of *Vogue.*[55]

Still, Miller grew increasingly impatient with covering the war from Vogue House. After the attack on Pearl Harbor, American servicemen arrived in droves in London. Their new Savile Row uniforms, not to mention the "cigarettes, canned goods, Scotch, Kleenex and goodies that the harassed British hadn't seen in four years", "drove poor Lee mad", according to Miller's friend and sometime lover, *Life* photographer, Dave Scherman. Miller was also unwilling to be "left out of the biggest story of the decade". In late 1941, Scherman "suggested that she too, a perfectly bona fide Yank from Poughkeepsie, apply for accreditation to the US forces as a war correspondent. She was an expatriate of twenty years and the thought had never occurred to her".[56]

Thus, in 1944 with Condé Nast's support, Audrey Withers hired Miller to be *Vogue*'s correspondent in Europe. Years later Withers explained her decision: "It was all very well encouraging ourselves with conventional patter about keeping up morale, but magazines – unlike books – are essentially about the here and now. And this was wartime".[57] By the summer of 1944, Miller was frustrated by the anodyne prose that often accompanied her photographs, and so she "badgered" Withers into allowing her to write the articles, as well.[58] Thus, Britain's premier fashion magazine, not only responded to the war like the other British women's magazines, with their complicated, double-edged "duty and beauty" agendas. *Vogue* employed its own war correspondent and published some of the most troubling and unique articles on the war in Europe. As we will see, Miller's roles as former *Vogue* model and artiste authorized her to pen prose that frequently transcended presumed boundaries between fashion magazine writing and front-line war reportage.

Withers described Lee Miller's first such submission as "the most exciting journalistic experience of my war", adding: "We were the last people one could conceive having this type of article, it seemed so incongruous in our pages of glossy fashion".[59] She had commissioned her to write a quiet picture story on U.S. Army field hospital nurses stationed in Normandy. What Miller produced was something altogether different. Entitled "Unarmed Warriors" in UK *Vogue,* fourteen of her photographs accompanied Miller's text. The piece appeared in a different format in the US edition under the title "USA Tent Hospital in France", and both articles were published in the September 1944 issues.

Second Lieutenant Herbert 'Bud' Myers recently recalled Miller's visit to the Normandy clearing station. Myers was the medical liaison staffer on the regimental commander's staff and he had been assigned to show Miller around and to keep her "out of mortar fire" – "the biggest danger to medical facilities".[60] He remembered how she had arrived in a jeep with a one star General, when they were "within earshot" of the Battle of the Falais Gap. Myers said that many journalists and photographers came through their three battalion aid stations, but that they were "all male" and they "showed very little interest in our end of it, most of them". Miller, in contrast, had a "high level of interest and a high level of understanding" of the operation. Most of the male correspondents just "wanted to be a part and be able to explain what it was like to be a GI Joe under fire, in a firefight, you know". But, Miller was "unusual" and conducted herself with "real class", as she moved respectfully and sensitively among the wounded men.[61]

Miller's repeated references in her report to Renaissance and medieval paintings, along with her particular portrayal of the soldiers, mark her distinctive voice, as well as vision. For example, at the Collecting Station, she wrote that she found that the "wounded were not 'knights in shining armour', but dirty, dishevelled stricken figures ... uncomprehending ... some exhausted and lifeless". She described a medical procedure, writing that:

> The doctor with his Raphael-like face turned to a man on a litter which had been placed on upended trunks. Plasma had already been attached to the man's outstretched left arm [...] his face was shrunken and pallid under dirt [...] by the time his pierced elbow was in its sling, his opaque eyes were clearing and he was aware enough to grimace as his splint was bandaged into place.[62]

Here the doctor was positioned as an artist, while the ordinary soldiers were rendered near-dead and grubby. Her denial of the knight-like qualities of the soldiers and her evocation of Raphael make Miller's work very different from much of the contemporary coverage of the Second World War, committed to gritty stories of heroism.[63-]

Lee Miller's are some of the most arresting articles ever to have appeared in *Vogue* magazine. She broke down barriers between fashion and news journalism, just as earlier in her career she had ignored the presumed boundaries between artist and model and fine art and commercial fashion photography.[64] Miller's pieces overflowed with rich, sensual descriptions of the scenes of war before her – sounds, smells and, especially, sights. Those scenes were frequently rendered in terms of high art, as well as the details of clothing, bodies and hair. For example, she wrote of a patient whose leg was being bandaged in the surgical tent: "In the chiaroscuro of khaki and white I was reminded of Hieronymus Bosch's painting, 'The Carrying of the Cross'".[65] Her references speak to her extraordinary eye, honed by her experiences of the previous two decades, where she had moved comfortably in the world of art and haute couture.

Withers reflected that when "you think that every situation she covered was completely outside her previous experience, it makes the sheer professionalism of her text even more remarkable".[66] Ironically, perhaps, these articles were generally positioned in British *Vogue*'s "pages of glossy fashion" as if they were not extraordinary. On the final pages of "Unarmed Warriors" the story is flanked by an advertisement for Scholl's "expert treatment", with a woman in an apron washing dishes and exclaiming to her husband, as he dries, "I've had my feet re-conditioned!". On the other side is an advertisement for Sirdar Wools, Ltd, Wakefield, featuring a photograph of an elegant, seated woman wearing a "Lace Ladder Rib Jumper".[67]

Similarly, Miller's 10,000 word article for the October 1944 issue accompanied by advertisements for the removal of "superfluous hair" "at the Tao Clinic" in Knightsbridge, for the Ostnath "elite baby carriage", and a Rayon producers' "hosiery homily" on how to take care of your precious stockings. The headline for the article read: "St. Malo: ... the siege and the assault ... covered by Lee Miller, of *Vogue*, ... only photographer and reporter there, under fire, throughout".[68] Written in three days of non-stop typing, the piece when published ran over eight pages, with thirteen of her photographs, two produced as half pages. Miller explained to *Vogue*'s readers that she "had thought that watching a battle from a hillside had gone out with the glamorous paintings of Napoleon" and had also "believed the newspapers when they said that St. Malo had fallen". In fact, the "Germans had merely been isolated from the main land", and the Army was actually fighting "bloody, heroic, tricky battles". She "organised" to stay on, realizing that she was "the only photographer for miles around" and that she "now owned a private war".

Amidst the vivid descriptions of the bombing and the arrests of female collaborators, are these signature Miller lines: "A company was filing out of St. Malo, ready to go into action, grenades hanging on their lapels like Cartier clips, menacing bunches of death".[69] Later in the article she wrote of gunfire bringing "more stones down in the street" and explained that she "sheltered in a kraut dugout, squatting under the ramparts". But there she entered a scene very much like the one from surrealists Luis Buñuel and Salvador Dali's 1929 film "Un Chien Andalou":

> My heel ground into a dead, detached hand and I cursed the Germans for the sordid ugly destruction they had conjured on this once beautiful town. I wondered where my friends that I had known here before the war were; how many had been forced into disloyalty and degradation – how many had been shot, starved or what. I picked up the hand and hurled it across the street, and ran back the way I'd come bruising my feet and crashing in the unsteady piles of stone and slipping in blood. Christ it was awful![70]

The combination of the image of her flinging a dead, detached hand across the street, with the evocation of her prewar French friendships is another example of Miller's unique voice – here, indignant, tough and personal.

The most interesting issue of wartime British *Vogue* is, unsurprisingly, the "Victory number" from June 1945. Perusing it today is slightly surreal. Sandwiched between articles entitled: "Colour in our Lives" (on artists' views "on the very exciting question: colour in the home") and "Softening Processes" (on the new "'shoulder cuff' sleeves" of one dress and the "soft rounded revers" of another) is Miller's "Germany – the war that is won". The article features ten photographs by Miller, including a very small one of a pile of bodies captioned: "Horrors of a concentration camp, unforgettable, unforgivable" (Figure 7.3). Dotted around the final pages of Miller's text are advertisements for the "fine cosmetics" of Roger & Gallet, and "the very charming Barri Maternity dress".[71] In the midst of this typical fashion magazine fare, Miller's article seems to explode. She wrote:

> Germany is a beautiful landscape dotted with jewel-like villages, blotched with ruined cities, and inhabited by schizophrenics. There are blossoms and vistas; every hill is crowned with a castle. The vineyards of the Moselle and the newly ploughed plains are fertile. Immaculate birches and tender willows flank the streams and the tiny towns are pastel plaster like a modern water-colour of a medieval memory. Little girls in white dresses and garlands promenade after their first communion. The children have stilts and marbles and tops and hoops, and they play with dolls. Mothers sew and sweep and bake, and farmers plough and harrow; all just like

Figure 7.3   Pile of Dead Prisoners, by Lee Miller, Buchenwald, Germany, April, 1945 ©. Lee Miller Archives, England, 2008.

real people. But they aren't; they are the enemy. This is Germany and it is spring.[72]

Within a paragraph she had moved on to Buchenwald and "the concentration camps", which she explained were not listed in her "fine Baedecker tour of Germany", "because no one in Germany ever heard of a concentration camp, and I guess they didn't want any tourist business either". "Visitors took one-way tickets only, in any case, and if they lived long enough they had plenty of time to learn the places of interest, both historic and modern, by personal and practical experimentation".[73]

She then recounted the horrors of slave labour and the camps, as well as her incredulity at the "slimy invitations to dine in German underground homes". "How dare they?", she wrote:

Who do they think we'd been braving flesh and eyesight against, all these years in England? Who did they think were my friends and compatriots but the blitzed citizens of London and the ill-treated French prisoners of war? Who did they think were my flesh and blood but the American pilots and infantrymen? What kind of idiocy and stupidity blinds them to my feelings? What kind of detachment are they able to find, from what kind of escape zones in the unventilated alleys of their brains are they able to conjure up the idea that they are liberated instead of conquered people?[74]

Miller's references to travel articles interpellate her female readers into a text where the righteous anger of the Allied victors is cast in terms of disdain for repression and an emphasis on the visual – or "eyesight".

Lee Miller continued her interpellation of her *Vogue* readers, along with her questioning of the humanity of the Germans, particularly the Nazis, in her feature for the next issue. In her quirkily titled "Hitleriania", published in British *Vogue* in July, 1945, Miller employed eerie juxtapositions, once again utilizing the language of an upmarket women's magazine.[75] The piece commences with a vivid account of Hitler's mountain retreat going up in smoke and ends with a detailed description of the interior of his mistress, Eva Braun's, Munich apartment. This is the article that included the now-famous photo of Miller in Hitler's Munich bathtub, taken by Dave Scherman.[76] Annalisa Zox-Weaver argues that the placement of Miller's naked body "in precisely the place where Hitler placed his" allows the photograph to interrogate "the limits of what is sayable and knowable of the Führer's corporeal experience".[77]

Zox-Weaver also acknowledges that this photograph "banalizes Hitler" to some degree, as well.[78] Certainly, the layout of the article in *Vogue* does so. This photograph of Miller in Hitler's bathtub, framed by a classical, kneeling female nude sculpture on her right and a photograph of the Führer himself on her left, along with her filthy flight jacket and combat boots, which have rudely tramped dirt all over the white bathmat, appears in a tiny 1/24th of a page format. On the same page, at the same size, there is a photograph of the "hausmeister" of the Sternecker Hofbrau Haus in Munich, where Hitler held regular Nazi meetings in one of the private drinking rooms, along with another, of an American serviceman lying on a divan, using the "Hotline" in Hitler's apartment, while reading a copy of *Mein Kampf*.[79] On the remaining half of the page appears an announcement from the Ministry of Food on how to bottle summer fruit.[80]

In the text, Miller told of how portraits of "Hitler tenderly autographed to Eva and her sister Gretl, who lived with her, were in plain view".[81] She went on to catalogue the apartment's "furniture and decorations", which, she said, "were strictly department store like everything in the Nazi regime: impersonal and in good, average, slightly artistic taste... " Miller described what remained of Braun's "envied wardrobe and equipment", and the "odds and ends" scattered on her dressing table: "tweezers, Elizabeth Arden lipstick refills..., a half bottle of Arden skin tonic, little funnels and spatulas for transferring beauty products", telling readers, "Nothing was grimy, everything looked new". Jean Gallagher has written that these "detailed verbal close-ups" allow Miller to "expose the very interiors of the body of the fascist regime itself – a body surrounded by an environment not at all unlike the one inscribed in *Vogue*'s advertisements and features".[82] According to Miller, Braun's bathroom was "supernormal", except for two "crammed" medicine chests, full enough of "drugs and patent preparations" "for a ward of hypochondriacs".[83] These descriptions somehow render Nazism banal, as they poke fun at Hitler and Braun's personal inadequacies.

When Miller reported that: "I took a nap on her bed and tried the telephones", the effect is to destabilize the text, bringing out the disturbing qualities of this account of the domestic fashions of a dictator. The idea of sleeping in Eva Braun's bed, with its connotations of making love to Hitler, is truly chilling. And as she did by using the bath, Miller was mocking and emasculating the now-dead Hitler through her "brazen engagement with and transgression of his own intimate spaces".[84]

She ends the article by describing "the large brass globe of the world" on "Eva's living room table", designed to hold "glasses and bottles for toasting... 'Morgen Die Ganze Welt'... 'Tomorrow, the Whole World'".[85] Her strange combination of the sort of detailed descriptive writing one could expect to find in an article on domestic interiors elsewhere in *Vogue*'s pages, along with the staggering reminder of Hitler's plan of

world domination, exemplifies her use of juxtaposition.[86] More importantly, these juxtapositions gesture towards the gruesome nature of any
sort of reporting on fashion or decorating in the face of Auschwitz,
Buchenwald and Dachau. How could we ever again blithely drink
liquors after learning of Hitler's globe-shaped holder? How was life to
return to normal for Miller or anyone after she had reported on the
Nazi atrocities? Not long after the war in Europe ended, British *Vogue*
wished to return to normality as far as possible under postwar conditions. And, of course, as in all the wartime issues, even within a few
pages of Miller's article on Hitler, there were features on: "Dresses worth a
straw" – "romantic", "flower and ribbon trimmed" straw hats "to wear
with these black dresses, enhancing their sleek formality yet giving an
ethereal look"[87] – and "showing a well-groomed leg" on how to achieve
"complete elimination of fuzz", even though depilatory and "abrasive
mitts" were in such short supply.[88]

Conclusion

Wartime British *Vogue* walked a tightrope, not only between the potentially contradictory demands of "beauty and duty" for British women, but
also over the internal conflicts of the British home front. There the ordinary and the extraordinary always had to be held in dynamic tension.
The tension between carrying on with "ordinary" life – be that "cleansing, toning and moisturising" or cooking hot, delicious meals, even
though ingredients and power were in short supply – and the truly extraordinary nature of wartime life had to be maintained here, as elsewhere. Given such a dynamic, it is hardly surprising that wartime British
Vogue sometimes seems rather "schizophrenic". This was true even before
Miller's war reports entered its pages. Audrey Withers and her team had
promised at the outbreak of war that *Vogue* would provide readers with
practical advice, but that it would also be a "tonic".[89]

Yet once the realities of the European theatre of war were starkly
and at times, shockingly, brought into the magazine through Miller's
coverage, this schizophrenia was further exacerbated. The contrast
between the usual pieces on fashion trends and beauty advice, with their
accompanying advertising, and Miller's wartime reportage can seem quite
bizarre for the reader today. Yet, at the same time, Miller's journalism
often managed to bridge the two worlds. As we have seen, Miller used
unique devices in her articles, frequently evoking the senses and high
culture, as well as gesturing towards the familiar terrain of upmarket
women's magazines – travel writing, interior decoration and cosmetic

advice. These devices rendered the war in Europe more accessible to *Vogue*'s readers, I would argue. Miller's articles brought the war home in a different, more intimate way. Teetering on the tightrope at times, British *Vogue* managed to engage with the "here and now" of the war – however harrowing or gruesome – while continuing to serve up standard fashion fare, albeit tailored to the new realities of wartime.

Acknowledgements

Thanks to Susan Grayzel and Philippa Levine for conceiving this book and asking me to contribute. I would also like to thank the London College of Fashion for my Senior Research Fellowship, as well as internal project funding for this chapter. I am grateful to Stephen Brooke, Christian Huck, and Adam Tooze, who have read and commented on versions of this chapter, and to Tony Penrose, Arabella Hayes and Carole Callow of the Lee Miller Archive, who have supported and facilitated all my work on Lee Miller, as have Harriet Wilson of Condé Nast and Brett Croft, Jooney Woodward, and Bonnie Robinson in the Vogue House Library, London. Don LaCoss provided some important conversations and citations on surrealism at a crucial moment in the revising of this piece. Similarly, Amy delaHaye offered insights into fashion and rationing in Second World War Britain.

Notes

1. "Beauty and Duty" comes from the title of a piece by Pat Kirkham, "Beauty and Duty: Keeping Up the (Home) Front", in *War Culture: Social Change and Changing Experience of World War Two*, eds. Pat Kirkham and D. Thom, (London, 1995), 13–28. See also Jane Waller and M. Vaughan-Rees, *Women in Wartime: The Role of Women's Magazines 1939–1945* (London, 1987); and Janice Winship, "Women's Magazines: Times of War and Management of the Self in Woman's Own", in *Nationalising Femininity: Culture, Sexuality and British Cinema in the Second World War*, eds. Christine Gledhill and G. Sawson, (Manchester, 1996), 127–39.

2. Sonya O. Rose, *Which People's War?: National Identity and Citizenship in Wartime Britain, 1939–1945* (Oxford, 2003), 135.

3. Quoted by Rose, 123.

4. Lucy Noakes, *War and the British: Gender and National Identity, 1939–91*, (London, 1998), 64; Jo Spence, "'What Did you Do In the War Mummy?': Class and Gender Images of Women", *Photography/Politics One*, 1977, 33; Winship, "Women's Magazines".

5. See Annalisa Zox-Weaver "When the War Was in *Vogue*: Lee Miller's War Reports", *Women's Studies* 32 (2003), 137; and Jean Gallagher, "Vision, Violence and *Vogue*", in her *World Wars Through the Female Gaze* (Carbondale, IL, 1998), 68–96.

6. Zox-Weaver, "When the War", 137.

7　*Vogue*, 20 September 1939, n.p. *Vogue* refers to British *Vogue*, unless otherwise stated.

8　*Ibid.*

9　*Vogue*, 20 September 1939, 23.

10　"Here and Now Resolve to Shop Courageously to Look Your Best", *Vogue*, 20 September 1939, 44.

11　*Ibid.*

12　"Power behind the Throne", *Vogue*, 20 September 1939, 25.

13　*Ibid.*

14　*Ibid.*, 26.

15　*Ibid.*

16　"*Vogue's* Thumb is Up, *Vogue's* Thumb is Down", *Vogue*, November 1939, 19.

17　Elizabeth Arden advertisement, *Vogue*, November 1939, 18.

18　*Ibid.*

19　"*Vogue's* Thumb is Up", 19.

20　*Ibid.*

21　Interestingly, in 1952 *Vogue* contained an article referring to the 1920s as a period of "decadence, neurosis, and futility" in which woman "denied her nature, cut her hair like a boy, [and] dressed like an immature child, avoiding her husband, home and children. (Joyce Carey, *Vogue*, October 1952, 126).

22　"Vogue's eye-view of no margin for error", *Vogue*, October 1940, 33.

23　*Ibid.* Hats were exempt from rationing, so women who could afford them could buy new ones to perk up their wardrobes, as well as their spirits. None of the sources explain why hats were not rationed, but British historians and curators, such as Kirkham and Amy de laHaye, speculate that it was due to a belief that they would boost morale. It may also have been in support of the British millinery industry. On hats and rationing, see Pat Kirkham, "Beauty and Duty", 22. See also Board of Trade Document, 'Clothing Coupon Quiz', HMSO, September, 1941: xiv: "Headgear is coupon-free, but scarves made into headgear require coupons'. See also, File Report 830, August, 1941, "Clothes Rationing", Mass Observation; File Report 791, "Clothes Rationing", July, 1941, Mass Observation, and File Report 1257, May, 1942, "Changes in Clothing Habits", in April 1941 and 1942, Mass Observation.

24　"Beauty Savings", *Vogue*, October 1940, 72.

25　*Ibid.*

26　Despite the Blitz, staff shortages and paper rationing, *Vogue's* wartime circulation climbed to 80,000. "A hopeful reader had to wait for a death to get on to the subscriber's list". (Jane Mulvagh, "Obituary, Audrey Withers", *The Independent*, 2 November 2001.) *Vogue* was a middle-class women's magazine, although we know that it was read in the doctor's office waiting room and the hairdressers, as it is today, and that it was passed from woman to woman during wartime. The most popular weekly wartime women's magazine, *Woman*, by contrast, was aimed at lower middle-class readers and had a readership of 750,000 in 1938 (Noakes, *War and the British*, 60). Newsprint production was limited during the war, with the weekly tonnage reduced from an average of 21,000–23,000 in 1938 to 4,320, at its lowest point in 1942. Advertising revenue fell as well. The Paper Control Order (no. 19) in June 1940 restricted the number of pages published. At some points in the war, for instance, *Woman* was restricted to only twenty small weekly pages. However, these restrictions seem not to have decreased the magazine's popularity and some speculate that the war increased readership (Noakes, 61). Mary Grieve, the editor of *Woman*, remembered how "a tremendous unsatisfied demand built up" during the war. "Copies were passed around three or four households with a readership of half a dozen per copy. Finally, the tattered remains were bundled off to a Service camp or hospital". (Grieve, quoted by Noakes, 61).

27 "Problem Hands", *Vogue*, February 1944, 34.
28 *Ibid.*
29 *Ibid.*
30 Pat Kirkham", Beauty and Duty", 16.
31 Noakes notes that although women's magazine editors "were quick to realise the potential the magazines held for transmitting information, idea and propaganda to their wartime audience", the government was slow to do so. She argues that the Ministry of Information, established in September 1939 to censor the press and produce wartime slogans and pamphlets, "barely registered the existence of women's magazines". This, she speculates, both reflected the magazines' low status, and the fact that the Ministry did not recognize the importance of imparting "information and morale-boosting propaganda to women" (60). Finally, in the spring of 1941, regular meetings were organized between the primarily female editors of Britain's women's magazines and that Ministry. Yet, "although the magazines incorporated much governmental advice into their editorial pages, they were never simply a mouthpiece for government policies" (60). Government authorities did ask for *Vogue's* editor, Withers, support "on matters affecting civilian life", including the Utility clothing scheme briefly discussed in this chapter. Carolyn Burke, *Lee Miller*, (London, 2005), 202. Once Miller became an official war correspondent, her articles were subject to government censorship. The original transcripts with their marks of censorship reside in her archive in East Sussex.
32 "Emergency Meals", *Vogue*, November 1939, 63.
33 *Ibid.*
34 "'Come When you can' Cooking", *Vogue*, March 1941, 70.
35 "General Economy", *Vogue*, May 1942, 21.
36 "Get Your Goat", *Vogue,* January, 1942, 74.
37 "No Nanny", *Vogue*, March 1942, 54.
38 *Ibid.*
39 "Doing things By Halves", *Vogue*, August 1944, 76.
40 "Stretch Your Wardrobe", *Vogue*, March 1942, 60, 61. "Make Do and Mend" was a government slogan launched in June, 1941.
41 "Cheerful Inside", *Vogue,* 20 September 1939, 47.
42 *Ibid.* Emphasis in the original.
43 Lesley Blanch, "Living the Sheltered Life", *Vogue*, October 1940, 47, 96.
44 "Here is *Vogue* in spite of it all", *Vogue*, November 1940, 19.
45 Lee Miller, 1940, quoted by Burke, *Lee Miller*, 206. Before the middle of 1944, the war "produced more deaths among civilians in Britain than among those who were in the fighting services". (Rose, *Which People's War?*, 1).
46 Angus Calder, *The People's War: Britain 1939–1945* (London [1969], 1992), 226.

47 Richard Titmuss, *Problems of Social Policy* (London, 1950), 324.
48 See for example, Audrey Stanley, "The Lay of the Land: The Girls of the Land Army", *Vogue*, May 1943, 56–7, 90; Lesley Blanch, "Night Life Now", on the Women's Services, *Vogue*, June 1943, 28–31; "Special Services", *Vogue*, July 1944, 50–1; Miller, "Unarmed Warriors", *Vogue*, September 1945, 35.
49 Condé Nast, telegram, 1939, quoted by Antony Penrose, *The Lives of Lee Miller* (London [1985], 2002), 98 and Burke, *Miller*, 202.
50 Penrose, *Lives*, 109.
51 Anonymous, "Thus Do Tastes Differ", *Vanity Fair*, May 1934, 51–2.
52 See Penrose, *Lives*, 16–96, and Burke, *Miller*, 39–193.
53 Anne Scott-James, "The Taking of a Fashion Magazine Photograph", *Picture Post*, 26 October, 1940, 22–5.
54 Kirkham, "Beauty and Duty", 23–4.
55 *Ibid.*
56 David Scherman, "Foreword", in *Lee Miller's War*, ed. Antony Penrose, (London, 2005), 9.
57 Withers, Interview, quoted by Burke, *Miller*, 222.
58 Penrose, *Lives*, 114.
59 Withers, quoted by Penrose, *Lives*, 118.
60 Herbert "Bud" Myers, interview with the author, at his home, Pennyroyal Farm, Collinsville, North Carolina, USA, 21 June, 2003.
61 *Ibid.*
62 Miller, "Unarmed", 85.
63 On Second World War reporting, see Paul Fussell, *Wartime: Understanding Behaviour in the Second World War* (Oxford, 1989). Although it is also true that in the last two years of the war photographs of injured and dead American soldiers appeared in the U.S. press. "According to Susan Moeller and George Roeder, [this] increasingly graphic depiction ... was aimed, in overtly articulated government policy, at reducing civilian complacency over the outcome of the war, producing greater agreement with the home-front sacrifices such as rationing and wage controls, and improving morale". (Gallagher, 80)
64 See my pieces on Miller's earlier work, "Lee Miller", *Fashion Theory*, 10 nos. 1&2, (2006): 97–126 and "Lee Miller's Simultaneity", in *Fashion as Photograph*, ed. E. Shinkle, (New York, 2008).
65 Miller, "Unarmed", 36.
66 Withers, quoted by Burke, *Miller*, 222.
67 Miller, "Unarmed", 82, 85.
68 Miller, "St. Malo", *Vogue*, October 1944, 51.
69 *Ibid.*, 84.
70 *Ibid.*, 86.
71 Miller, "Germany – the war that is won", *Vogue*, June, 1945, 84, 89.
72 *Ibid.*, 41.
73 *Ibid.*
74 *Ibid.*, 42, 84.
75 Lee Miller, "Hitleriana", *Vogue*, July, 1945, 36–7, 72–4.
76 Miller took a similar photograph of Scherman in Hitler's tub which has never been published. It appeared in the V&A Museum's *Lee Miller Centenary* exhibition in autumn 2007 for the first time.

77   Zox-Weaver, "When the War", 156.
78   *Ibid.*
79   Miller's text describing the "hausmeister" was edited out of the published version of "Hitleriana". The entire text appears in Penrose, *Lee Miller's War,* chap. 12. The photograph of the serviceman is reproduced in Mark Haworth-Booth, *The Art of Lee Miller,* (London, 2007), 198.
80   Miller, "Hitleriana", 73.
81   *Ibid.,* 74.
82   Gallagher, "Vision, Violence", 91. Gallagher also claims, citing an article from the *New Yorker* June 9, 1945, that "Miller's description of these domestic spaces and consumer objects is part of a larger pattern of American reportage on the end of the Third Reich" (Gallagher, n. 15, 168). This would be very interesting to explore further.
83   *Ibid.*
84   Zox-Weaver, *"When the War",* 157.
85   *Ibid.*
86   Some would argue that Miller's use of juxtaposition is in keeping with what Max Ernst described in 1934 as the surrealist "procedure": "the exploitation of the fortuitous meeting of two distant realities on one plane" (Max Ernst, *Une Semaine de Bonté, ou les Sept Eléments Capitaux* (Paris, 1934). Whitney Chadwick, for instance, states that Miller's photographs "show the surrealist love for evocative juxtaposition" (Chadwick, *Women Artists and the Surrealist Movement* (New York, 1985, 39). Many scholars of surrealism are quick to point out that surrealism did not attempt to merely highlight juxtapositions such as beauty/ugliness, sense/nonsense, etc, like some other twentieth century modern movements, but rather it aimed to reconcile them through insisting on a higher reality, especially through a "dialectical resolution of the contradiction between conscious and unconscious". (Penelope Rosemont, "Introduction", *Surrealist Women: An International Anthology* (Austin, 1998, xxxiii). André Breton proclaimed in "Manifesto of Surrealism" (1924, 23–4): "I believe in the future resolution of these two states, dream and reality, which are seemingly so contradictory, into a kind of absolute reality, a surreality".
87   "Dresses worth a straw", *Vogue,* July 1945, 34–5.
88   "Showing a well-groomed leg", *Vogue,* July 1945, 30.
89   *Vogue,* 20 September, 1939, n.p.

8
"Fighting for the Idea of Home Life": *Mrs Miniver* and Anglo-American Representations of Domestic Morale

Susan R. Grayzel

I.

First appearing as the title character in a column by Jan Struther [the pseudonym of Joyce Maxtone Graham] in the London *Times* in the late 1930s, "Mrs. Miniver" went on to achieve iconic status as a trans-Atlantic image of stoic womanhood in the face of the traumas of World War Two.[1] The book version of *Mrs Miniver* was a bestseller in both Britain and the United States, and the Hollywood film version, which opened in June of 1942 in the United States and a month later in Britain, went on to win the Academy Award for Best Picture. Such acclaim for a story about war (both anticipated and then experienced) that focuses mainly on family life and the so-called home front suggests that it may tell us something significant about how Anglo-American culture constructed women at home as active wartime participants. By examining the popular images of gender and class during World War Two through an analysis of *Mrs Miniver*, this essay participates in the ongoing project of rethinking what is meant by "the people's war" and by the "myth of the Blitz" as key elements of the war's cultural experience. It further explores how these two notions interacted with the ways in which women became held responsible for maintaining domestic morale.

As a good deal of the literature on women and war has shown, women's contributions to war have most often been limited to the waged and unwaged active labour of working for the armed forces or in civilian capacities that directly influence the war effort.[2] The military has grown to include women, yet governments waging modern wars have sought to involve civilians in other capacities. The production of war material, from shells to uniforms to food, in industrialized war has required the participation of women in factories, workshops and fields. From the Crimean and Civil Wars of the nineteenth century, medical services also drew upon the allegedly special traits of women that rendered them unfit for combat but quite suited for the caretaking duties associated with wartime nursing. This visible activity, understandably perhaps, receives the bulk of attention, but maintaining the support of civilians has become one of the fundamental aspects of modern, total wars – a task often bequeathed to women with mixed emotions and mixed results.

The *Oxford English Dictionary* traces the origins of the word "morale" to the nineteenth century, defining it as "[m]oral condition; conduct, behaviour; esp. with regard to confidence, hope, zeal, submission to discipline, etc. Said of a body of persons engaged in some enterprise, esp. of troops".[3] Most of the examples, and indeed the common understanding of "morale" applied to military personnel. The notion of civilian morale was largely an invention of the First World War. Concern about how those at home would respond to wartime hardships as well as how they might influence the military can be found throughout Allied wartime media. The role of women was seen as especially central to this effort. From the outbreak of war in 1914 onward, print media and informal as well as official propaganda emphasized the need for women to be cheerful as they sent their men off to war. Wartime women received both visual and verbal cues about how to persuade men to keep fighting and to show themselves worthy of their sacrifices by making some of their own.

As an article in Britain's *Evening Standard* put it in August 1914: "it is not too much to ask that the women who have bid God-speed to those they love with a cheery word and smile should take the fortunes of war with an equally serene and calm confidence".[4] In addition to maintaining this calm serenity themselves, middle and upper-class women were also called upon to set examples for their presumably less "calm" working-class counterparts. As the war continued, a variety of charitable and voluntary organizations came to rely on female labour to sustain troop morale in canteens, rest huts or via the auspices of the YMCA. However, propaganda aimed at encouraging women to support men in uniform could also backfire. Both the British and American governments became concerned with the "dangers" that young women suffering from what the British called "khaki fever" could pose to military men and thus emphasized the need for sober and restrained, i.e. non-sexual, interaction between men and women.[5]

Propaganda focused on women and also created by them was thus a feature of war as it returned to Europe in the 1930s in Spain. Moreover, this took shape against a backdrop of women's international protest against war and militarism (and fascism). By not only mobilizing women but also focusing on them as key components of the war effort, governments in the prelude to World War Two and its duration followed patterns previously established in the First World War. They linked a variety of behaviours and qualities – thrift, serenity, steadfastness, cheerfulness – that could be exhibited by women with the maintenance of good, civilian morale and the successful outcome of the war.

In Britain, agencies such as Mass Observation took note of morale, especially among women, and a report issued in 1940 sheds some important light on this:

> The word 'morale' has been used widely by press and Government propaganda to describe the state of the public mind about the war and the principles for which we are fighting. An official definition of morale has yet to be given.... Though many of them are now doing a man's job, sharing with men danger and hardship, the morale of women cannot be judged by the same standards as that of men and soldiers. The housewife, though she has not the direct leadership and discipline that the soldier experiences, may have to undergo more danger and put up with more inconveniences than her husband. It is the propaganda of her everyday life which determines whether she accepts war and sacrifice willingly or not.[6]

After spending some time illustrating how women across Britain are facing the war, the report concludes that "the majority are accepting the inevitable, not with a fervour that accepts sacrifice as a duty, but with a quiet endurance and passivity that conserves their energies for the humdrum, everyday tasks necessary for holding together what remains of ordinary life and habit".[7]

The desire to allow the maintenance of "ordinary life and habit" emerges across participant nations, and so too does concern with how women would face such threats to "good" morale as the arrival of air raids (again something set in motion in World War One). The Mass-Observation report just quoted noted that while raids did affect women at first – "[t]here are recorded very few instances of women's morale being seriously affected by raids".[8] Yet, there is contradictory evidence that the threat of raids, as well as the experience of them, could become a serious threat to morale. Even American women in the service, allegedly prepared to face enemy fire, could recall fright during an air raid. When working in Iwo Jima, Mary Dahl describes that "our lowest morale point" came during air raids: "we were really scared".[9] Women's ability to sustain morale despite the hardships imposed by war – be they military dangers or economic and material deprivation – thus emerges as something to be actively cultivated.

It is within this context that it may be worthwhile to explore some of the multiple ways in which women's roles as the keepers of morale were constructed and received on both sides of the Atlantic immediately before and during World War Two through an analysis of one significant work of popular culture, *Mrs Miniver*. As the discussion of the literary and cinematic versions of this far from ordinary fictional character that follow will suggest, providing an emblematic heroine who faces the hardships of war without flinching offered a model to its female audiences – especially to wives and mothers rather than mobilized single women – of how they too should ideally react to the exigencies of World War Two.

Facing up to war without allowing one's emotions to intervene became part of a parcel of behaviours that wartime governments expected their civilians to exhibit, and this expectation transcended national borders. Yet in Britain, as the postwar "myth of the Blitz" enshrined such virtues as being exhibited across class, gender and ethnicity, it elided numerous differences, not only ones of temperament.[10] As Sonya Rose has so thoughtfully explored, the notion of the unified nation fighting a "people's war" begs the question, "which people's war?"[11] Kay Miniver's fictional experiences are meant to reflect those of "everywoman" facing war and thus to mask class tensions, but this may have been accepted across the Atlantic in ways that were more difficult at home in Britain.

II.

When war seemed imminent in Europe in the late 1930s, governments had already prepared appeals to "ordinary" women. The British government had laid the groundwork for how to instruct the civilian population to respond to future wars during the 1920s and 30s, including plans for providing shelters from air raids in both private homes and public spaces and protection from chemical weapons by issuing gas masks. They made arrangements for evacuating children and mobilizing men and, wherever possible, women as well. Along with these practical preparations, they tried to ensure that these actions would proceed calmly and not unduly upset the civil population. If the government could issue posters and pamphlets, those supportive of these efforts could pass along similar messages through other cultural means. One example of how this could be done by taking already popular figures through this process can be found in the depictions of *Mrs Miniver*.[12]

By the time readers reach the end of Jan Struther's 1939 *Mrs Miniver* – just as the audience of the *Times'* columns upon which they were based had previously done – they have been able to go inside a lovely English family of five, seeing them celebrate Christmas and walk in the countryside on holiday. Readers have seemingly eavesdropped upon an upper-class mother's thoughts on everything from shopping to parenting. Furthermore, the placement of Struther's pieces alongside the court circular announcements, notices of engagements and marriages and advertisements for women's fashions attests to its associations with an idealized world of traditional national, familial and gender concerns.[13] When this chatty, domestic woman then turns to look at a world preparing for war, the stoic courage that is emblematic of transcendent, good civilian morale takes over. The sense of a larger, looming crisis beyond the boundaries of the home emerges gradually but Mrs Miniver provides a role model for how to address it.

One of the earliest indications of the growing threat to her comforting domesticity comes when she describes the task of fitting herself, her children (and her servants, an indication of her class status) with gas masks. Mrs Miniver reflects on the stack of masks "covering the floor like a growth of black fungus" that "it was for this ... that one had boiled the milk for their bottles, and washed their hands before lunch". The inability to protect one's children is part of what this new warfare brings and yet, Struther through Miniver points out, women also have the responsibility to guard against blind nationalism and hatred, that "was the most important of all the forms of war work which she and other women would have to do: there are no tangible gas masks to defend us in war-time against its slow, yellow, drifting corruption of the mind". When the danger of imminent war seemingly passes, she recounts her family "poorer by a few layers of security" but enlarged by a sense of "looking at each other, and at their cherished possessions, with new eyes ... by a sudden clarifying of intentions".[14]

A bit later, Mrs Miniver describes her own willingness to take in as many evacuated children as possible at the family's home in Kent; she is eager to perform this bit of wartime service. She then satirizes a titled woman complaining about the entire scheme and recounting the lady's command to the billeting surveyor that "if the worst does come to the worst, you must make it quite clear to the authorities that I can only accept Really Nice Children".[15] Then, in London in August, she meets a woman in a park practicing knots for First Aid, and her thoughts take in the fact that "the ever-present contingency of war" has some positive effect: "almost everybody you meet is busy learning something".[16] There is an idealism to Mrs. Miniver in her desire to see good and reject bias whether based on class or national distinctions. A kind of simplified internationalism appears when she describes the similarities between children, regardless of their nationality, and thinks of what could be accomplished if "all governments would spend the price of a few bombers on exchanging for the holidays, free of charge, a certain number of families …" so that they could get to know one another as people first and foremost.[17]

The trans-Atlantic bestselling book – and its selection by the Book-of-the-Month Club testifies to its middlebrow appeal in the United States – ends with a "letter" from Mrs. Miniver dated 25 September 1939, with Britain now officially at war. She describes her husband's battery quartered in a girls' school, and her own children adjusting to "our seven tough and charming évacuées". She then summarizes the mood: "we're all so buoyed up just now with the crusading spirit, and … burningly convinced of the infamy of the Government we're fighting against (this time, thank goodness, one doesn't say 'the nation we're fighting against')". Once again, Caroline (Kay) Miniver expresses a broadly humanitarian appeal to her fellow citizens, to keep in mind that it is a government they are preparing to fight, not a people, and yet the ability to express this sentiment shows what is different about "our" side. Yet she continues, "it oughtn't to need a war to make a nation… give all its slum children a holiday in the country … to make us … live simply, and eat sparingly, and recover the use of our legs, and get up early enough to see the sun rise".[18]

Reviewing the collection of vignettes published as *Mrs Miniver* in *The Times*, a critic took note of the fact that the character was not universally popular, "a correspondent recently wrote to *The Times* to say that he (or she) loathed her and wished she might be hit by a bomb because she is so invariably successful and right". The critic added, however, that what "Mrs Miniver does possess and what is no little comfort in these times is a combination of serenity and humour … common sense and calm". All qualities that "these times" – the outbreak of war – required.[19] A short review in *Punch* also offered a positive assessment, that the last chapter "has something to say about the things that it has needed this war to teach us and that no peace must make us forget, which are very well worth saying".[20] The potentially inspirational power of Mrs Miniver was further noted in a letter to the editor of *The Times* in September 1939 asking if her reactions to the war would be forthcoming: "her peculiar brand of commonsense idealism would be more than ever comforting" under the current circumstances.[21]

In a rather critical review of the book, novelist Rosamond Lehmann claims to speak for the minority who find that Mrs Miniver, despite her tact, kindness, tolerance, humor and contentment, "exercises an oppression of spirits" upon her audience. Her gleaming home and charming children belie "sentimentality masquerading as sensibility". And now that "war is upon Mrs. Miniver, as it is upon all of us", she concludes "whoever is defeated, she'll come through ... she will be adaptable, and come up, shaken but intact, whatever new society emerges".[22] Lehmann seems to suggest that an apolitical domestic woman (with a naive politics of just wanting everyone to get along and if not they need to appreciate the simple things life offers us – sunrises and the countryside) could survive as easily under fascism or democracy. This is the dangerous undercurrent to the promotion of domesticity as apolitical and therefore stable; confining women to an untarnished separate sphere of home and family during wartime itself carries risks to the successful outcome of the war.

It would take a film version of Mrs. Miniver both to broaden her audience and change her into a more political creature, whose belief in transcending differences among people clearly does not blind her to the horrors of what Nazi Germany contains. Meantime, Struther would continue to represent British women as possessing an ability to hold on to essential values by writing the introduction to a collection of letters, entitled *Women of Britain*, published in the United States in 1941. In it, she hoped to help provide "a true picture of wartime life in Great Britain", and began by acknowledging what was different about this new war, "in which the entire domestic life of one of the most domesticated countries in the world [has been] turned inside out and upside down .... In war, our upbringing had led us to suppose, the men would go away to fight in order to defend their homes .... We certainly never imagined a war in which the homes themselves would be changed almost beyond recognition".[23]

Struther emphasizes that she refers here not merely to the "comparatively few homes which have been physically destroyed by fire or high explosive", but the nearly universal way in which those occupying homes from villas to tenements have "been forced to change the whole rhythm and pattern of ... daily life".[24] She explains further: "when a nation has already had the greater part of its home life disrupted, transplanted or indefinitely suspended, and it still goes on fighting and enduring, than we know that it is fighting for something more precious than bricks and mortar, more precious even than its own home life – that is, it is fighting for the *idea* of home life, for the right of all human beings to live how and where they like".[25] Yet the positive lessons to be learned from all such changes, in family life, children, and the home, are what Struther ultimately emphasizes, continuing to show an American audience not only what Britons fight for – the very idea of home life – but also what they too might learn in preparation for entering a war-torn world.

III.

By the fall of 1941, four screenwriters, including George Froeschel, an Austrian refugee, along with William Wyler (himself a German Jewish immigrant) were working on a film adaptation of Struther's *Mrs Miniver*; the film itself being the brainchild of Hollywood producer Sidney Franklin. Between the American publication of the book in 1940 and the appearance of the completed film in mid-1942, a great deal had changed in the American context: war was underway in all its facets. In Europe, Britain had endured the onslaught of aerial attacks in the autumn of 1940 that became known as the Blitz and by the time of the film's release, the United States had experienced the attack on Pearl Harbor. Thus, while the original intent may have been to show Americans (and especially American women) how to respond to the possibility of a war that might directly affect their home lives, the film ended up being avidly consumed by a wartime audience both American and British.[26]

When the literary figure of Mrs Miniver was transformed in the 1942 film, her heroism took on both more inspirational and practical forms. Interestingly enough, the military war experiences of both Mr Minivers (Clem, the husband, and Vin, the eldest son) take place off-screen. The father goes to Dunkirk in the mythic expedition to rescue stranded troops after the fall of France; the son joins the RAF. It is the Mrs Minivers (the mother and eventual daughter-in-law) who are portrayed as facing the enemy directly. First and foremost, however, the story adapts the "lovely English family of five" into one now facing blackouts, bombs and, ultimately, the death of loved ones.

The film begins by establishing a portrait of the Minivers, especially of the parents, and of a deceptively simple life in suburban England, whose inhabitants are preoccupied with growing roses, buying hats and the domestic pleasures of an idyllic home life. A hint of politics first appears when the eldest son Vin returns from Oxford, full of radical ideas about class inequality and how it might be overcome, but he is portrayed as a bit of a young idiot, at best naïve, so his views are clearly not meant to be taken seriously. Unlike the book, where we are witnesses to the build up to war, the film depicts it occurring without warning (something for which British reviewers would be quick to take it to task).

We see some of the wartime adjustments with comic effect – an air raid warden who is also the town's grocer both inspects the family's precautions and tries to sell provisions at the same time – but gradually, war transforms the family. Vin achieves a purpose in life by becoming a pilot, and, as mentioned earlier, Clem Miniver joins a group of local men (and their boats) to voyage to an unknown location. We see his boat join others in a huge flotilla – and we see his disheveled appearance upon his return – but of the actual rescue at Dunkirk, we see nothing. Instead, while Clem is away, in one of the film's most famous scenes, the unarmed Kay Miniver confronts and ultimately defeats a fallen German pilot.

The first sign of something wrong comes when she spots boots in the grass and then a gun, but before she can reach the gun, the young German gets up and chases her into her home, into the kitchen (its symbolic and literal heart) and then demands, in mono-syllables, "bread", "milk" and "meat". While she confesses her fear, asking him to stop pointing his gun at her because it "frightens" her, there is a kind of maternal sympathy as she watches him devour food and observes the debilitation caused by his wound. Finally, he collapses; she is able to grab the gun and rushes to telephone the police.

When she returns to the kitchen and he regains consciousness, she helps him up from the floor and ministers to him, assuring him that he'll be well looked after in the hospital and that after all, "the war won't last forever". In response, the German reveals the fanaticism of the enemy. He admits to his failure but declares that others will come to finish it off: "you will see ... we will come. We will bomb your cities". And, he continues, England will be like other places that have fallen to the Reich. When Mrs Miniver protests that the war has thus far entailed the bombing of "innocent people" and of "women and children", he declares that there will be "the same thing here". At this, Kay Miniver turns from the maternal everywoman to the female patriot and slaps him across the face. The police and a doctor then arrive to take the airman away, and the scene closes with her reassuring the doctor that she's perfectly "all right".

The scene reveals the core of steel in this wife and mother but without making her any less maternal or domestic. She is quick to be sympathetic, even to an enemy – who is clearly meant to be akin to her pilot son – but just as quick to be outraged by the viciousness of his ideology. She never panics, and she ends up in control of the situation, if not, understandably, of all of her emotions. Our final glimpse of her in the kitchen, after she herself has finally sat down to breathe after the ordeal, reveals her cradling her youngest child, restraining her tears, as he asks "who was here Mummy?" If the enemy has been in her home, she has protected it, her family and herself from harm.

Shortly thereafter, we witness the entire family under fire as they endure an air raid from within their backyard's Anderson shelter. By focusing on the family, and particularly by foregrounding Mrs Miniver, the film allows the audience to vicariously experience the raid in all its noisy and fearful uncertainty. It is a sentimental yet highly effective moment; the mother has just finished reading *Alice in Wonderland* and tucked her two small children in. The father goes out to have a last smoke on his pipe and both parents watch distant explosions as if they were fireworks before settling themselves into the shelter for the night. While she is knitting and he has his tea and biscuits, they discuss their elder son Vin's return from his Scottish honeymoon with his new (aristocratic) wife Carol. All so cosy and, if not for the setting, so far-removed from war. Then, the sound of planes and bombs grows louder and louder, but we never leave the cramped interior of the shelter. It begins to shake, objects fall off shelves, we see the gas mask containers for the entire family; the explosions grow louder, the door swings open – flames vaguely appear outside – the children awaken, and the mother tries to comfort them over the deafening sound of the aerial onslaught. The camera focuses on Mrs Miniver throughout; she remains the centerpiece as the child in her arms cries out the scene's last line, "they nearly killed us this time Mummy". Yet once again, the emotions of Mrs Miniver are displayed on her face, not in any panic-stricken words or gestures. She holds her child close, offers comfort, and does not express fear.

It is not until the next morning, when the elder Mr and Mrs Miniver return from picking up the newlyweds at the train station that we see the material effects of the previous night's raid. The house has been hit directly; war has literally come home, and yet Mrs Miniver carries on as if a hole in her roof were only a minor inconvenience. The scene in the shelter also underscores the words of the downed pilot, lest we have forgotten. More enemy fliers have come, and they have bombed "women and children". Yet if Kay Miniver cannot deliver a literal slap in the face to those who have wrecked her home, she can deliver (and implicitly so too can all women) a metaphorical slap in the face by ignoring the devastation and carrying on.

In what is arguably the film's tragic denouement, the junior Mrs Miniver is killed during an air raid as her mother-in-law tries to drive them both to safety. Once again, here is an intrusion of war without warning, disrupting the annual flower show, symbolic of an idealized England. The perspective of the two women in the car becomes ours as they watch a flaming plane sink to the ground, followed by another that sprays gunfire across the roadway. Carol is hit; an innocent civilian, female victim of the war, and we feel the sense of horror and violation by looking into Kay Miniver's face. Yet even in this instant, and its immediate aftermath, we witness too the strength of those waging, as the Minister's sermon in his bombed-out church reminds us, "a people's war". The enemy may attack these ordinary people and kill women and the young, but they will not surrender.

It is the main character's actions after the culmination of all these traumatic events that are so striking. Despite the intensity of these experiences, Mrs Miniver exudes calm stoic acceptance and certainty that in the end Britain will prevail – in other words, the essence of good morale and the embodiment of the people's war. While the final words of encouragement are left to the minister to deliver at the funeral service, the film makes clear the essential heroism of its (and potentially all) women.

It is one thing to analyse a cultural text for its overt and hidden messages. It is another to recover what contemporaries made of such messages. The film was a success in the United States and Britain; a survey conducted by Britain's Mass Observation found that it was the most popular box-office film of 1942.[27] Popular opinion and critical opinion, however, diverged, largely along national lines.

The *New York Times'* Bosley Crowther began his response to the film as follows:

> It is hard to believe that a picture could be made within the heat of present strife which would clearly but without a cry for vengeance, crystallize the cruel effect of total war upon a civilized people. Yet that is what has been magnificently done in ...'Mrs. Miniver.' ... For this is not a war film about soldiers in uniform ... This is a film about the people in a small, unpretentious English town on whom the war creeps up slowly, disturbing their tranquil ways of life, then suddenly bursts in devastating fury as the bombs rain down and the Battle of Britain is on. This is a film of modern warfare in which civilians become the front-line fighters and the ingrained courage of the people becomes the nation's most vital strength.[28]

From the outset then, the film became more than a woman's film and more than a war film; it was seen as revealing the transformation in modern war that "turned" civilians like Mrs Miniver into "front-line fighters". This was the startling aspect – after all there was nothing unusual about turning male civilians into "front-line fighters". Yet, as we have seen, Mrs Miniver is a particular kind of "front-line fighter", neither aggressive nor passive. She responds to crises without betraying either her essential femininity or the most outward emblems of fear.

Other American responses in the mass media tended to agree with Crowther's positive assessment. "Whether or not the screen story was contrived as propaganda for our side, the Metro-Goldwyn-Mayer release happens to pack a more persuasive wallop than half a dozen propaganda films pitched in a heroic key", stated the review in *Newsweek*. The review went on to offer the following praise "every sequence, humorous or grim, has been written with good taste and intelligence".[29] *The Commonweal* extolled it as a film that few could surpass in its portrayal of "people caught in total war ... Through misty eyes we see why England survived".[30] *The New Yorker*'s reviewer described the film as "stupendous" ... "the final say on the superb and hellish struggle of English families from the beginning of the war until today". In particular, it singled out that the picture depended upon the performance of Greer Garson as "Mrs. Miniver", as it summarizes her war experiences at the end of the film as follows: "She has seen her son off to the air corps; she has waited while her husband ran their launch on some strange errand, which turned out to be Dunkerque; she has had to deal with a wounded German found hiding in her garden; she has had to spend a night with her two younger children and her husband in an air-raid shelter while bombs blew half her house to pieces above them; and she has had to see her son's young bride die from a gun wound".[31] Throughout all these activities, she has also, implicitly, remained both maternal and steadfast.

Time magazine offered both an enthusiastic review of the film and appraisal of the director. Like other magazines, *Time*'s critic celebrated "that almost impossible feat, a great war picture that photographs the inner meaning, instead of the outward realism of World War II .... With reticence, good taste, and an understanding of events, [Director Wyler] reflects the war's global havoc without ever taking his cameras off the Minivers' quiet corner of England". It made some of the implied messages of the film obvious to Americans, by singling out the scene where the war is "reduced to the compass of an Anderson shelter when the Minivers and their well-scrubbed youngsters ride out an air raid in their own backyard. It is anybody's backyard, anywhere". Noting the improvement over "the bathetic whimsey" of Struther's best-seller, the review concludes by praising "womanly Greer Garson's Mrs. Miniver.

She had to be, and is, exactly right". This review further attributes the film's success to its director, William Wyler, and his understanding of war through experiencing World War I in a zone that changed hands between the French and Germans many times, "Wyler spent considerable time underground. His most vivid memory: crawling out of the cellar after each conflict, wondering whether he was French or German".[32] This offers a reminder of the relationship between the filmmaker and the conditions of modern war; Wyler may be able to convey what it is like to be bombed at home because he has himself endured it.

A longer reflection in the Sunday *New York Times* offered the main film critic's views on what the film meant for American audiences: "a clear compelling picture of the impact of war upon civilisation – a picture made all the more credible by the plainly essential fact that it shows that impact upon people who might just as soon be you". While it might not depict the range of suffering inflicted by aerial warfare on Britain, it offered something more: "we who are still enjoying comparative security on our own home front are much more affected by a picture which shows a sudden violent disruption of pleasant life than we would be say, by a picture which showed the peacetime underprivileged handed more woe". Moreover, Crowther stressed that the film illustrates "the spiritual test of an entire nation" and "the obligation of courage which strife impels", the singular importance of domestic morale for all home fronts.[33]

Nor were British audiences long to be kept in the dark about the outpouring of critical and popular acclaim for the film. The day after it opened in New York, the *Times* of London's correspondent sent a special report on the American reactions quoting Crowther's line about this "most exalting tribute to the British, who have taken it so gallantly ... Two years ago yesterday Winston Churchill gave his memorable address, 'We shall go on to the end ... we shall never surrender,' It was most propitious that *Mrs. Miniver* should open on that anniversary. One seeing it can understand why there was no doubt in Mr. Churchill's mind".[34]

The Times of London began its own reflection after the film's British debut, a month later, by noting the differences between the book and the film, seeing the latter as using the Minivers as "a means of illustrating to America the way in which the English behave under the impact of war". Yet "the picture of England at war suffers from that distortion which seems inevitable whenever Hollywood cameras are trained on it. It is absurd to show an English village... caught unprepared for the news of the declaration of war". Even if such mistakes are tangential to the film, they "nag at the natural sense of gratitude for an American film which is generous and whole-hearted in its desire to offer tribute to the courage and character of ordinary people attacked by a force they are determined to resist".[35]

Other British critics had harsher things to say about how "their war" had been reinterpreted by Hollywood. In other British reviews, the class biases of the film were brought to the forefront. Writing in the *New Statesman and Nation* in July 1942, William Whitebait begins by commenting that "Most American films about England ... at war, have a blithe inaccuracy that soars at times into fantasy". While noting that some aspects of the film are less "calamitous" than one might imagine, he assails the film for at most achieving "an easy pathos; sentimentality (and class sentimentality at that) takes on a tone of holiness, of smug simplicity, which personally I found it rather difficult to bear. 'This is a people's war', says the vicar delivering a sermon in his bombed church; but it isn't, it is only (look round at the faces, look back over the story!) the best people's war".[36] Nor can Whitebait resist a dig at Mrs Miniver's creator, "the fact that Miss Jan Struther ... saw the Blitz from America probably also accounts for the grace with which her heroine weathers the war".

In a similar vein, the reviewer in the *Documentary News Letter* of August 1942 described it as being in many ways "just repulsive". Yet, "[y]ou can sit in the Empire [theatre] and hear practically the whole house weeping – a British audience with three years of war behind it, crying at one of the phoniest war films that has ever been made".[37] In part the critic attacks Wyler for portraying members of the working class as "morons" and generally failing to "make the forty-seven odd million people in Britain just a little more realistic". Yet, even this suggests something of the film's appeal – as its critics stated over and again – it is one based on emotion and sentimentality despite what an audience might know about the "real" nature of warfare and its "real" victims, and in particular, about the effects of the war on those without the class privileges of the Minivers.

Edgar Anstey's response in *The Spectator* begins by describing the first half hour of the film as "intolerable". If the Minivers are supposed to represent "'ordinary' people whose fortitude in luxurious adversity" is meant to be "symbolic of the British war effort", then only one conclusion can be drawn "by the transatlantic victims of such well-meaning but unconsciously pro-fascist propaganda – that the world revolution which is visible to the people of every other country in the world has manifested itself in Britain only as a defence of bourgeois privilege".[38]

Anstey refuses to let the "Hollywood" origins of the film excuse such inaccuracies. As he points out, the physical details of the Anderson shelter are accurate so why couldn't "the historical and psychological milieu" be presented in a similarly authentic manner? Although he sees the film as being fundamentally about "puppets" not "people", Anstey does find some redeeming moments – the "frightened family in the shelter, each member suppressing or communicating terror in the most convincing manner" – and goes on to assert that there is no doubt the film will be popular. Such popularity had at its root the transcendent appeal of maternal fortitude as a cornerstone of domestic morale.

IV.

Other successful women's war films reflected the contributions of women in realms more usually associated with "war work". Few, however, highlighted the "quiet" heroism of wives and mothers as effectively as *Mrs Miniver*. Although the character lives a life made easier by her class status (she has servants, a nice home and clothes and things), her situation as wife and especially as mother – to a son in uniform – is meant to rise above these differences and speak to a very widespread female audience. Like the women watching her exploits in the dark theatre, Kay Miniver does all she can to protect those she loves and to maintain the essence of domestic well-being despite the war. She comforts her children, supports her husband, runs her household and does not let material losses bother her. That she is unable to safeguard her family entirely speaks to the vulnerability of "all of us" in a wartime world. But who is meant by "all of us?" By comparing the Miniver family under threat in the book with the way the family was transformed cinematically and also exploring the varied responses to the film, embraced as being "the true story of Britain at war" in the American press while receiving a much more critical response in Britain, this essay has tried to show that uniting across class, gender and national lines was no easy task despite its mythic significance.

British commentators were aware that the main targets of the Blitz lived in the poorer neighbourhoods of London, not its posh suburbs, and that "the grace" exhibited by Mrs Miniver perhaps belonged more to the realm of fantasy. But the image of grace under fire as *the* desired way for women to respond to total war and for societies to understand the stakes of "modern" war, something that began with the First World War, became part of this decisively Anglo-American take on morale and the "home front" in World War Two. *Mrs Miniver* – in its various incarnations – tells the middle of a long story about modern warfare and how two intertwined societies would use it to see themselves – as providing ways to transcend gender, class and nation – the point of emphasizing that bombs could, although of course, did not, fall on "anyone's backyard, anywhere".

Lest we think that the lessons of *Mrs. Miniver* have no resonance in a world of women not only in uniform but also constantly under fire, consider an essay by right-wing Anglo-Canadian Barbara Amiel that appeared in *Macleans* magazine in September 2002. Entitled "A New *Mrs. Miniver* for Modern Times", Amiel described the ultimate lesson of Mrs Miniver as serving to counter "the hardship and suffering of war with resilience and humour ... to turn terror into a force that ennobled human beings rather than making them cower". Comparing the attacks of September 11, 2001 to those of the London Blitz, Amiel argues that "just as the Germans achieved the very opposite of what they intended with the Blitz terror and only succeeded in turning every housewife into *Mrs. Miniver*, so 9/11 cast the iron of America's soul into steel".[39] Such reflections continue to buy into the mythic aspects of Mrs Miniver, the notion that the upheavals of war caused all women to display ordinary heroism – to maintain good morale. In this way, "war" still can be seen as "ennobling" those far from the so-called front lines.

One can read this essay as an updated form of propaganda for a new war (which of course it is), but the endurance of Mrs Miniver as a metaphor for how civilians (women) should face modern, indiscriminate warfare is itself suggestive. Despite the changes in women's lives and in the nature of the work they can perform in wartime, the ability of ordinary women (and men) to "carry on" unquestioningly shows the undiminished significance of the need to maintain domestic morale and the ongoing power of the myth of the Blitz.

Acknowledgements

Earlier versions of this essay were presented at the 2004 conference on "Crosstown Traffic: Anglo-American Cultural Exchange since 1865" at the University of Warwick and the conference on Women, War, and Work held at the Massachusetts Historical Society. I am grateful to the organizers, participants and audiences at both for their feedback. For assistance with its later incarnations, I appreciate the criticism offered by Nancy Bercaw, Erin Chapman, Angela Hornsby, Theresa Levitt, Noell Wilson, Joe Ward, and Philippa Levine, and the inspiration of Sonya Rose.

Notes

1 For more information on her un-Miniver like life, see Ysenda Maxtone Graham, *The Real Mrs Miniver* (London, 2001).

2 There is now a vast literature on this, for the First World War alone, see the bibliography in Susan R. Grayzel, *Women and the First World War* (Longman, 2002). For American women in particular, see Lottie Gavin, *American Women in World War I: They Also Served* (Niwot CO, 1997); Dorothy and Carl J. Schneider, *Into the Breach: American Women Overseas in World War I* (New York, 1991) and Susan Zieger, *In Uncle Sam's Service: Women Workers with the American Expeditionary Force* (Ithaca, NY, 1999). For the Second World War, see the classic studies of American women, Susan M. Hartmann, *The Home Front and Beyond: American Women in the 1940s* (Boston, 1982) and D'Ann Campbell, *Women at War with America: Private Lives in a Patriotic Era* (Cambridge, MA, 1984). For important studies of British women during the Second World War, see James Hinton, *Women, Social Leadership and the Second World War: Continuities of Class* (Oxford, 2002) and Penny Summerfield, *Reconstructing Women's Wartime Lives* (Manchester, 1998). For work on wartime media and culture, including film, among many others, see Christine Gledhill and Gillian Swanson (eds.), *Nationalising Femininity: Culture, Sexuality and British Cinema in the Second World War* (Manchester, 1996); H. Mark Glancy, *When Hollywood Loved Britain: The Hollywood "British" film 1939–45* (Manchester, 1999); Antonia Lant, *Blackout: Reinventing Women for Wartime British Cinema* (Princeton, NJ, 1991); and Susan M. Schweik, *A Gulf So Deeply Cut: American Women Poets and the Second World War* (Madison, WI, 1991).

3 "Morale", *Oxford English Dictionary* Concise Edition, col. 654.

4 *Evening Standard*, 26 August 1914.

5 See the discussion of this in Grayzel, *Women and the First World War*, 9–10 and 62–77. See also Nancy K. Bristow, *Making Men Moral: Social Engineering during the Great War* (New York, 1996) and Angela Woollacott, "'Khaki Fever' and Its Control: Gender, Class, Age, and Sexual Morality on the British Homefront in the First World War", *Journal of Contemporary History* 29 (1994), 325–37.

6 "M-O Report No. 520: Women and morale, December 1940", in Dorothy Sheridan (ed.), *Wartime Women: A Mass-Observation Anthology 1937–45* (1990, Rpt London, 2000), 110–11.

7 *Ibid.*, 122.

8 *Ibid.*, 118.

9 Mary Elizabeth Dahl Jorgensen, "It Was the Patriotic Thing to Do: From Montana to Iwo Jima", in Pauline E. Parker (ed.), *Women of the Homefront: World War II Recollections of 55 Americans* (Jefferson, NC, 2002), 142.

10 For one of the clearest articulations of this idea, see Angus Calder, *The Myth of the Blitz* (London, 1991).

11 Sonya O. Rose, *Which People's War? National Identity and Citizenship in Wartime Britain, 1939–1945* (Oxford, 2003).

12 In her important study, *Forever England*, Alison Light places *Mrs Miniver*, the book, in the context of the domestic conservatism of the 1930s, but she, like others, pays scant attention to its foreshadowing of war and to the interplay between the prewar book and the wartime film. See Alison Light, *Forever England: Femininity, Literature and Conservatism between the Wars* (Routledge, 1991).

13 See the original columns in *The Times* from October 1937 through "Letters from Mrs. Miniver" written in the fall of 1939 after the war's outbreak.
14 Jan Struther, "Gas Masks" in *Mrs Miniver* (New York, 1940), 149, 157–8.
15 Jan Struther, "A Pocketful of Pebbles", in *Ibid.*, 206–7.
16 Jan Struther, "London in August", in *Ibid.*, 261.
17 Jan Struther, "Back from Abroad", in *Ibid.*, 271.
18 Jan Struther, "From Needing Danger …", in *Ibid.*, 286.
19 "Life and Family", *The Times*, 27 Oct. 1939.
20 "The Promotion of Mrs Miniver", *Punch* 197, 15 Nov. 1939.
21 Dorothy Vincent and Cyril Falls, "Letter to the Editor", *The Times*, 28 Sept. 1939.
22 Rosamond Lehmann, "A Charming Person", Review of *Mrs Miniver*, *The Spectator*, 163 (1939).
23 Jan Struther, *Women of Britain: Letters from England* (New York, 1941), 6–8.
24 *Ibid.*, 6.
25 *Ibid.*, 10.
26 Factual information about the film's background was gleaned from a number of sources, see Michael Anderegg, *William Wyler* (Boston, 1979); Michael Druxman *One Good Film Deserves Another* (South Brunswick, 1977); Roger Manvell, *Films and the Second World War* (South Brunswick, 1974); and Andrea Walsh, *Women's Film and Female Experience, 1940–1950* (New York, 1984). For information about the film's popularity in America, see Hartmann, *The Home Front and Beyond*, 191, which describes audiences "flocking" to it in 1942; and for British popularity, see the appendix on "British Box Office Information, 1940–1950" in Lant, *Blackout*, 231, which lists *Mrs. Miniver* as having the biggest box office in 1942. All descriptions and direct quotes are taken from the 2004 Turner Entertainment DVD of *Mrs. Miniver*.
27 Janet Thumim, "The Female Audience: Mobile Women and Married Ladies", in *Nationalising Femininity*, 248.
28 Bosley Crowther, "The Screen in Review", *The New York Times*, 5 June 1942.
29 "Mrs. Miniver's War", *Newsweek*, 19, 15 June 1942.
30 Philip T. Hartung, "There'll Always Be", *The Commonweal* Vol. 36, Apr.–Oct. 1942.
31 John Mosher, "Over There", *The New Yorker*, 18, 6 June 1942.
32 "Cinema: New Picture", *Time*, 39, 29 June 1942.
33 Bosley Crowther, "Tribute to Human Courage", *The New York Times*, 14 June 1942.
34 "'Mrs. Miniver' in the War", *The Times*, 6 June 1942.
35 "Mrs. Miniver", *The Times*, 8 July 1942.
36 William Whitebait, "The Movies", *The New Statesman and Nation*, 18 July 1942.
37 "Film of the Month: Mrs. Miniver", *Documentary News Letter*, August 1942.
38 Edgar Anstey, "The Cinema", *The Spectator*, 17 July 1942.
39 Barbara Amiel, "A New *Mrs. Miniver* for Modern Times", *Maclean's*, 115, no. 37 (2002).

9
Film and the Popular Memory of the Second World War in Britain 1950–1959

Penny Summerfield

Film can be a powerful interpreter of the past. Whether it fosters nostalgia or adopts a critical stance towards history, it plays an important role as a "vector of memory".[1] The 1950s saw the release of over eighty films about the Second World War in Britain, thirty of which were listed as top box office successes.[2] Since the earning power of films indicates their resonance with the public, and since, in the 1950s, cinema was still the most popular form of mass entertainment in spite of declining audiences due to television, these high-earning films can be considered key components in the formation of the popular memory of the war in Britain in the 1950s.[3] This essay focuses on what the most successful 1950s war films contributed to the popular memory of the Second World War in Britain between 1950 and 1959. It builds on interpretative readings of the postwar war film by a number of scholars, notably Geoff Eley, Christine Geraghty, Andy Medhurst and Neil Rattigan.[4] Adapting the question which Sonya Rose poses in relation to the social and cultural history of the war in *Which People's War?* it explores whose memory of the war the 1950s films privileged, by examining the influences on their production, the derivation of their stories and their resulting representations of the national war effort.

In an effort to explain the popularity of the war films, Lewis Gilbert, who directed four of them, claimed that "after the war Britain was a very tired nation, worn out by five or six years of war, and this was a kind of ego boost, a nostalgia for a time when [the British] were great, because they were rapidly overtaken economically by other countries, particularly by Japan and West Germany, whom they had just defeated".[5] Gilbert was not alone in believing that the purpose of British film-makers in depicting the war was consolatory. The head of production at Ealing Studios from 1937–1959, Michael Balcon, insisted that postwar films should contribute to the restoration of Britain's international prestige.[6] However, while twenty-five of the popular war films were made by British studios, three were American and two were Anglo-American productions, and American approaches were different from those of British film-makers especially in terms of historical accuracy and respect for British military leadership. Whatever their nationality, though, producers and directors of the thirty most popular war films represented the war effort predominantly through the fighting men of the battle front rather than civilians on the home front: fifteen films concerned military campaigns; eight were about prisoners-of-war; five were tales of espionage and resistance; and two were comedies of military life.

The Armed Forces thus occupy a central place in these films. In terms of the films' content the Services constitute the settings for explorations not only of military prowess and (through representations of the Axis powers, the erstwhile Allies and Britain's wartime imperial relationships) of the politics of war, but also of key aspects of the wartime social fabric such as national identity, social class and gender. In addition, Service chiefs sought to exercise some control over the memory of the military war effort that the films communicated, as did other groups with a stake in the way their part in the war was remembered. Tensions at times flared between such attempts to influence production and the creative, artistic and commercial demands of film-making. The different approaches of film-makers and members of the Armed Forces, and of British and American producers, as well as changes in the treatment of the war over time, gave rise to contestations that have been overlooked by historians as well as considerable ambiguities in the version of the war offered in the films. The memory of the Second World War communicated by the most popular 1950s war films was not only highly selective but, contrary to the aspirations of Gilbert and Balcon, not consistently reassuring.

British film-makers of the postwar period placed a high value on authenticity. Balcon explained in 1952 that wartime films had addressed issues arising from the war, and that postwar "audiences in Britain wanted this type of realistic entertainment".[7] Most of the narratives on which he and other film-makers based their war films came from autobiographical publications. In this way individual accounts that had already reached the public domain travelled even further on the cultural circuit as films: among the bestselling books made into films were Eric Williams' *The Wooden Horse* (1949), Nicholas Monsarrat's *The Cruel Sea* (1951) and Pat Reid's *The Colditz Story* (1952). Even when there was no personal account on which to base a war narrative, British producers and directors insisted that realism prevail. During the making of

Malta Story (1953), about the Axis siege in 1943, Thorold Dickinson said "we take a slice of history and determine the policy of how to handle that slice of history … In the Malta film … we intend to subordinate fiction by history".[8] As this suggests, British film-makers of the 1950s made bold claims for truth: "This film shows how three British officers carried out an actual escape from a German camp in the last war" stated the introductory title of *The Wooden Horse*. Audiences were regularly told, as they were in the case of *The Colditz Story*, that "Every incident in the film you are about to see is true".

Of course realism is never unmediated. Williams admitted fictionalizing some aspects of *The Wooden Horse*, in which he wrote of himself in the third person. His account and that of Reid were shaped by the narrative models of First World War escape stories, notably A. J. Evans' *The Escape Club*, and, like them, presented escape as a mixture of duty and sport.[9] Monsarrat spent five years at sea in Atlantic convoys during the war, but his novel *The Cruel Sea* expressed what he felt war had done to men like himself, rather than providing an exact documentary record of his experiences. Another best-selling book, Pierre Boulle's *Bridge on the River Kwai* (1954), was set in the geographical and historical realities of the River Kwai in Siam where British prisoners built a bridge under the command of a Senior British Officer. It was written from experience: the author, a Frenchman, had been a rubber planter in Malaya who had worked with the British and French against the Japanese until he was taken prisoner. Yet it was presented neither as history nor autobiography, but rather as an interpretation of British character.

Film adaptations took the transformative process further, conflating characters and events, extending the selectivity and shifting the emphasis of the interpretations they offered. American and Anglo-American productions went beyond British ones: in the case of *Bridge on the River Kwai*, produced by the American Sam Spiegel and directed by the Briton David Lean, the character of the Senior British Officer, Colonel Nicholson (Alec Guinness), who decides that the prisoners should build a superb bridge, is transferred faithfully from the book to the film, but that of Shears (William Holden) is transformed. The upright British commando officer of the book becomes a cynically self-centred American who, when required to join the British commando team, provides a critical commentary on the rule-bound and war-obsessed Britons. Other American productions also used wartime events as settings for the development of dramatic stories that moved away from historical fact. For instance, *Stalag 17* (1953), also starring William Holden, was based on a play set in a German prison camp for American airmen. In contrast to British-made prisoner-of-war films it does not attempt to reconstruct escape attempts that actually happened. Its focus is the developing tension between a suspected traitor and the other American prisoners and its genre is the thriller rather than the documentary.

In contrast, purported historical veracity was the hallmark of British productions of the 1950s and the impression of authenticity was enhanced by the official involvement of the Armed Forces. This was particularly important for military campaign and prisoner-of-war films, whose producers depended on the Services for the loan of tanks, aircraft, battleships, military camps, personnel, the provision of technical advice and in some cases military training for the actors.[10] For example, *Above Us the Waves* (1955) was the "true" story of the attack on the German battleship "Tirpitz" by British midget submarines in 1943, based on a memoir written by two of the submarine crew. The Admiralty provided the film-makers with "human torpedoes", submarines, hitherto secret British and German film records of underwater operations, and an expert adviser, and it also allowed the naval water tower in which submariners practised underwater escapes to be used not only to train the actors, but also to appear in the film.[11] Such assistance, repeated many times over, represented a considerable commitment on the part of the War Office, the Admiralty and the Air Ministry, but it was apparently given willingly in the expectation of a positive portrayal of their part in the war. Among the thirty best-selling 1950s war films only one, *Private's Progress* (1956), to which we shall return shortly, was publicly refused official assistance.

Producers were charged for the costs of Service personnel and facilities; thus Michael Balcon received a bill for £36,561 in 1958, for "personnel, transport and some incidental facilities provided by the War Office" for use in the making of *Dunkirk*.[12] However, the Forces stood to make a variety of gains from their involvement. All three Services' recruitment figures fell annually throughout the 1950s, partly due to full employment. To reach their required complement the Forces depended on compulsory National Service, which, however, was phased out from 1958. The amount the Services spent on publicity rose steadily.[13] Popular war films provided immediate recruiting opportunities and lent military enrollment a special glamour. They also perpetuated and enhanced military prestige and with it the Forces' political influence.[14] For example, in 1955 the Admiralty advocated full naval co-operation with the premiere of *Cockleshell Heroes* on the grounds that "the recruiting value of participation is probably as great as could be obtained from a function of this kind".[15]

On their side, film distributors advised cinema managers to use the Forces' recruitment needs for promotional purposes. Thus in 1950 exhibitors were told that *The Wooden Horse* "is realism of the most faithful order, and has the earnest backing of the Air Ministry, which sees in the film a means of stimulating national pride in a great force. The Ministry is, therefore, linking its recruiting campaign with the film, and will give material aid to the publicizing of the film. Every showman will want to make full use of this powerful factor in presenting the entertainment".[16] Managers were regularly advised to call upon local senior officers to help launch a film with military parades, demonstrations of equipment and the presence of uniformed personnel at their cinemas.

The high level of military involvement reinforces the sense in which the films should be seen as contributing to "popular" or "public", rather than "collective", memory. The concept of collective memory originally referred to the role of shared memories in promoting social cohesion and identity in families and communities.[17] But theorists have emphasized that the issue of how the past is remembered is also a product of power dynamics. Thus Pierre Nora suggests that the production of "national memory" is the result of interactions between pluralistic groups with competing agendas.[18] Marc Ferro argues further that states seek to control collective memory in their interests because the popular view of the national past matters.[19] The 1950s war films might appear to be just such officially-managed versions of the past. However, unlike certain wartime productions, they were not propaganda films. None of them was state financed and controlled, and film-makers were insistent on their creative independence. All the same, direct government intervention was not necessary to persuade many British producers and directors to present positive images of Britain at war.

All the military campaign films stress procedures and discipline, key aspects of Armed Forces' identity. Officers' insistence on these qualities is frequently portrayed uncritically, as in *Above Us the Waves*, when Commander Frazer (John Mills) on meeting his crew for the first time, dresses down its Australian member for wearing a non-uniform pullover under his jacket. To paraphrase the script, getting the uniform right symbolized getting everything else right, and so would lead to winning the war. There are also films in which the military effectiveness of correct modes of address, attire and behaviour is questioned; however, in British films, apart from *Private's Progress*, it is always validated. For example, in *Sea of Sand* (1958), about a commando raid on an enemy ammunition dump in the desert, Cotton, an officer who has enlisted only for the duration, derides the commitment to regimental rules of Williams, a regular officer who joins his team. Yet as the mission lurches from crisis to crisis, Williams exhibits the training and authority that count in military terms. It is difficult to see this treatment as substantiating the argument, made by Nicholas Pronay, that British war films of the fifties were informed by a loathing of conscription and the "insanity" of soldiering.[20] Rather, most of the popular British films emphasize the rectitude of the military traditions to which recruits must learn to conform.

The portrayal of military ingenuity and technological effectiveness in the films was also designed to enhance the Forces' prestige. There are lengthy and didactic explanations of a variety of techniques, including new ways of waging war such as ASDIC, a method of detecting submarines using sound waves, in *The Cruel Sea*, and bouncing bombs in *The Dam Busters*. The films also depict ingenious ways of overcoming practical problems, such as constructing a gym horse that will carry and conceal two men, their digging equipment and bags for the removal of excavated earth in *The Wooden Horse*, and how to get a military ambulance up a sand-dune, in *Ice Cold in Alex*. Some of this technology proves less than perfect. In *The Cruel Sea* the inability of ASDIC to differentiate between submarines and other underwater objects leads directly to the depth-charging of a non-existent submarine, tragically killing the survivors of a torpedoed ship who are struggling in the water above the supposed contact point. However these are narratives of technological progress: over the whole timeframe of *The Cruel Sea*, developments in both ASDIC and radar are shown to improve the British Navy's capacity for underwater detection.

Some contemporary reviewers tired of the technological emphasis of the films. For instance, critics regarded the "almost exclusively technical conversation" and the "repeated details of naval technicalities" in *Above Us The Waves* as robbing the film of "humanity".[21] However, ingenuity and technological proficiency are made more exciting by their connection with rebellion. Innovators are seen campaigning against the scepticism of those in authority for the effectiveness of a particular technique, whether it is the "human torpedo" in *Above Us the Waves*, a new type of bomb in *The Dam Busters* or a tactical fighter formation in *Reach for the Sky*. These innovators are thus presented as both idealists and rebels, although this is, to use Christine Geraghty's phrase, "managed rebelliousness".[22] It never goes too far, and ultimately it reinforces national pride. British individuals are shown to be clever, ingenious and persistent, and British military leadership can be trusted to recognize the value of innovative ideas – eventually – and to accept the alterations to strategy that they demand.

These qualities are relentlessly masculine, and their portrayal in the films communicates a strong message about gender. The association of technology with masculinity echoes and reinforces the postwar gender divide in education and paid employment, whereby mechanical and technical subjects and related types of work were considered inherently male, in spite of ample evidence that women had done them success-fully in the war years. Women's roles in war work and defence had been depicted in wartime films such as *Went the Day Well?* and *Mrs Miniver* (both 1942) and *Millions Like Us* and *The Gentle Sex* (both 1943). These popular 1940s Home Front films suggested that the mobilization of British women had destabilized (although not overturned) the conven-tional "gender contract" of earlier wars, under which men fought to protect women and children, who supported them in doing so, watched and waited for their return and did not interfere. The rapidity with which women's wartime roles were expunged from public memory is indicated by the consensus among 1950s reviewers that there was no place for women in war films. Women characters were included in British films only by virtue of a romantic sub-plot, and women were introduced even more gratuitously to American (co-) productions, as scantily-clad sex objects. Either way, British reviewers regarded these female appearances as unwelcome intrusions. The *Manchester Guardian* reviewer's comment on *Above Us the Waves* stands for many: "the women at home are mentioned but never appear. So much to the good".[23]

There are just three war films among the thirty box office successes of the 1950s (which were all directed and produced by men) in which women play central roles – *Odette* (1950), *A Town Like Alice* (1956) and *Carve Her Name with Pride* (1958). *Odette* and *Carve* focus on espionage and resistance: as Ken Worpole argues in relation to popular war liter-ature of the 1950s, such themes make space for socially marginal char-acters – including women.[24] *A Town Like Alice* is a prisoner-of-war film with a difference, in that the women and children captured by the Japanese in Malaya are forced into a three-year trek since no camp commander will admit them. In contrast to the male prisoner-of-war dramas, this is a story of survival rather than escape. The agency which these films give women disturbs the "contract" between fighting men and supportive civilians; however in all three films, this potential female power is offset by vivid and lengthy depictions of the victim-ization and degradation of the women, such as the torture which Odette Sansom suffers in the film *Odette*.[25]

The remaining films' commemoration of wartime masculinity is characterized by a focus on male bonding and the "othering" of women. They commonly feature pairings of men that Raymond Durgnat has described as those between the "eternal cadet" and the "effective father".[26] These pairings were between men of the middle and upper classes: their centrality to 1950s war films is seen by recent commentators, such as Neil Rattigan, as a reassertion of the conventional social order in response to the rising power of the working class during and after the war.[27] The bond is at its strongest in *The Cruel Sea*: Lockhart is recruited from his civilian occupation as a journalist, with little experience of the sea, to serve in naval escorts to Atlantic convoys. Under the stern guidance of Captain Ericson, a former merchant seaman, he becomes the efficient First Lieutenant of a corvette and then a frigate, and Ericson's "Number One". He remains the "eternal cadet", however, in that he opts to continue to serve under Ericson rather than accept promotion and take command of a ship of his own. The closeness of the two men, and their single-minded devotion to their work, enable them to survive and succeed while other men are defeated.

Where women are not completely excluded, their relationships with men are problematized. In one version, the problematic is whether it is morally right to allow the "normal" processes of attraction, engagement, marriage and family to take place in wartime. Control over such developments is depicted as resting with men, who are also those at greatest risk. In *Malta Story* (1953) Flt. Lt. Peter Ross (Alec Guinness) postpones his marriage to Maria until the end of the war, only to confirm the reason for doing so by dying in action on a special mission. In an alternate version, the problem is not men's responsibility towards women and children, but the ways in which women potentially undermine the capacity of men to wage war. In *The Cruel Sea*, a wife saps the strength of her naval husband by her infidelity. This is an extreme case, but in all instances, men's commitment to women serves actually or potentially to distract them from the war effort. Understanding this, Lockhart decides that he must give the war all his attention, even though he is attracted to a Wren, Julie Hallam. The resolution in the film affirms the gender order: Julie will wait faithfully for Lockhart; good women subordinate their own desires to the demands of war on men.

There is, however, a counter narrative to this apparent heterosexual normalization in *The Cruel Sea*. Lockhart's relationship with Julie lacks depth; in contrast the film portrays the development of the tie between Ericson and Lockhart almost provocatively strongly. Reviewers approved of the Ericson-Lockhart relationship in 1953, seeing it as a natural and authentic part of the "brotherhood of those who sail together", and some complained that, in contrast, the romantic relationship on land was "handled in a regrettably stiff, over-detached manner".[28] They were not necessarily unconsciously applauding a homosexual relationship; but they were recognizing that heterosexual love stories deflected the ideological project of the 1950s war film, since, to quote Andy Medhurst, "it is a love between men that is a major force propelling that project".[29]

Yet these films were also famous for male suppression of outward signs of emotion. Reviewers referred critically to the abundance of "stiff upper lips" which actors such as Jack Hawkins, Kenneth More, Richard Todd and John Mills managed to give their characters. "That stiff upper lip. Does it never relax?" asked the *Evening Standard* of *Malta Story* in 1953.[30] The stiff lip had become a powerful signifier of what it meant to be British. It ensured understatement: immodest and triumphalist claims did not escape from under it; it permitted only the driest humour; it disabled expressions of grief. Above all it signified control of the self and hence of others, and thus it had overt class, military and colonial implications. To paraphrase research by J. A. Mangan and John MacKenzie, from the mid-nineteenth century the attitudes that fostered it were taught in public schools to successive generations of upper- and middle-class English boys as part of a code of chivalry and fair play that marked them as superior and prepared them for leadership in the professions, the military and domestic and colonial government. It distinguished the British from foreigners and especially from colonial subjects, who were by definition less rational and more hysterical than their "natural" rulers. It was central to military discipline and ethos. To some 1950s critics, the stiff upper lip was symbolic of the close relationship between the war films and the Armed Forces. "British films continue to play safe with the Services" complained William Whitebait in the *New Statesman*, reviewing *Above Us The Waves* in April 1955. "Corporate feeling may be assumed, jargon and stiff upper lip provide the packing, and every glimpse of the man behind the uniform is a point gained".[31]

Whitebait viewed the stiff upper lip as "packing" that, like the uniform, concealed the man behind it. In most of the popular war films, no layers of wrapping are removed: protagonists struggle – successfully – to maintain their self-control in the face of tragedy. But there is a protracted moment of instability in *The Cruel Sea* when, following the disastrous depth-charging of the non-existent submarine, Ericson consumes a large quantity of alcohol and weeps. This impressed reviewers, both as an acting feat and for the humanity it restored to Ericson and to Lockhart who subsequently makes a brief affectionate speech to the now comatose Ericson as he settles him in his cabin.[32] The meaning of the incident is expressed by Monsarrat in the book. Lockhart, observing Ericson, sees that: "Incredibly there were tears in his eyes which glittered like bright jewels starting from a mask, proclaiming his weakness and his manhood in the same revealing moment".[33] The "mask" of manly control has slipped; the stiff upper lip has been forced to relax; the tears – which are compared to precious stones – reveal the human being. These infrequent displays of emotion support Medhurst's view that these are "films about repression, rather than ... hopelessly repressed films".[34] Nevertheless, in *The Cruel Sea* as in the other British films, control is always restored; the problem is not named or discussed; it is subsumed in cigarettes, alcohol and action.

If the female characters in the few films that give women central roles disrupt the military-civilian relationship, so too does colonialism. Coverage of the position of colonial populations occurs infrequently in fifties war films. *Malta Story*, however, depicts the islanders' suffering due to the Axis powers' regular aerial bombing, which destroys their homes, and the naval blockade that deprives them of essential supplies. The question arises of why they, as colonial subjects, should put up with the miseries brought upon them by the presence of the British garrison. Anglophile Maria works for the British, but Maria's mother listens to Italian radio and is partly persuaded of the wisdom of surrender, and Maria's brother, Giuseppe, is caught spying for the Italians. Before he is executed, he makes an impassioned speech to his British captors about colonial injustice. He is not a traitor, he is loyal to the Maltese people, who will be better off surrendering to the Axis powers, and in any case the British have no right to the island.

The film does not provide a direct answer to Giuseppe. Indeed, the position of the British as a colonial power is emphasized by the "otherness" of the Maltese, marked by accent, religion, dress and housing; but the British apparently treat the Maltese benignly – awarding the George Cross to the whole island. The film implies that the British deserve Maltese loyalty simply by being British and standing for fair play and decency, in the same way that escaping prisoners-of-war in *The Wooden Horse* "deserve" the help given them, at huge personal risk, by French forced labourers and Danish seamen in Northern Germany. Furthermore, 1950s audiences "knew" that the Maltese were right not to give in: surrender, as in France in 1940 and Singapore in 1942, was shameful. In any case, the Allies would be victorious in the end. In

1953, the instability of the British Empire made the depiction of doubting colonial subjects "realistic": resolving the problem with a victory for the "good" colonial power offered a consoling message for the British and a cautionary one for the colonies.

Malta Story also illustrates one of three different ways in which the enemy is represented. In the *Malta Story* version, the enemy as a human being is virtually invisible: the technology of warfare (ships, planes and bombs) is all that is seen of the Germans and the Italians. In a second version, the enemy, usually German, is "the goon in the block", the title of Eric Williams' first memoir: tyrannical and sadistic. Prisoner-of-war escape stories in particular cast German guards in this way, and also as superficially cunning but ultimately stupid. *The Colditz Story* excelled at turning German camp personnel into comic figures with monocles and no sense of humour, who could be mocked and outwitted. However, in a third type of representation, the enemy is neither invisible nor an idiotic tyrant, but an equal. In *Above Us the Waves*, the captain of the *Tirpitz* salutes the "brave men" of the British Navy who have blown up his ship; in *The One That Got Away*, we are encouraged to respect Von Werra, the sole German to escape from British captivity and return to Germany, for doing exactly what British prisoners-of-war were trying to do; and in *Ice Cold in Alex*, the German spy becomes a valued member of the British team. In any case, in *Ice Cold*, it is not the Germans but the desert that is the "real" enemy, just as in *The Cruel Sea* we are told "the only villain is the cruel sea". This depoliticization was considered by some contemporary reviewers to be a healthy sign of anti-war feeling, and by others a necessary aspect of accommodating Germany as an economic and political partner in the postwar world. Only the communist paper, the *Daily Worker*, worried about the implications of such "display[s] of sympathy ... for ... Nazi[s]".[35]

Whatever the representation of the enemy, however, the numerous Allied and Commonwealth troops who joined the British in tackling the enemy remained practically invisible in British-made films. Aside from the inclusion of an occasional Australian accent and the background presence of the Americans, British film-makers preferred to represent the Second World War as one that Britain fought alone. An American production, *The Desert Rats* (1953), on the other hand, highlights Britain's dependence on imperial forces, and does so critically, depicting the exposure of an Australian division to extreme dangers when it is required by the British high command to defend Tobruk. Neither American nor British films ever addressed the roles of non-white colonial soldiers.

Until 1956, the military authorities did not, apparently, regard any of the popular war films with which they were asked to co-operate as inappropriate representations of the British war effort. In as far as there were any official anxieties about the war films released in Britain, they appear to have focused up to this point on the revelation of secrets concerning the security services. However, in 1956 John Boulting directed *Private's Progress*, a comedy of wartime military life based on Alan Hackney's novel of that name. *Private's Progress* is in part a skit on a serious wartime film, *The Way Ahead* (1944), which shows a group of recalcitrant civilian conscripts becoming loyal and effective soldiers. In contrast, in Boulting's film, a naïve undergraduate fails his officer's training, and, returned to the ranks, learns the tricks of the old sweat's trade. Through a crooked Brigadier uncle, he later gets a commission, but becomes an unwitting accomplice in this man's scheme to plunder art treasures looted by the Nazis. During the war, the Boulting brothers had worked with the Army Film and Photographic Unit on films such as *Desert Victory* that glorified the front line, and in 1955, when John Boulting approached Antony Head, Secretary of State for War, he was allegedly assured of the usual assistance. But a few days later he was informed that co-operation was impossible because his film was "not likely to assist recruitment". As a consequence, the Boultings had to build their own army camps and hire vehicles and armaments, adding to their costs.[36] *Private's Progress* did not directly question the capacity of British military leaders to wage an effective modern war against the Nazi enemy. Its most radical suggestions were that some recruits never conformed, and that some of those leading them were inept and corrupt. However, this representation of the Army was unacceptable to the War Office.

The promotion of the film capitalized on the War Office's disapproval: *Private's Progress* was introduced as "The film THEY didn't want made", and, in contrast to the credits for Armed Forces assistance in other films, the producers "gratefully acknowledge[d] the co-operation of absolutely nobody". In part because of this, *Private's Progress* was the third biggest box office success of 1956. The film-makers believed that the five million wartime conscripts as well as the postwar generation of National Servicemen appreciated its jokes, even if the "brass hats" did not. With the exception of Campbell Dixon in the *Daily Telegraph*, reviewers rejoiced in *Private's Progress* as a welcome respite from the formulaic war film.[37] Dilys Powell in the *Sunday Times* regarded it as "the perfect antidote to high-falutin about war ... the unheroic record of ... the man who never wanted to have "much of a war"; ... it is a relief to find this deplorable character celebrated on the British screen, which has given so long an innings to steel nerves and iron jaws".[38]

It is tempting to regard 1956, the year of the Suez Crisis, as a turning point in the public memory of the Second World War, on the grounds that after that international disaster, British political and military judgement could never again be represented uncritically, whatever period of history was under scrutiny.[39] Even if *Private's Progress* was made before Suez, a growing number of popular comedies about service life followed it, in film, television and radio, which questioned lower ranks' discipline and officers' competence. However these shows featured not 1940s war service but 1950s National Service, and the popularity of celebrations of the wartime stiff upper lip and all it represented was not abruptly reversed. The top box office success in 1956 was *Reach for the Sky*, and the successes of *Battle of the River Plate* (1957), *Sea of Sand* (1958), and *Sink the Bismarck* (1960) continued the tradition. Audiences evidently enjoyed both comic and serious representations of war, and could doubtless distinguish between the meanings communicated by the different genres.

Yet although there was continuity, there was also change. Two films released in 1958 asked more searching questions about British military and political leadership than previous serious war films had done. *Dunkirk* features the efforts of a working-class corporal, Binns (John Mills), separated from his unit with a small group of men due to the German advance, to fill the leadership vacuum in which he finds himself in the retreat of the British Expeditionary Force to Dunkirk in 1940. It also emphasizes the importance of the contribution of (male) civilians to the war effort through the small boats rescue of the stranded soldiers: one of the rescuers, Charles Foreman (Bernard Lee), delivers a critical commentary on the debacle. The Ealing Studios production team (Michael Balcon, Michael Forlong and Lesley Norman) was one of the most patriotic working in Britain in the fifties. However, there were still moments of tension with the military authorities over the interpretations of British history that the film offered.

Initially there seemed to be few problems: Forlong received a supportive letter in response to the script from the War Office's Director of Public Relations in March 1957.[40] Yet, in April 1957, Lt. Col. Earle advised Sir Gerald Templer, Chief of the Imperial General Staff, that the script presented "a travesty of a major campaign", and Templer objected to Balcon that the emphasis on the stragglers underplayed "the success of the British Army in maintaining cohesion in the last days of withdrawal".[41] The stakes were high. 1950s military leaders wanted this key moment in the Second World War to be remembered as a major triumph, not a disgraceful defeat. Ealing Films needed to make the film with extensive service "facilities": tanks, artillery, destroyers and 3,000 serving soldiers. Balcon explained the demands of creativity to Templer: "No film or novel can be uncritical if analysed in detail", and assured him that the film showed that "the withdrawal to Dunkirk and the subsequent evacuation succeeded gloriously, and that ... the heart of the British Army is sound to the core".[42]

The production team modified the script to strengthen the portrayal of the "performance and spirit of the British Expeditionary Force (B. E. F.)", and the War Office was reassured.[43] The film was given a Royal Premiere in March 1958. It had not been "officially managed" but the readiness of the film-makers to self-censor ensured that the evacuation from Dunkirk was presented as "an epic chapter of British history",[44] and was not, in the eyes of some contemporary film reviewers, "rescued from folk lore".[45] Nevertheless, *Dunkirk* was based on different dynamics from the "steel nerves and iron jaw" films that preceded it, not least in giving its central role to a working-class character. While it presented some of the dilemmas of the British class structure, military ethos and political history, its criticism was muted. Outspoken critique was the preserve of another of the most popular films of 1958.

The Bridge on the River Kwai was an Anglo-American production. Its producer, Hollywood's Sam Spiegel, had no stake in promoting the British Armed Forces, and its director, Britain's David Lean, was more interested in exploring the Shakespearean dimensions of the theme than in making a film that enhanced Britain's prestige. The social-class dynamics of the British Army provide a crucial point of dramatic tension and censure in this film. Its central character, Colonel Nicholson (Alec Guinness), represents colonial military leadership. He suffers torture and risks death rather than allow his officers and himself to join the other ranks in manual labour, as the Japanese commander of the prisoner-of-war camp, Colonel Saito (Sessue Hayakawa), requires. When Saito eventually concedes, Nicholson determines to demonstrate to the oriental "barbarians", as he sees them, the superiority of British workmanship by building a superb bridge in record time. The working-class men under his command do not impede him: they admire their Colonel for his manly courage in standing up to the Japanese on a point of principle, even though it underlines the class difference between officers and men, and they agree to work hard. However, Nicholson's commitment to the bridge-building project turns him into a collaborator, for the bridge will transport troops and supplies for the Japanese war effort. Moreover, his insistence that even the sick must work blurs the distinction between him and the sadistic Saito. In a parallel plot, a British-led commando group is arranging to blow up the bridge: but in this group, too, adherence to the British military code is taken to obsessive extremes. The American in the group, Shears (William Holden), explicitly opposes his own values of pragmatism and hedonism to those of the leader, Major Warden (Jack Hawkins), yelling at him in the jungle: "you make me sick with your heroics. All you know is how to die by the rules, when the only important thing is to live like a human being". The Shears-Warden conflict disrupts the "effective father"/ "eternal cadet" relationship of the fifties war films, and Shears' accusation challenges the modest heroism of a succession of British officers, including numerous escaping prisoners-of-war. Voiced by an American, it suggests that the British class structure and imperial code are outdated, and even hints that the British are spent as a world power.

As in the case of *Dunkirk,* the War Office was asked to support the film. Its P.R. department had doubts from the outset on three main grounds: no British commanding officer would have acted as Nicholson did; prisoners-of-war would not have helped the enemy war effort in the way depicted; and the film "shows up the British Army generally in a bad light".[46] However, although the War Office excused itself from providing "facilities",[47] and thus ensured that the film carried no acknowledgement of official Army co-operation, it did not try to stop the production from going ahead. There were two linked reasons. Firstly, officials were wary of making their disapproval public after their experiences with Boulting: "The refusal of War Office approval and facilities to a Film Company, as was the case in "Private's Progress" will cause inevitable repercussions".[48] Secondly, the Air Ministry had already agreed to provide RAF facilities on condition that the War Office approved. Desperate to avoid publicity, a War Office official wrote to the producers objecting to the film on the grounds that it did not "authentically portray the behaviour and conduct of British Officers", but stating, "we have no intention of placing stumbling blocks in your way and we are prepared for you to assure the RAF that we have no objection to the proposed filming".[49]

This was not, however, the end of the story. Lt. General A. E. Percival, President of the National Federation of Far Eastern Prisoners of War Clubs, objected strongly during the making and after the release of the film, on the grounds that it implied that British prisoners helped the Japanese war effort.[50] He drafted a statement to be shown at the beginning of the film to the effect that "the action of the British Officers and men in building a good bridge over the River Kwai for the Japanese has no foundation in fact and would have been contrary to the high standards of duty and loyalty maintained by the British troops who were forced to work as prisoners-of-war on the Siam-Burma Railway".[51] Spiegel agreed only to a watered-down version, and Percival later complained that this was shown at no more than a few screenings in London and then dropped, presumably because Spiegel was not committed to it.[52]

At stake were issues of fact and fiction, authenticity and dramatic licence. The War Office and the Federation of Far Eastern P.O.W. Clubs worried that audiences would take the representation literally, especially since details of the Japanese treatment of prisoners-of-war on the Burma-Siam railway were, they claimed, common knowledge by the late fifties. Such sensitivities continued for years. Lt. Col. Philip Toosey, the Senior British Officer at the actual prisoner-of-war camp on the Kwai, rebutted the implication of the film that he was a collaborator in an interview in the seventies, explaining "you couldn't refuse to do what the Japs ordered", but nevertheless "we did our damnedest to sabotage nearly everything about us". After his death in 1975, his daughter and Professor Peter Davies of Liverpool University did their best to restore his reputation.[53] The status of most war films, which apparently presented true stories, predisposed them to do so. The makers of *Bridge on the River Kwai* were impatient with such arguments, responding that of course this was a fictional representation. But the origins of the War Office's half-hearted stand on *Bridge*, and the ex-prisoners-of-war's more vehement one, were the same: they did not wish the British Army, its officers and men, in and out of captivity, to be remembered in this way.

What did the war films of the 1950s that large numbers of people chose to see contribute to the popular memory of the Second World War? Although only a tiny number of British and American films struck an explicitly questioning note, all the films contained internal contradictions. They depicted a just war that the British Armed Forces won against incredible odds, but they could only do so by ignoring allied and imperial involvement. They emphasized the daring, ingenuity and technical acumen of self-controlled upper- and middle-class officers in charge of well-disciplined and loyal lower-class servicemen, but if the inevitable social tensions were admitted, they were resolved so as to secure the social order. Rebelliousness was never threatening because it was channelled to positive ends. Bonding between men helped them survive, but it also put men's heterosexuality in question, especially since women were represented as a potentially disruptive presence and had to be subordinated. Women's contributions, apart from those of an exceptional few, were ignored. The British Empire signified rectitude, but it could not be depicted as altogether secure. The enemy, whether German, Italian or Japanese, was in the wrong, especially when guarding prisoners-of-war, but the German enemy might be discovered to be an equal in adversity so long as Nazism was forgotten. No interest was taken in the experience of black troops, persecuted minorities, the Soviet former ally or German and Japanese victims of saturation and atomic bombing.

Although British war films of the 1950s were not officially managed, most British directors did not wish to damage the reputations of the Forces' chiefs and ex-servicemen. With a few notable exceptions, filmmakers were prepared to try to avoid the offence of deviation from the officially preferred memory of the British war effort in spite of the contradictions noted above, even when their response to Service sensibilities involved curtailing their creative independence. The films' alleged authenticity, which was closely associated with Armed Forces backing and provision of military facilities, endowed them with considerable authority as vectors of memory. So powerful were the truth claims of the majority of the films that the fictionalized versions favoured by some American producers were deeply distrusted not only by Service chiefs but also by groups of ex-servicemen who feared that these films too would be received as historical fact. There was no doubt in the minds of those whose experiences were depicted in ways they did not like, that 1950s war films did indeed shape the popular memory of the Second World War.

Acknowledgements

The research on which this article is based was supported by a Leverhulme Trust Research Fellowship. Previous versions were presented at academic gatherings in Boston, London and Manchester. Grateful thanks to participants for their comments; they are not implicated in the outcome.

Notes

1 Henry Rousso, *The Vichy Syndrome* (Cambridge, MA, 1991), 226.
2 80–100 films featuring the Second World War were released 1945–1963. Nicholas Pronay, "The British Post-bellum Cinema: A Survey of the Films Relating to World War II made in Britain between 1945 and 1960", *Historical Journal of Film, Radio and Television* 8, no. 1 (1988), 39; John Ramsden, "Refocusing 'The People's War': British War Films of the 1950s", *Journal of Contemporary History*, 33, no.1 (1998), 45. *Kinematograph Weekly* listed annual box office successes every December 1950–1959.

3   Pronay, "Post-bellum Cinema", 39: weekly cinema attendance 1950 30m.; 1953 23m.; 1960 11m.

4   Geoff Eley, "Finding the People's War: Film, British Collective Memory, and World War II", *American Historical Review*, 106, no.3 (2001); Christine Geraghty, *British Cinema in the Fifties* (London, 2000); Andy Medhurst, "1950s War Films", in *National Fictions*, ed. Geoff Hurd (London, 1984); Neil Rattigan, "The Last Gasp of the Middle Class: British War Films of the 1950s", in *Re-viewing British Cinema 1900–1992*, ed. Wheeler Winston Dixon (New York, 1994). Useful context is also provided in Sue Harper and Vincent Porter, *British Cinema of the 1950s: the Decline of Deference* (Oxford, 2003) and S. P. MacKenzie, *British War Films 1939–1945: The Cinema and the Services* (London, 2001).

5   Brian McFarlane, *An Autobiography of British Cinema* (London, 1997), 221.

6   Michael Balcon "Let British Films be Ambassadors to the World", *Kinematograph Weekly*, 11 January 1945, 31.

7   British Film Institute Library [BFI], H/22, MB, 7 November 1952.

8   BFI, Thorold Dickinson, Rediffusion Malta, 30 November [1952].

9   P. R. Reid, *The Colditz Story* (London [1952] 2003), 9; Eric Williams, *The Wooden Horse* (London [1949] 2005), 14–15.

10   S. P. MacKenzie, *British War Films 1939–1945: The Cinema and the Services* (London, 2001), 129–58.

11   BFI, *Above Us the Waves*, Premiere Programme, 31 March 1955.

12   BFI, MEB I/146g, 19 September 1958.

13   Hansard, *Parliamentary Debates*, vol. 536, cols. 28–9, 26 January 1955.

14   Ramsden, "Refocusing", 53–4.

15   The National Archives [TNA], ADM 1/26411, 30 September 1955.

16   BFI, *The Wooden Horse*, Press Book.

17   Maurice Halbwachs, *On Collective Memory* (Chicago, 1992), 53.

18   Pierre Nora, *Realms of Memory*, 3 vols. (New York, 1998), 3: 616.

19   Mark Ferro, *The Use and Abuse of History* (London, 2003), x–xii.

20   Pronay, "Post-bellum Cinema", 48.

21   *Spectator*, 1 April 1955; *Manchester Guardian*, 2 April 1955.

22   Geraghty, *British Cinema*, 193.

23   *Manchester Guardian*, 2 April 1955.

24   Ken Worpole, *Dockers and Detectives* (London, 1983), 60.

25   See Penny Summerfield, "Public Memory or Public Amnesia? British Women on the Second World War in Popular Films of the 1950s and 1960s", *Journal of British Studies*, forthcoming 2009 or 2010.

26   Durgnat, *A Mirror for England* (London, 1970), 142.

27   Neil Rattigan, "The Last Gasp", 143–53.

28   *Glasgow Herald*, 13 April 1953; *Monthly Film Bulletin*, 20:228/239 (1953), 65.

29   Medhurst, "1950s War Films", 37.

30   *Evening Standard*, 26 June 1953.

31   *New Statesman*, 16 April 1955.

32   *Daily* Mail, 25 March 1953.

33   Nicholas Monsarrat, *The Cruel Sea* (London, 1951), 199.

34   Medhurst, "War Films", 38.

35   *Daily Worker*, 28 June 1958.

36   *Daily Mail*, 8 September 1955.

37   *Daily Telegraph*, 18 February 1956.

38 *Sunday Times*, 19 February 1956.
39 Peter Hennessy, *Having It So Good* (London, 2006), 458.
40 TNA, WO 32/16917, 13 March 1957.
41 *Ibid.*, 25 April 1957; 30 April 1957.
42 *Ibid.*, 2 May 1957.
43 *Ibid.*, 6 May 1957.
44 *Daily Sketch*, 21 March 1958.
45 *Daily Mail*, 21 March 1958.
46 TNA, WO 32/16237, 20 September 1955; 26 July 1956.
47 *Ibid.*, 11 July 1956.
48 *Ibid.*, 26 July 1956.
49 *Ibid.*, 31 July 1956.
50 *Ibid.*, Percival correspondence, April 1957–June 1958.
51 *Ibid.*, 11 June 1957.
52 *Ibid.*, 26 May 1958.
53 *Sunday Times*, 26 October 1997.

Part III

Gender, Race and the Aftermath of War and Empire

10
Men of the Royal Air Force, the Cultural Memory of the Second World War and the Twilight of the British Empire

Martin Francis

In an influential article which appeared in 1996, Bill Schwarz provocatively asserted that, in the postwar reconfiguration of Englishness, "the external determinations were primary, and that from the ruins of the colonial empires across the globe there emerged, among the white populations themselves, a recharged, intensified self-consciousness of their existential presence as white". The rhetoric of embattled white settlers in Kenya, Rhodesia and South Africa was, in the 1950s and early 1960s, rearticulated in the populist language of politics in the metropole itself. In both domains, a common discourse emerged in which a vulnerable and increasingly victimized white community were betrayed by a political elite who were indifferent to the prospect of imminent racial suicide. With mass immigration into postwar Britain from the Caribbean and South Asia, the colonial frontier not merely came home, but "the language of the colonies was reworked and came with it".[1] Schwarz's claim for a common structure of thought among whites in both metropole and colony has been taken up by Frank Mort's study of moral change in postwar London, in which he notes that press coverage of the Mau Mau insurgency in Kenya encouraged a "symbolic interaction between images of the disintegration of British colonialism and the domestic world of inner-city areas like north Kensington".[2] Even if the projection of white fantasies about African culture back to the metropole was somewhat uneven (historians remain divided as to how resonant the Kenyan emergency was in metropolitan popular culture[3]) there were undoubtedly many who felt there were definite analogues between the racial politics of home and abroad during the years of imperial disengagement. Ian Smith, whose bloody-minded campaign to maintain white supremacy in Rhodesia had led to a unilateral declaration of independence (UDI) from Britain in 1965, had a loyal following in the metropole among some backbench Conservative MPs, newspaper column-ists, businessmen and the general public.

Some of Smith's more devoted admirers in Britain were responsible, in February 1966, for sending the beleaguered Rhodesian premier the gift of a painting, accompanied by a special dedication, boasting that it was "presented to the Honourable I. D. Smith MP, Prime Minister of Rhodesia, at an epic period in her history, on behalf of many British people who remained true despite the misguidance of government". The painting itself was of two Spitfire fighter aircraft, taking off on a wartime mission at dawn.[4] At one level, the choice of illustration was unremarkable. During the Second World War Smith had been a fighter pilot with 237 (Rhodesia) Squadron, flying both Hurricanes and Spitfires in the Mediterranean theatre, and his war service had been widely pub-licized, not least by the premier himself.[5] However, the image of a Spitfire clearly had profound and extensive associations, which could not be, nor – in this case – were ever intended to be, contained within the para-meters of individual biography. Well before 1966, this formidable, yet profoundly elegant, aeroplane had become inseparable from the myth of Britain's "finest hour" during the Battle of Britain in 1940, and had come to attain a symbolic power, possibly only matched by Churchill's radio broadcasts, as the emblem of Britain's resistance to, and ultimate victory over, the evil of Nazism. Both Smith and his supporters would have understood the subliminal message of the painting: that the betrayal of white Rhodesia provided yet another distressing example of how a powerful nation, triumphant in war, had become abject, com-promised and defeated in peace. The values of western civilization which young men such as Smith had safeguarded in the skies over Europe two decades earlier were now again under threat, this time from the mur-derous atavism of black insurgency, on both the imperial frontier and within the decaying urban spaces of Britain itself.

The deployment of the cultural myth of the Second World War – and the Battle of Britain in particular – to support the discourses of postwar white racial resistance has been singled out for condemnation in Paul Gilroy's dissection of what he termed "postcolonial melancholia". Gilroy argued that Britain's "continued citation of the anti-Nazi war", even into the twenty-first century, was essentially pathological, in that it prevented a willingness "to face, never mind actually mourn, the pro-found change in circumstances and moods that followed the end of the empire and consequent loss of imperial prestige". For Gilroy this potent grip of the war on the nation's culture and self-understanding created a myth that in 1940 Britain had attained a sense of national integration and purpose, to which "the chaotic, multicultural present" would always be compared, and forever be found wanting. "This", he declared, in an allusion to the appearance of two preserved Battle of Britain fighter planes in the pageantry which accompanied the funeral of the Queen Mother in 2002, "is the point at which the comforting rumble of Spitfires and Hurricanes can be heard approaching in the distance".[6]

This essay also hears that thunder of Spitfires and Hurricanes overhead. Using as its entry point the freedom struggle in Rhodesia-Zimbabwe of the 1960s and 1970s, it seeks to explore how the cult of the wartime RAF flyer might help illuminate the intersection between the cultural memory of World War Two and the end of empire. It argues for a more nuanced approach to the way the memory of the air war came to be deployed in the discourses of postcolonialism than that offered in Gilroy's brief reflection. The visual presence of the Spitfire in a gift to Ian Smith or as part of the Queen Mother's internment might suggest that the history of the wartime RAF was ultimately required to do the cultural work of those who failed to come to terms with either national decline or postwar multiculturalism. However, even if this were the case, the annexation of the flyer to the discourses of recidivism and white resistance was a process, not a given fact. Such an outcome was not predetermined, and other possible readings of the wartime flyer were, and still are, available. At times, the wartime RAF seemed less suited to the strictures of white supremacy than it did to embodying the ideals of a postwar Commonwealth, which should not be simply dismissed as a refurbished version of classic imperialism. The cult of the flyer had to be fashioned in a particular way, requiring a selective memory, especially given men of colour had made a significant contribution to the RAF's war effort. Moreover, if the wartime flyboys were to ventriloquize the values of white civilization, it was necessary to emphasize their chivalric and domestic qualities, and to obscure their role as savage agents of destruction.

The broader implication of this case study is, in one sense, an obvious one, that we need to appreciate that there was no singular memory of World War Two in postwar Britain and its Empire-Commonwealth. However, it also requires us to align the emerging study of the memory of 1939–1945 with the increasingly rich literature on the complex process of cultural negotiation by which a range of subjective "experiences" became transformed into the dominant national "memory" of 1914–1918.[7] To date, studies of the memory of the Second World War in Britain, with the notable exception of an intervention from Geoff

Eley,[8] have lacked sophistication, and many authors have been guilty of ultimately reifying the myths they claim to interrogate.[9] Moreover, with the exception of an analysis by Lucy Noakes of how the discourses of World War Two were redeployed during the Falklands-Malvinas War in 1982, the memory of the World War and the end of empire have been treated as two separate scripts which rarely come together on the same page.[10]

Metaphors relating to Britain's "finest hour" were ubiquitous in the rhetoric of Ian Smith and his supporters during the Rhodesia-Zimbabwe crisis of the 1960s and 1970s. Munich and the Battle of Britain were regular reference points in the lexicon of white supremacy. Despite its title, the text of Rhodesia's Unilateral Declaration of Independence in 1965 possessed a familiarity with the precedents of 1938 or 1940, rather than 1776. White Rhodesians, it asserted "have rejected the doctrinaire philosophy of appeasement and surrender". An American admirer was adamant that "no country has 'stood alone' with quite such phlegm since the Battle of Britain".[11] The appeasement analogy served a double purpose. It not merely granted white Rhodesia's resistance equivalence with the great anti-fascist crusade of World War Two, but also allowed Smith's regime to court anti-communist opinion in the United States, where, of course, the unhappy precedent of Britain's initial failure to stand up to Hitler in the 1930s was being regularly pressed into service by those demanding America remain resolute in its commitment to the war in Vietnam. When, in 1976, Umtali became the first Rhodesian city to suffer mortar bombardment from Patriotic Front guerillas, the city's Cecil Hotel became an evacuation centre, where, according to the white Rhodesian press, the white population adopted the nonchalant "spirit of the Blitz", dedicating themselves to making placards which declared "Umtali Can Take It". Churchill, who had died less than a year before UDI was declared, was regularly appropriated to the cause of white Rhodesia. Smith insisted that "If Churchill were alive today I believe he'd probably emigrate to Rhodesia – because I believe that all those qualities and characteristics of the British we believed in, loved and presented to our children, no longer exist in Britain".[12] Memories of the war were also employed on behalf of a notion of solidarity between white Rhodesians and the mother country which had been cruelly dishonoured by Britain's postwar political leaders.

In all of this, narratives of the war in the air were central. No white Rhodesian kitchen in the sixties and seventies was complete without an illustrated dishcloth featuring "Good Old Smithy" and his trusty Spitfire. Tributes to the Rhodesian security services always included prefatory chapters which reminded readers that between 1939 and 1945 a total of 2,409 Rhodesians joined the air force, of whom 498 were killed. During the war, three RAF squadrons were awarded the designation "Rhodesia" – 237 and 266 Squadrons of Fighter Command and 44 Squadron, which flew Lancaster bombers and was famed for the raid on Augsburg and the precision bombing of the German warship *Tirpitz*.[13] However the emphasis on the flyer did more than register Rhodesia's not insubstantial contribution to the war effort and permit reference to Smith's personal credentials as a war hero. It also allowed Rhodesia's white resistance campaign to identify itself with the particular esteem and public affection which had attached itself to the RAF's wartime flyboys. Poignant memories of fresh-faced young flyers, living life to the full, in the precious intermissions between combat duty, carefree sensualists under constant sentence of death, had become one of the most enduring images of Britain's struggle for survival during the Second World War. The RAF's glamorous slate-blue uniform, with a set of silvery white fabric wings sewn on the breast pocket, made its wearer an object of (often unwelcome or embarrassing) hero-worship. The fact that these young men had waged war thousands of feet above the earth in an unfamiliar and surreal world only added to their romantic allure.[14]

Smith was able to reinforce the association of white Rhodesia's struggle with the cult of the wartime flyer (and more specifically the Battle of Britain) through the support he received in the metropole from former fighter ace Group-Captain Douglas Bader. Bader was a controversial figure. He had been a career officer, rather than one of the volunteer reserve who made up the bulk of the celebrated heroes of the Battle of Britain, and he never entirely shook off the snobbery and public-school heartiness which characterized the prewar RAF. He was capable of legendary insensitivity and arrogance, verging on megalomania, and his swashbuckling disposition often alienated colleagues and senior officers. However, Bader was a hero in the eyes of millions of Britons between the 1950s and 1970s, not simply on account of his valour and leadership in commanding a fighter squadron during the Battle of Britain, but because all this had been achieved in spite of the loss of both his legs in a flying accident in the early 1930s. Bader's energetic postwar campaigning on behalf of the disabled and the appearance in 1954 of a hagiographic biography by Paul Brickhill (subsequently made into a feature film) added to his canonical status.[15] From the late 1950s he became a regular newspaper columnist, airing his views first in the *News of the World* and later the *Daily Express*. Here he revealed himself to be an unapologetic reactionary, his hostility to black majority rule in Rhodesia part of a depressingly familiar litany of established diehard bugbears, including Commonwealth immigration, the creation of the Race Relations Board, the EEC, the repeal of the death penalty and the failure to take draconian measures against the terrorists of the IRA. In the case of Rhodesia, Bader was disgusted that Britain's leaders were destroying "our gallant ally of two world wars". As his biographer points out, unintentionally echoing Schwarz's "common syntax of white ethnicity", this desperate cry from the heart to save a nation which, "in his view was utterly British in thought and action", was also a "sad lament for his own nation".[16]

Smith and Bader were inevitably guilty of considerable self-delusion. For a start, Rhodesia's wartime relationship with Britain had not been entirely free of tension. Female servicewomen had been astonished to observe Rhodesian aircrew file off the crown on the Rhodesian lion cap badge which they sported, an action prompted by their anger at Britain's unwillingness to grant Rhodesia full Dominion status.[17] Smith must have been aware that commonalities between white Rhodesians and the mother country might be more imagined than real. Smith himself had been born in Rhodesia and did not visit territorial England until late in life, while a significant minority of white Rhodesians were of Afrikaner or Greek descent, and therefore lacked any British ancestry. More specifically, the war in the air would require manipulation and modification if it was to unproblematically corroborate the racial fantasies of Smith and Bader. The wartime RAF was a genuinely multinational service. In addition to recruits from the White Dominions of New Zealand, Australia, Canada and South Africa, there were exiles from Nazi-occupied Czechoslovakia, Poland, France and Norway, and volunteers from neutral countries as diverse as the United States, Switzerland, Turkey, Argentina and – in the form of Spitfire pilot Prince Varananda Dhavaj Chudadhuj – Thailand. Ken Adam, a Typhoon pilot with 609 Squadron, had previously been Klaus Heine, a German Jew who had fled Nazi persecution. Many of these men had no ties of kinship or heritage with Britain, while renowned Battle of Britain pilots such as Al Deere (New Zealand), Johnnie Kent (Canada) and Adolph 'Sailor' Malan (South Africa) often personified the more open and less deferential frontier cultures of dominions that were moving towards young nationhood, rather than the more hidebound traditions of the mother country.[18] Eight Irish fighter pilots fought in the Battle of Britain, despite being condemned by the de Valera administration. One of them, Brendan "Paddy" Finucane was the son of a staunch republican and Sinn Féin activist.[19] The Battle of Britain may have been fought over "deep England", the coast houses and apple orchards of Kent and the gently rolling hills of the South Downs, but, in terms of personnel, it was certainly not an exclusively English (or even British) affair. The extraordinary cosmopolitanism of the wartime RAF would have to be disregarded if its heroism was to provide a precedent for the defence of a narrowly constituted "island race".

It has been estimated that around forty per cent of the RAF's wartime aircrew came from the white Dominions. It was not uncommon for a single Lancaster bomber to have an Australian pilot, an English navigator, a New Zealand flight engineer, a South African radio operator and a Canadian rear gunner.[20] At one level, this might appear as a fellowship of white men, in which racial commonality had transcended national difference. However, not merely would such a conceit require disregarding the complex ethnic variations which existed under the rubric of "whiteness". It also fails to account for the possibility that this international interaction and solidarity might have been understood, less in terms of race, and more in terms of the notion of the Commonwealth, that peculiar hybrid of tradition and modernity which became increasingly pertinent in official and popular discourses in the war and immediate postwar decades. The Commonwealth was presented by its advocates, both in Britain and overseas, as an international community of equal nations that sought to sustain 'Britishness' in the former empire, while at the same time reconciling it to multiracial diversity and mutual, voluntary co-operation.[21] This is not to say that the idea of the Commonwealth was not informed by racialized understandings of the world, even as it emphasized partnership and democracy and repudiated the previously hierarchical relationship between metropole and colony. However, as discussions of the coronation and the Everest expedition in 1953 or the death of Smuts in 1950 have revealed, the Commonwealth, a peculiar amalgam of past and present, was a space in which a broader range of understandings about race and nation could play out than those which had been permitted in the real and imagined worlds of traditional imperial authority.[22] It might be interesting to consider, in this context, the appointment of glamorous Battle of Britain ace Peter Townsend (as opposed to the fusty peers who usually received such positions) as equerry to King George VI in 1945, a move applauded at the time as welcome evidence of the royal family's desire to introduce an element of youthful informality into the court, thereby aligning it with the modernizing and democratic impulses which were accompanying the shift from Empire to Commonwealth.[23]

If the flyer's status within the discourses of the end of empire is coupled to the more progressive connotations of the Commonwealth, not least its prospect (albeit rarely realized in practice) of partnership and equality, then it once again becomes obvious that there was nothing inevitable about the association between the memory of the wartime RAF and those uncompromisingly monoracial fantasies of the national past offered up by Smith and Bader. Furthermore, those same imperial ties that had made the young Ian Smith eager to volunteer for the RAF, had also brought men of colour into the fraternity of flyers. A memorandum prepared for the Air Ministry in early 1945 estimated that around 422 "coloured" men (the blanket term used to include West Indian, West African and South Asian flyers) had served as aircrew during the war, with a further 3,900 acting as groundcrew. This did not imply a challenge to notions of racial difference and racial hierarchy, but it did require, at least at the level of propaganda and public rhetoric, an opportunity for non-white subjects of the British crown to participate in (and be acknowledged as participating in) the fight against fascism.

How far, in the course of furthering this end, the RAF was able, or even intended, to overcome (or at least mitigate) racial divisions is questionable. The use of air power against civilian populations in Iraq in the 1920s exposed an unapologetic racial arrogance within the RAF, which was reiterated in the grotesque re-enactments of the bombing of "native" villages at the annual Hendon Air Pageant in the early 1930s.[24] Racist assumptions were certainly in evidence in confidential assessments of the capabilities of non-white aircrew produced by the RAF hierarchy. A survey of the performance of "coloured aircrew" suggested that, overall, non-white trainees attained the same level of success as their white equivalents, and that they possessed the qualities "necessary to take their place in operational aircrew". However, the report then shamelessly backpedaled from this apparent ringing endorsement of the competence of flyers of colour:

> In spite of the satisfactory standard of the technical and other abilities possessed by coloured officers and airmen who have qualified as members of aircrew, experience has shown that the appointment of any of this class of personnel as a Captain of Aircraft has not met with success. However good the individual may be the mere fact that he is coloured may induce a feeling of lack of confidence in the members of the crew. It is a matter entirely beyond the Captain's control and though the feeling may only be subconscious, it will tend to lower the efficiency of the crew as a whole.

Conversely, the report also felt promoting black aircrew to the position of captain might lead "a coloured airman to regard himself as a privileged person and to show resentment when certain breaches of conduct and behaviour were pointed out to him by superior officers". In the early part of the war, the RAF had actively sought to recruit aircrew from the colonies, but by 1943 it was only interested in enlisting ground crew. This decision not merely reflected the racist assumptions of the RAF hierarchy, but also a desire to appease the Americans, who were troubled by the presence of black cadets among those aircrew being trained on RAF training schemes operating in the USA.[25]

However, non-white flyers, while a distinct minority among aircrew, certainly did make a significant contribution to the war effort, despite such barely-disguised racial prejudice. Organizations committed to racial equality such as the League of Coloured Peoples were keen to promote the achievements of black flyers, while remaining vigilant towards incidents of discrimination and prejudice. The pages of the League's newsletter recorded with pride the granting of a commission to Pilot Officer Peter Thomas from Sierra Leone, the award of DFC and DSO to Flying Officer Ulric Cross of Trinidad, and mourned the loss of Pilot Officer Victor Tucker, a Jamaican fighter pilot with four kills to his credit, lost over France.[26] Official British propaganda (especially that associated with the Colonial Office) was also keen to publicize the activities of non-white colonial aircrew, although this was always circumscribed by anxieties about alienating white settler populations in Britain's imperial possessions. Ulric Cross appeared in the documentary *West Indies Calling*, while a Maori flyer featured in *Maximum Effort*, a movie about the New Zealand crew of a Lancaster bomber.

Given alarm at the apparent increased militancy of Indian nationalism during the war, official propaganda was eager to promote the contribution of South Asian flyers to the conflicts in both Asia and Europe. Among those Indian flyers singled out for publicity purposes were Pilot Officer Shir der Singh, who had taken part in the famous bombing raid on Brest, and Hari Chaud Dewan who had flown twice over Berlin "to bomb the very heart of the country which stands as much a scheming enemy of India's future as of this country's".[27] In October 1940 the BBC broadcast a radio programme which featured an interview with a Sikh flying officer from the Punjab who had joined the RAF after a prewar career with Imperial Airways.[28] Such propaganda sought to counter attempts by both Germany and Japan to exploit anti-British and anti-imperial sentiments in India, most notably the creation of Subhas Chandras Bhose's Indian National Army. Inevitably, Indian flyers tended to be deployed in the defence of India and the campaign in neighbouring Burma. However, F. Yeats-Brown, who had served in the Bengal Lancers before the First World War, reminded readers of his

celebration of the finest traditions of "martial India" that, at the outbreak of war in 1939 100 Indian students, rather than returning home,
had volunteered to join the RAF. Forty of them became aircrew and
several served in the Battle of Britain. "Strange", mused Yeats-Brown,
"how few of us know this, either in England or India".[29]

The fact that non-white aircrew have been largely erased from the
dominant cultural memory of the wartime RAF is not just about the
triumph of the monoracial refashioning of World War Two that was
offered up by Smith and Bader, and others like them, in the 1960s.
It also says something about the limitations of how the history of cultural memory has been conceptualized and written. While wartime
propaganda films featuring flyers of colour may be dismissed as a
smokescreen, an alibi for a war effort which made no attempt to question racial and imperial hierarchies, it is important to remember that
the men featured in them were not merely ciphers, but were possessed
of individual agency and subjectivity. Official testimony can offer only
a limited reconstruction of their contribution to the war effort, but
more grassroots forms of historical recovery can bring these men back
into the historical record and compensate for their absence from the
conventional archive. Oral history has proved important in this regard,
for example the interviews with West Indian aircrew carried out by the
Guyanan RAF veteran Robert Murray. Murray's interviews disclose
both the virtually ubiquitous racism non-white flyers had to negotiate,
but also their sense of pride in what they had achieved during the
war.[30]

Recovering the presence of the flyer of colour requires us to be imaginative in our choice of evidence, to read between the lines and
against the grain, to try and make linkages between sources which initially appear piecemeal, incomplete and devoid of context. We need to
register more effectively the brief, fleeting references which appear in
the memoirs of white aircrew, men like Miles Tripp who recalled that
the tail gunner of his Lancaster bomber was Harry, a black Jamaican
who could swear and fight but also "appreciate delicacy and nuance in
conversation".[31] We need to be impertinent, to stop and pause at
anomalies in the conventional record which others have passed over
without comment. For example a biography of "Sailor" Malan includes
a posed photograph of Malan with black Jamaican Spitfire pilot Vincent
Bunting. Bunting fails to feature in the text of the book, despite the
fact that one might have expected the question of the relationship of
Malan, an Afrikaner, with a fellow flyer who was black to have aroused
his biographer's curiosity.[32] However, that doesn't preclude a historian

with a very different agenda from trying to pursue this lead further. Equally, we need to discover why a photograph of Sikh Hurricane pilot Mahinder Singh Puji appears to reveal that he had inscribed the word "Amritsar" on the side of his aircraft.[33] Was this merely an innocuous reference to his home city, or an impudent reference to the massacre there in 1919 which had energized the freedom movements of the Indian subcontinent? By adopting Geoff Eley's demand to question the "superior languages of objectivity" and to adopt a "far more mobile agenda" with "a much richer repertoire of legitimate methods and approaches", it might be possible to restore a more ecumenical understanding of the wartime flyer, in contrast to the circumscribed and parochial memory of the war in the air which became dominant in the postwar era, and which was to prove so readily amenable to the discourses of white resistance and national chauvinism.[34]

Moreover, in southern Africa's other last redoubt of white supremacy, the cult of the wartime flyer fitted much less comfortably into the specific political configurations which enforced racial difference than it did in Ian Smith's Rhodesia. In South Africa, public opinion had been deeply divided over the dominion's support of Britain during the war, with many Afrikaners feeling they had more in common with Nazi Germany than with the supposed mother country. Many veterans returning from wartime service found themselves shunned by their fellow countrymen, a sense of alienation that deepened when the Nationalist Party swept to power in 1948, committed to a programme, not merely of intensified racial segregation, but of hostility to the Anglophile sentiments of the Smuts era. Among those ex-servicemen was Group-Captain Adolph Gysbert Malan, DSO and Bar, DFC and Bar, a veteran of the Battle of Britain and generally regarded as one of the greatest fighter pilots of all time. While an Afrikaner, "Sailor" Malan was disgusted at the Nationalist Party's malicious wrecking of the historic ties which had encouraged young men like himself to fight alongside Britain during the war. Initially, his response was to retreat into farming, but in 1951 he entered politics, provoked by the decision of the administration headed by his namesake, D. F. Malan, to disenfranchise the "coloured" voters of the Cape, without observing the terms laid down in the 1909 South African constitution. Malan, sporting his wartime flying jacket and medals, mobilized thousands of his fellow veterans into what became known as the Torch Commando movement, its name derived from the torchlight processions which accompanied its meetings.[35] Malan had little interest in, let alone commitment to, racial equality. His movement was more concerned with the discontent of white veterans than it was with the political rights of coloured voters, his challenge effectively being directed at "the state's allocation of the privileges of whiteness". Unlike more radical veterans' associations, such as the Springbok Legion, Malan certainly had no desire to include either coloured or black veterans in Torch, and his movement developed within the racial parameters of the colonial order. As he made clear to a rally in Johannesburg in May 1951, "Who has the greatest claim to talk about saving white civilization? The moles who now pay lip service to it, or the men who fought for it?"[36] However, while Torch was complicit in a racialized conception of South Africa, Malan's campaign made it impossible for the exclusive Afrikaner nationalism which was the engine of apartheid to appropriate unproblematically the myth of the flyer into its particular fantasy of the ongoing defence of white civilization. In Pretoria, unlike Salisbury (or indeed Enoch Powell's Wolverhampton) the defenders of the laager would have to battle on without the reassuring sound of the Spitfire overhead.

The repertoire of white resistance required a rendering of the flyer which was highly partial. Not merely was it necessary to expunge flyers of colour from the memory of the wartime RAF, but it was equally imperative to sever white flyers from various negative associations that would compromise their status as tribunes of a morally superior white nation. In the 1930s airmen had regularly been identified with the politics of fascism and authoritarianism, and as late as 1941 Rex Warner could still portray men of the RAF as sinister and narcissistic strongmen in his terrifyingly dystopian novel *The Aerodrome*.[37] Such promethean associations were dissipated by the RAF's central role in the struggle against Nazism, but residual anxieties remained that the flyer's sense of other-worldliness and elitism might be a potential danger to postwar democracy. Indeed, some representations of the flyer in the immediate postwar years were far from flattering, ranging from the inconsiderate and vacuous Freddie Page in Terence Rattigan's play *The Deep Blue Sea* to the cruel and murderous Wing Commander Glennon in the 1950 movie *Cage of Gold*.[38] Those who wished to draw a dividend from the myth of the wartime flyer needed to emphasize the lover of flight rather than the lover of war, the gentle and sensitive poet – encapsulated in David Niven's portrayal of Flight Lieutenant Peter Carter in Powell and Pressburger's 1945 cinematic fantasy *A Matter of Life and Death* – and not the violent agent of destruction.[39] At a time when the process of imperial demission had seen, not a retreat from, but a reiteration of, the violence that underpinned white authority in the colonial context (most notably, in the Kenyan emergency of the

1950s, but also in a series of other counter-insurgency campaigns whose bloody intensity is only now coming under public and historical scrutiny)[40] it was vital to identify the flyer with a chivalric gentleness and the romance of the air.

For this reason, much of the postwar cult of the flyer focused on fighter pilots as opposed to bomber aircrew, since the latter's reputation was beginning to suffer from growing squeamishness among both politicians and public that the strategic bombing campaign had seriously compromised Britain's claims to have fought a "good war". The raid which destroyed Dresden in February 1945 became especially troubling to the national conscience, possibly because, unlike the atrocities committed against colonial peoples in the empire, it had brought destruction to a city that was believed to exemplify the achievements of western, Christian, civilization.[41] Significantly, the iconic postwar text of Bomber Command heroism, the 1955 movie *The Dambusters*, concentrated on the precision bombing of the Ruhr reservoirs in 1943, rather than on the area bombing which created firestorms in cities across Germany during the war. It is perhaps not inconsequential that both Bader and Smith were fighter pilots, and their beloved Spitfires were free of the taint of civilian slaughter that might have compromised the equation of white resistance with the preservation of "civilized" values against the onslaught of the barbaric other.

Certainly, if Ian Smith and Douglas Bader were to be successfully incorporated into the dominant myth of the wartime flyer, they would, to some extent, have to be made over. Neither Bader, the belligerent hearty nor Smith, the charmless puritan, in their radically different ways, fitted the image of the dashing and romantic flyer. Smith's notoriously sour countenance – his "poker face" – was now attributed to a skin graft he received to cover the injuries he had sustained when his Hurricane had crashed in North Africa. Smith's relatively undistinguished war record was transformed into a heroic narrative, which related how, after being shot down over Italy, he served with anti-fascist partisans.[42] While the story lacked any obvious love interest, it certainly recalled two popular romantic narratives of the downed flyer on the run, H. E. Bates' middlebrow novel *Fair Stood the Wind for France* and the feature film *The Glass Mountain*. Even if it were unintended and subliminal, Smith surely benefited from having the public's understanding of his wartime story refracted through the lens of popular culture, especially if it was in the form of texts which promoted idealized and romanticized imaginings of the wartime flyer.[43] In the case of Bader, the relationship to popular cultural texts was much more overt and personal. He was involved in the cinematic adaptation of his own life story, *Reach For the Sky*, which was released in 1957, and remained a regular fixture of British cinema (the most successful film shown in Britain since *Gone With the Wind*) and television for decades afterwards. Bader was fortunate that the actor chosen to play him, Kenneth More, provided a sympathetic and attractive rendering of the flyer's personality, emphasizing not just ebullience and breeziness, but a quiet tenderness which actually embellished, rather than detracted from, his more obvious manly virtues.[44] If the real Douglas Bader did not always match the stipulations of modesty and gentleness required by the cult of the flyer, the reconfigured Douglas Bader of *Reach for the Sky* had sufficient purchase in the British imaginary that the potential dissonance was rarely noticed.

What ultimately made it impossible for either Bader or Smith to deploy the myths of the British war effort unproblematically, and 1940 in particular, was that those myths could just as easily be appropriated by their critics and opponents. As the *Sunday Mirror* pointed out in a profile of Bader: "Here is a man who risked his life a hundred times in a war which was fought against tyranny, censorship and racism – the very stuff the Rhodesian rebels are made of. If Bader's views on such matters were the same in 1940 as they are today, what was he fighting for? It is a curious predicament to feel grateful to someone whose views one finds so repulsive".[45] While the association of the wartime flyer with the triumph over Nazi racism could serve as a credible alibi for the racial prejudices of Smith and Bader, it could just as easily function as a highly convincing witness for the prosecution.

In her study, *Which People's War?* Sonya Rose demonstrated how the dominant social, political and cultural understandings of the Second World War in Britain were deeply inflected by gender, social class and racial difference.[46] This essay has provided a case study of how Rose's insistence on the absence of a singular meaning attached to the *experience* of war can also be applied to the way the war was *remembered* from the 1950s to the 1970s, and beyond. The RAF's wartime story played an important role in the cultural memory of the Second World War in Britain, but it also revealed the complexity and contestation surrounding the war's meaning, especially since it became entwined with the end of empire. If the myth of the wartime flyer was to be deployed (as it was by Ian Smith and Douglas Bader) in order to reassert racial hierarchies in both the disintegrating empire and the metropole itself, this required a process of selective denial and extensive refashioning, not least the expunging of non-whites from the dominant memory of the RAF at war. Here we seem to have a classic illustration of the claim of the French ethnographer Marc Auge, that "memories are shaped by forgetting, like the contours of the shore by the sea".[47] Of course, forgetting in regard to war is not necessarily to be condemned. For many it has been an understandable strategy of psychological survival and emotional restitution.[48] However, in the case of the mythic afterlife of the flyer, it is difficult not to conclude that forgetting operated as a political instrument, a means to ensure the preservation of the authority of whiteness, both on the frontier and in the metropole.

Paul Gilroy demands that Britain move beyond its neurotic obsession with World War Two in order to remedy "the mysterious evacuation of Britain's postcolonial conflicts from national consciousness".[49] In contrast, this essay has suggested that such a paradigm shift is an impossibility, since memories of the anti-Nazi struggle and the twilight of empire are irretrievably linked, at the levels of both the real and the fantasized. A fuller scrutiny of the scripts surrounding the wartime flyer make it clear that there was nothing preordained or straightforward about them being obliged to perform the cultural work of discourses which denied the credibility and viability of a multicultural vision of postcolonial Britain. Beneath the "comforting rumble" of the Spitfire and Hurricane, one might be able to detect a less harmonious cadence, the sound of alternate fading and swelling which constitutes the pulsing of an aircraft engine. Likewise, under the surface of the dominant cultural myth of the flyer, lies an intricate matrix of experience and memory, one in which subaltern and less exclusionary registers are no less significant than those which have provided succour for the politics of post-imperial self-delusion and racial re-homogenization. The culture of national consolation offered by the myth of the flyer appears increasingly vulnerable when that myth is unpacked and the stories behind it are retold in their unabridged versions. Next time vintage aircraft thunder overhead as part of the pageantry of national commemoration, we might just about be able to discern, albeit in a minor key, the dissonant, discomforting sound of the return of the repressed.

Acknowledgements

This essay is an extended version of a paper presented at the annual meeting of the North American Conference on British Studies, Boston, Massachusetts in November 2006. I wish to thank the audience and my fellow panelists – Penny Summerfield, Janet Watson, Nicoletta Gullace and Fred Leventhal – for comments and suggestions. My participation at this conference was made possible by the support of the Charles

Phelps Taft Memorial Fund of the University of Cincinnati. Thanks are also owed to Brenda Assael, Stephen Brooke, Chris Waters, and Maura O'Connor.

Notes

1   Bill Schwarz, "'The Only White Man In There': The Re-Racialisation of England, 1956–1968", *Race and Class* 38, no.1 (1996): 65–78.

2   Frank Mort, "Scandalous Events: Metropolitan Culture and Moral Change in Post-Second World War London", *Representations* 93 (2006): 127–30.

3   See, for example, Joanna Lewis, "Daddy Wouldn't Buy Me a Mau Mau: The British Popular Press and the Demoralization of Empire", in *Mau Mau and Nationhood: Arms, Authority and Narration*, eds. E. S. Atieno Odhiambo and John Lonsdale (Athens, 2003), 227–50 and Stephen Howe, "When (if Ever) did Empire End? 'Internal Decolonisation' in British Culture since the 1950s", in *The British Empire in the 1950s: Retreat or Revival?* ed. Martin Lynn (Basingstoke, 2006), 223–6.

4   Reproduced in Ian Douglas Smith, *The Great Betrayal* (London, 1997), opposite 274.

5   Peter Joyce, *Anatomy of a Rebel: Smith of Rhodesia* (Salisbury, 1974), 48–60.

6   Paul Gilroy, *Postcolonial Melancholia* (New York, 2005), 87–95, 116.

7   For example, Janet S.K. Watson, *Fighting Different Wars: Experience, Memory, and the First World War in Britain* (Cambridge, 2004).

8   Geoff Eley, "Finding the People's War: Film, British Collective Memory and World War Two", *American Historical Review* 105, no.5 (2001): 818–38.

9   For example, Mark Connelly, *We Can Take It! Britain and the Memory of the Second World War* (Harlow, 2004).

10   Lucy Noakes, *War and the British: Gender, Memory and National Identity* (London, 1998). This unfortunate lacuna in the literature stands in marked contrast to the literature on memory in postwar France. Here, the recovery of how the war was remembered has come to be understood as requiring, not just the ending of amnesia surrounding the Vichy regime, but also an appreciation of how the legacies of wartime collaboration and resistance came to inform the nation's understanding of the violent struggles surrounding decolonization in Indo-China and Algeria.

11   Holmes Alexander, quoted in Anthony Harrigan, *One Against the Mob* (Arlington, VA, 1966), 13–14.

12   David Caute, *Under the Skin: The Death of White Rhodesia* (London, 1983), 47, 90.

13   John Lovett, *Contact: A Tribute to Those Who Serve Rhodesia* (Salisbury, 1977), 20.

14   Martin Francis, *The Flyer: Men of the Royal Air Force and British Culture, 1939–1945* (Oxford, forthcoming).

15   Paul Brickhill, *Reach for the Sky: The Story of Douglas Bader* (London, 1954), John Frayn Turner, *Douglas Bader* (Shrewsbury, 1995), Laddie Lucas, *Flying Colours: The Epic Story of Douglas Bader* (London, 1990).

16   Robert Jackson, *Douglas Bader: A Biography* (London, 1983), 147–62.

17   Pip Beck, *A WAAF in Bomber Command* (London, 1989), 35.

18 Paul Addison, "National Identity and the Battle of Britain", in *War and the Cultural Construction of Identities in Britain*, eds. Barbara Korte and Ralf Schneider (Amsterdam, 2002), 225–40.

19 Richard Doherty, *Irish Men and Women in the Second World War* (Dublin, 1999), 97–124, 176–200.

20 Ashley Jackson, *The British Empire and the Second World War* (London, 2006), 38–40.

21 Wendy Webster, *Englishness and Empire, 1939–1965* (Oxford, 2005), 7–8, 61–2.

22 "Introduction", in *Moments of Modernity: Reconstructing Britain, 1945–1964*, eds. Becky Conekin, Frank Mort and Chris Waters (London, 1999), 1–3; Peter H. Hansen, "Coronation Everest: The Empire and Commonwealth in the 'Second Elizabethan Age'", in *British Culture and the End of Empire*, ed. Stuart Ward (Manchester, 2001), 57–64; Bill Schwarz, "Reveries of Race: The Closing of the Imperial Moment", in Conekin, *Moments of Modernity*, 189–207.

23 Peter Townsend, *Time and Chance: An Autobiography* (London, 1978), 120, Sarah Bradford, *George VI* (London, 1991), 549–51.

24 Priya Satia, "The Defense of Inhumanity: Air Control in Iraq and the British Idea of Arabia", *American Historical Review* 111, no.1 (2006): 16–51; David Omissi, "The Hendon Air Pageant, 1920–37", in *Popular Imperialism and the Military, 1850–1950*, ed. John M. MacKenzie (Manchester, 1992), 198–220.

25 National Archives, [TNA], AIR 2/6876 "Coloured RAF Personnel: Report on Progress and Suitability", n.d. [February 1945].

26 *The League of Coloured Peoples Newsletter*, 33 (June 1942): 75, 37 (October 1942): 9, 60 (September 1944): 97, 63 (December 1944): 59–60, 63.

27 TNA, AIR 2/6552 "Indians in the RAF: Press Publicity", n.d.

28 "In It Together", *The Listener*, 17 October 1940, 559–60.

29 F. Yeats-Brown, *Martial India* (London, 1945), 167.

30 Robert N. Murray, *Lest We Forget: The Experiences of World War II West Indian Ex-Service Personnel* (Nottingham, 1996).

31 Miles Tripp, *The Eighth Passenger: A Flight of Recollection and Discovery* (London, 1969), 11.

32 Norman Franks, *Sky Tiger: The Story of Group Captain Sailor Malan* (London, 1980), 163.

33 This photograph appears (without any textual comment) in Christopher Somerville, *Our War: How the British Commonwealth Fought the Second World War* (London, 1998), after 140.

34 Geoff Eley, "Foreword", in *War and Memory in the Twentieth Century*, eds. Martin Evans and Keith Lunn (Oxford, 1997), ix–x.

35 Oliver Walker, *Sailor Malan: A Biography* (London, 1953), 159–75.

36 Neil Roos, *Ordinary Springboks: White Servicemen and Social Justice in South Africa* (Aldershot, 2005), 129–57.

37 Robert Wohl, *The Spectacle of Flight: Aviation and the Western Imagination, 1920–1950* (New Haven, 2005), 305–38; Rex Warner, *The Aerodrome* (London, 1941). There are other interwar portrayals of flyers as harbingers of destruction, see I. F. Clarke, *Voices Prophecying War: Future Wars, 1763–3749* (Oxford, 1992).

38   Terence Rattigan, *The Deep Blue Sea* (London, 1953, 1999), British Film Institute Library, London, Pressbooks and Cuttings: *Cage of Gold* (1950).

39   Ian Christie, *A Matter of Life and Death* (London, 2000), 13–14.

40   Caroline Elkins, *Britain's Gulag: The Brutal End of Empire in Kenya* (London, 2005).

41   Donald Bloxham, "Dresden as a War Crime", in *Firestorm: The Bombing of Dresden, 1945*, eds. Paul Addison and Jeremy A. Crang (London, 2006), 180–208.

42   Peter Godwin and Ian Hancock, *"Rhodesians Never Die": The Impact of War and Political Change on White Rhodesia, c.1970–1980* (Oxford, 1993), 61.

43   H. E. Bates, *Fair Stood the Wind for France* (London, 1944); *The Glass Mountain*, dir. Henry Cass (1950).

44   Kenneth More, *Happy Go Lucky: My Life* (London, 1959), 152–61.

45   Quoted in Jackson, *Douglas Bader*, 153.

46   Sonya O. Rose, *Which People's War? National Identity and Citizenship in Wartime Britain, 1939–1945* (Oxford, 2003).

47   Quoted in Susan Rubin Suleiman, *Crises of Memory and the Second World War* (Cambridge, MA, 2006), 215.

48   This has obviously been a key theme in discussions of historical memory and the *Shoah*, for example, Saul Friedlander, *When Memory Comes* (New York, 1979).

49   Gilroy, *Postcolonial Melancholia*, 89.

11
Disturbing the People's Peace: Patriotism and "Respectable" Racism in British Responses to Rhodesian Independence

Alice Ritscherle

On the morning of November 11, 1965, the Rhodesian Broadcasting Company enjoined listeners to stand by for a radio address from Ian Smith, head of the Rhodesian Front Party and Prime Minister of the self-governing British colony that would become Zimbabwe in 1979. That afternoon, at 1:15, Smith went on the air and announced that his cabinet had just issued a Unilateral Declaration of Independence (UDI) from Britain. Citing a "paralyzing state of uncertainty" created by nationalist agitation and communist insurgencies throughout Africa, Smith declared that there could be "no future" for Rhodesia while it drifted in "constitutional twilight".[1] Unlike Britain's Labour government, committed in Smith's view to the steady transfer of power to Soviet-backed African nationalists throughout the continent, the Rhodesian Front (RF) "rejected the doctrinaire philosophy of appeasement and surrender".[2] Rhodesians, he asserted, would stand in defence of European civilization, democracy and free enterprise (these often conflated in Smith's UDI address and other RF pronouncements), "fortified by the same strength and courage" that had distinguished Rhodesia's founding pioneers.[3]

While emphasizing his party's disaffection from the British government, heightened by the Labour Party's failure to stem the tide of African nationalism threatening "civilization" in Rhodesia, Smith repeatedly appealed to metropolitan whites by delineating Rhodesia's historical connections with Britain. Hours after signing a Declaration of Independence under a portrait of Queen Elizabeth II, Smith insisted that Rhodesians had no quarrel with "the people" of Britain, "kith and kin" who shared "Rhodesians' concept of justice and civilization", but only with politicians who had compromised the interests of Britain's loyal subjects. To the strains of "God Save the Queen", he concluded his UDI address by invoking an inviolable bond between Rhodesians and Britons who "had fought shoulder to shoulder against a common enemy in two world wars".[4]

In issuing UDI, the Rhodesian Front spat into the winds of change. Pressured by Westminster to expand Rhodesia's franchise – a franchise based on property and educational qualifications that excluded almost all of Rhodesia's 4,000,000 Africans – the RF upheld the privilege of 200,000 whites in what was effectively an apartheid state. In Britain, public denunciations of Smith in the editorial pages of newspapers and during rallies led by organizations such as Movement for Colonial Freedom were matched, if not overshadowed, by expressions of sympathy for Rhodesia's white minority.

This essay explores the ways that Rhodesia's UDI shaped the terms of an incipient conservative backlash in Britain. It first considers metropolitan support for Smith's regime, focusing on the most evocative and populist terms of its expression. As Britain's imperial epoch drew to a close and its "civilizing mission" lost credibility, the most resonant terms for supporting the Smith regime referenced Rhodesians' heroic sacrifices for the Allied cause during World War II. Second, it considers Rhodesia's recurrent role in British public debates about immigration control and the social democratic settlement established by the "People's Peace". Ultimately, metropolitan whites' patriotic identification with Smith's regime, committed in the most contradictory fashion to both white supremacy and "free" market capitalism, ultimately broadened the populist dimensions of conservative and racial politics in the critical years preceding the rise of the New Right.

Reflecting the influence of innovative scholars, most notably Bill Schwarz and Wendy Webster, who have accounted for the impact of decolonization on metropolitan whites' racial subjectivities, this essay considers the contradictory legacies of the "People's War" for British political culture.[5] During the mid-1940s, the "People's War" produced an alignment between patriotism and left politics, elevating popular expectations that, following victory, the state would reward citizens with a wide range of welfare benefits, defined as social rights.[6] The war also conditioned a new dispensation in race relations, insofar as awareness of Nazi genocidal atrocities delegitimized race as a source of political mobilization and curbed open reference to "race" in public debate. If the war produced a leftward shift in Britain's political culture and certain forms of racial egalitarianism, it nevertheless elicited powerful nationalist sentiments, with all of their chauvinistic and exclusionary overtones. As Geoff Eley has noted, the "collectivist momentum" produced by wartime mobilization had, by the 1960s, shaded into "conservative forms of patriotism" and "assimilated to militarism, imperialism and more traditional interpretations of British nationalism".[7] Metropolitan reactions to UDI provide stark evidence of this transvaluation. In Britain, whites who defended the actions of a regime committed to both white privilege and "free" market capitalism often predicated support for UDI on the presumably inviolable wartime bonds forged during the struggle to defend democracy, not to mention England.

In 1965, associations between Rhodesian militarism and the defence of democracy were rather strange, to say the least, even if such associations had deep roots in a shared Commonwealth effort to defeat German fascism between 1939 and 1945. By 1965, Rhodesia was anything but a seat of democracy. As Doris Lessing wrote of the 1950s, the Mau Mau insurgency in Kenya served as "a burglar alarm in a rich house", hardening white supremacist and anti-communist attitudes among whites throughout Africa. Following Mau Mau, Rhodesian whites, riveted by events in Kenya, increasingly obsessed about "[R]eds like Iain McLeod" riding "rough-shod over [the] rights" of whites in Africa and cast dire predictions about what their fate might be if Labour returned to power in Britain.[8] The secessionist and militaristic inflections of white Rhodesian nationalism became even more pronounced following the eruption of violence in the Congo in 1960, when bars began appearing on the windows of whites' homes in Rhodesia, and a volunteer Home Guard began patrolling white neighbourhoods after dark.[9] Conditions were ripe for the electoral success of the newly-formed Rhodesian Front, the spearhead of a grassroots white nationalist movement. Formed in 1962, the RF all but displaced liberal opinion from mainstream Rhodesian politics, garnering wide support with pledges to uphold Rhodesia's 1931 Land Apportionment Act, which had designated the most fertile land for European ownership and consigned Africans to tse-tse infested "Native Purchase Areas". The popularity of the RF also rested upon the party's declared intent to enforce Rhodesia's restrictive voting qualifications, occupational colour bars, pass laws, curfews in African townships and racial segregation in most public facilities.

After winning the general election in 1962, the RF did little to contain its most rabid supporters, who verbally abused and physically assaulted their opponents at public meetings with impunity. After sweeping the 1964 election, the RF stepped up its hard-line efforts, imprisoning political dissidents, censoring newspapers and banning African nationalist organizations.[10] In 1965, the RF won its third election – interpreting victory as a mandate for UDI – after circulating posters featuring the mingled legs of black and white schoolgirls and the caption: "Rhodesia is not ready for this!"[11] During the month preceding UDI, the RF imposed a state of emergency, ostensibly to prevent the infiltration of Soviet-trained insurgents from Zambia.[12] Police assumed powers to arrest without warrant and to disband public gatherings of more than three persons.[13] With the leaders of dissident movements imprisoned or otherwise silenced, the stage was set for UDI.

In Salisbury, Rhodesia's capital, white workers in a number of offices danced around their desks following the announcement of UDI; throughout RF supporters uncorked champagne bottles festooned in RF colours at evening "Independence Parties".[14] In an immediate sense, however, UDI did little to disrupt life in white Rhodesia. The same could hardly be said for life in African townships. In Gwelo, thousands of Africans defied curfews, taking to the streets in public demonstrations that resulted in mass arrests and over 200 caning sentences.[15] The worst clashes between Africans and police took place in late November, in the Mpopoma township, where police used tear gas and armoured cars to disperse 3,000 protestors.[16] In other townships, police fired tear gas and ammunition into crowds, killing at least one individual.[17]

The Soviet Union, its satellites and various "third-way" countries responded to UDI and state violence in Rhodesia with unqualified condemnation. The Soviet Union, for one, immediately pledged to support the "national liberation struggles of the Zimbabwean people" and condemned Anglo-American collusion in propping up apartheid states as bulwarks against communism.[18] In the UN, which imposed mandatory sanctions against Rhodesia in December of 1966, Kwame Nkrumah and other leaders of independent African states challenged the British government to deploy troops, as it had during Mau Mau, to suppress the rebellion. In Delhi and Dar Es Salaam, hundreds of students protested Britain's "support for another South Africa" by stoning British embassies and burning Union Jacks.[19]

In Britain, UDI also elicited swift and emotional, albeit less violent, reactions. In the House of Commons, general bi-partisan agreement quickly emerged around the desirability of avoiding military conflict with Rhodesia. Most peers agreed that a strike could unleash anarchy in an already volatile situation, and that soldiers ordered to attack "kith and kin" in Rhodesia might stage a "Curragh Mutiny".[20] In lieu of military force, Harold Wilson's Labour Government imposed political and economic sanctions on Rhodesia. On November 11, the government ineffectively asserted jurisdiction over Rhodesia's internal affairs, claiming to exercise authority through special Orders of Council to be implemented by Rhodesia's Crown-appointed Governor.[21] In subsequent days, it invalidated passports issued in Rhodesia, stating that only (white) individuals fleeing political persecution could freely enter Britain.[22] Finally, it excluded Rhodesia from Commonwealth trading preferences, froze Rhodesian assets in Britain and banned all trade between Britain and Rhodesia.[23]

By mid-1966, bi-partisan agreement over the means of bringing Rhodesia back to constitutional rule had broken down.[24] However, challenges to the Wilson government's Rhodesia policy emerged much earlier. In mid-November of 1965, about two dozen far-right Tories defied Edward Heath's leadership of the Conservative Party by opposing sanctions and calling for immediate negotiations with Smith. This splinter group had its most vocal representative in 72 year-old Lord Salisbury, an early and unswerving critic of consensus politics and decolonization, whose waning political career received a significant boost in the months surrounding UDI. Speaking in the House of Lords on November 15, Salisbury invoked the spectre of violence in the Congo to defend Smith, a traitor only by virtue of legal "technicalities". Sanctions, Salisbury declared, represented a "supine repudiation" of those "kith and kin" keeping the "British way of life alive in Central Africa".[25] Outside Parliament, Salisbury's followers in the Anglo-Rhodesia Society and Monday Club rallied public support by circulating pamphlets, distributing "Support Rhodesia" bumper stickers (some of which began to appear on cars parked at Westminster) and organizing public meetings that ended with enthusiastic cheers for Smith.[26]

Smith's metropolitan supporters were, by no means, confined to conservative fringe groups. Immediately following the announcement of UDI, whites flocked to Rhodesia House, home to Rhodesia's High Commission in London, to inscribe a visitors' book with hundreds of congratulatory messages such as "We will fight for you as you fought for us".[27] In December 1965, the *Times'* classifieds carried numerous Christmas wishes for Smith, as well as solicitations from a London committee operating on a "purely non-political basis" to create a "Save Rhodesia Fund" for families affected by sanctions.[28]

While some metropolitan whites supported UDI on explicitly racial grounds – one woman interviewed by *Panorama* explained her support for Smith by stating simply, "he's white like us" – *overtly* racist expressions of support for Smith's regime were rare.[29] More precisely, metropolitan whites rarely made reference to biological or phenotypical differences between Europeans and Africans to explain their support for the Smith regime. That said, ideas about race, however obliquely expressed, crucially shaped metropolitan opinions and debates about

UDI. Metropolitans who supported the Smith regime often expressed racialized (and racist) forms of identification with white Rhodesians in terms of national characteristics and cultural attributes that ostensibly formed the basis of a transcontinental community of (white) Britons. One aim of this essay is to consider the contours of racial identity and popular conservatism among metropolitan whites at the end of the imperial epoch, when reconfigurations of the literal and imagined boundaries of the nation precipitated redefinitions and reinscriptions of race in Britain's political culture. As Paul Gilroy and others have argued, the fiction of "race" and the imagined community of the "nation" are often inseparably bound, both products of parallel historical trajectories and entangled genealogies. Based upon principles of inclusion and exclusion, each posits notions of cultural, inevitable and even natural and primordial bonds.[30] In debates about UDI, discredited ideas about "race" and racist sentiments typically found expression through the process of articulation with more acceptable ideas about British "culture" and "character", and through celebratory narratives about Britain's national and imperial history.

Particularly in the weeks preceding UDI, before the RF severed Rhodesia's constitutional connection to Britain, effectively negating the subject status of Rhodesians, metropolitan whites often inscribed Rhodesians into nostalgic and sanitized narratives about Britain's imperial past. At the Conservative Party Conference in October of 1965, Lord Salisbury argued that, by bending to the winds of change, the Labour government had betrayed white émigrés who had brought "British ideas of peace and justice to remote and primitive lands".[31] Equating nineteenth-century pioneers and mid-twentieth-century Rhodesians, Salisbury described Smith's supporters in the present tense as "ordinary decent British men and women, people very like ourselves", who had converted Rhodesia from "a stretch of country riddled with disease in its most terrible form and racked with warfare between tribe and tribe" into a prosperous country.[32] The popular press also conflated Rhodesia's founders and contemporary Rhodesians, as when the editor of the *Daily Express* attacked sanctions as a means of forcing constitutional change. "Those who attack Rhodesians", he argued, are "not referring to some faraway exotic land peopled by barbarians, but their own kinsfolk who have carved a modern, prosperous State out of a profitless wilderness".[33]

Accounts of contemporary Rhodesian grit were, at best, ill-informed. The majority of Rhodesians who voted Smith into office had followed a well-paved path to privilege. Between 1946 and 1960, Rhodesia's white population increased from 82,000 to 221,000, due largely to an influx of lower middle-class immigrants hoping to capitalize on acute labor shortages created by rapid industrial and corporate growth in Rhodesia.[34] White immigrants generally enjoyed rapid upward social mobility due to low taxes and occupational colour bars that artificially inflated their wages; most joined Rhodesian-born whites in ostentatious displays of wealth and privilege. By the 1950s, and in contrast to Britain, most white families owned at least one car – contributing to massive suburban sprawls around Salisbury and Bulawayo – and employed African servants to dust sparkling new appliances, tend expansive lawns and gardens and clean private swimming pools.[35]

Despite the advantages that propelled their social advance, most postwar émigrés related their experiences to Rhodesia's founding myths, joining their compatriots in commemorating Cecil Rhodes and the "founding pioneers", and celebrating the enterprising spirit said to define Rhodesian character. Such stories allowed British émigrés to refashion themselves as (not-so-rugged) individualists contributing to an ongoing civilizing mission. Often "products of the British labour movement, with its traditions of brotherhood", émigrés seduced by the material benefits of white supremacy typically justified their newfound wealth with racist pronouncements about the abilities of "kaffirs".[36] During the 1960s, most threw in their lot with the reactionary RF, despite its lack of support for social welfare programmes and unswerving commitment to "free" market capitalism. As Roy Perott of the *Observer* noted in October 1965, at least half of Smith's most fervent supporters were recent immigrants, skilled or semi-skilled workers who likely would have voted Labour in Britain.[37]

Partly for this reason, the RF actively recruited British whites to Rhodesia throughout the 1960s. In ads placed in a number of periodicals including *Punch*, the *Sunday Telegraph* and the *Daily Express,* the Rhodesian Immigration Board depicted Rhodesia as a land of opportunity or more accurately, opportunism for whites hoping to escape the congestion, inclement weather and rigid class system of England. In June 1965, a full-page *Daily Express* ad promoted Rhodesia as a country with a pleasant climate, booming economy and "champagne feeling" that lasted "all year round".[38] Those "stuck in a rut" and "sick of waiting for 'dead men's shoes'", the advertisement promised, could realize their potential in a "young progressive country" where competition was "keen but not overpowering", and where "go-getters" could easily obtain promotions, servants and swimming pools. Beneath photos of pristine beaches, shimmering glass skyscrapers and cheerful white moviegoers, a caption assured a warm welcome in a thriving country where "the only direction

[was] up".[39] The only allusion to the grim realities of white supremacy was a brief assurance that Rhodesia had "a stable and responsible government" committed to protecting Rhodesia's "standards and way of life".[40]

The contradiction between "free" enterprise and the brutal suppression of Africans was not lost on metropolitan critics of the Smith regime. Lower middle-class émigrés' privilege and awkward embrace of nouveau riche lifestyles provided their critics with endless fodder. In the lead-up to UDI, one contributor to *Punch* defined Rhodesia as "a first-class country for third-class whites",[41] while the *Guardian's* Clyde Sanger caustically described the "light-headed state" of "country club revolutionaries" preparing for rebellion.[42] Shortly after UDI, the *Sunday Telegraph's* Douglas Brown derided befuddled whites "lost in the bush", emptying champagne bottles and playing "an historical charade to relieve the monotony of their affluent but empty existence".[43] In the House of Commons, Labour MP Merlyn Rees ridiculed expatriates in Rhodesia as lower middle-class "subtopians from England" who had "come face to face with African nationalism and been found wanting".[44]

Clearly, white Rhodesians' ostentatious displays of privilege could easily belie paeans to Rhodesian grit and enterprise. For this reason, Rhodesia's contributions to Britain's war effort between 1939 and 1945 generally provided the most resonant terms with which metropolitan whites could extol the character of Rhodesian society and express support for UDI. This was evident in the British media's depictions of Smith, a celebrity of sorts, followed by the press and cheered by well-wishers when he visited London for negotiations in October of 1965. Covering negotiations and then UDI, the British press almost invariably noted Smith's war record and included the appellation "former RAF fighter pilot" after nearly every mention of his name. In writing about Smith, British journalists consistently provided stock descriptions of his crooked smile and drooping eyelid, evidence of injuries sustained during a 1943 runway accident in Alexandria.[45]

In tributes to Smith, celebrations of masculine virility and heroism – once staples of imperial adventure stories – entered into public dialogue about wartime camaraderie without entirely muting the imperial hues in projections of national identity.[46] In December 1965, Lord Fraser of Lonsdale denounced the Labour Government in the House of Lords for withholding the war pensions of 2,000 Rhodesians until Rhodesia returned to legality. Wilson, he stated, "could not know much about war pensions or battles", if he thought it possible to intimidate a "former war pilot", adding that, if he "had to go lion shooting", he would "rather go with Mr. Smith".[47]

More generalized tributes to Rhodesians' contributions to the war effort revealed the depth of emotion surrounding what Smith called Britain's "Great Betrayal" of former allies. As early as October 1965, mainstream British newspapers began dedicating ample space to editorial letters pledging support for UDI, explained as repayment for Rhodesians' wartime contributions – or rather, the contributions of 9,000 whites, as references to 15,000 African veterans were practically non-existent.[48] One letter to the *Birmingham Post* urged Wilson to recall "the magnificent war record of Mr. Ian Smith and his colleagues" in the struggle to prevent "Hitler's domination of Britain" and warned of the "eternal disgrace" that would haunt Britain if it "forced black domination upon Rhodesians under the guise of a spurious democracy".[49] On November 11, 1965, the staff of Rhodesia House mounted photos and brief biographies of veterans in the RF cabinet in the windows of Rhodesia House. For days, the photos attracted the admiration of small crowds gathered before Rhodesia House to demonstrate support for Smith's government.[50]

Public dialogue about economic sanctions only broadened the populist dimensions of support for white Rhodesians, widely viewed as "ordinary" people courageously enduring deprivation in ways that recalled the homefront during the "People's War". In the short-run, sanctions boosted Rhodesia's economy, encouraging diversification, import substitution and, by extension, a boom in construction. The importation of oil through Mozambique, as well as ongoing trade with South Africa, Portugal, the United States and, to a lesser degree, British interests acting illegally through "neutral" third-party distributors in Johannesburg, sustained Rhodesia's economy until the late 1960s.[51] Nevertheless, the effects of sanctions were undeniable. Hardest hit were agricultural and industrial producers reliant on Commonwealth markets and small retailers whose stocks and sales diminished with rationing.[52] In June 1966, with declining capital investment and trade portending long-term economic downturn, the *Economist* described Rhodesia as a structurally unsound house, in which "the bricks are falling down, leaving the wallpaper standing".[53]

The comparison was apt. To buoy a listing economy, the RF deviated from "free" market principles by instituting state controls over the dismissal of employees in the iron, steel, tobacco-packing and auto industries, primarily to stem unemployment and an exodus of whites to South Africa. Ordered to maintain personnel levels, many manufacturers curbed expenditure by staggering production, so that it was not uncommon to see factory workers playing cards beside silent assembly lines.[54] At the same time, Smith's government subsidized farmers through the state purchase of unsold tobacco, and by advancing loans to sugar producers unable to secure credit from private banks.[55] Nevertheless, by late 1966, tobacco farmers, the backbone of Rhodesia's agricultural export economy, had consigned most of their crops to rot in warehouses, while sugar producers had opened fields of uncut cane to grazing cattle.[56]

Immunized from paralysing insecurities by press censorship, most white Rhodesian consumers continued "business as usual". Shortages of non-essential items such as golf-balls did impinge upon leisure pursuits, while inflation soared due to the rationing of certain imported foods, as well as the hoarding of luxury items, including cosmetics and gin. (Immediately following UDI, white women overran Salisbury department stores and bought "enough lipsticks and face cream to last for years").[57] By the end of 1966, mounting credit card debt was causing anxiety among many whites, to the degree that the *Daily Mail*'s Donald Wise described Rhodesia as a formerly "gay, sunkissed place" that had become "humourless – bitter and twisted by hatred for Whitehall".[58] That said, most consumers maintained their status quo to the best of their abilities (or credit limits).

In private exchanges, Harold Wilson derided the grasping materialism of white Rhodesians ill-prepared to weather a genuine crisis, suggesting that "laissez-faire" principles would ultimately undermine the rebellion, as Smith lacked the experience of "organizing and directing the whole economic life" of a country.[59] To those publicly disposed towards the Smith regime, the "suffering" caused by sanctions engendered a great deal of sympathy for white Rhodesians and a corresponding hostility towards the Labour Government. In the House of Lords, the Earl of Perth argued that sanctions imposed on former allies only revealed the extent of Britain's own moral degeneration. "Hitler lost the war", he declared, but "we were all the losers and have been for the last fifteen years", adding "Rhodesians fought against Hitler and are not the sort of people who, at this time, are going to throw their hand in when, once again, they feel that their way of life is at stake".[60] A contributor to the *Birmingham Post* asserted that Rhodesians were representative "of the toughest British stock" and, endowed with "the determination that saw us through 1940", and were "defending their homes, as any other worthwhile person of British blood would".[61]

The rhetorical equivalence of Rhodesian rebels and survivors of the Blitz often implied a corresponding equivalence between fascism and African nationalism. According to the Conservative peers who mustered behind Lord Salisbury, Britain was, as in the 1930s, engaging in "appeasement", this time by sacrificing a vulnerable white minority to an African majority bent on subverting British traditions. Lord Grimston of Westbury put forward this view in the House of Lords, condemning those who thought it "intolerable" that a "few white Rhodesians should stand in the way of the great march of African nationalism". Appeasers' disregard for minorities, he suggested, had benefitted Hitler "when he overran the whole of Europe", only to be stopped by "this wretched little Island which had the nerve to stand out against him". Rhodesians, he concluded, were not "going to have it, any more than we were going to have it from Hitler".[62] An editorial in the *Observer* stated simply that Britain could not "afford another Munich in Africa".[63]

As Martin Francis demonstrates in this volume, the role of wartimé memories in shaping metropolitan reactions to UDI was by no means clearly defined. Critics of Rhodesia's white supremacist regime often invoked memories of the Second World War, citing the racial and political inequalities that structured Rhodesian society as gross betrayals of the democratic values defended between 1939 and 1945. Ultimately, however, Smith's supporters effectively countered such critics with rejoinders that Rhodesians had crucially contributed to the defeat of Hitler, and with damning charges that any attack on Smith or his supporters implied disrespect for war veterans.

This became most clear on Remembrance Day, which elicited some of the most emotional outpourings of support for white Rhodesians. Reporting on Remembrance Day observances in Salisbury, Terry Finchley of the *Daily Express* described sombre veterans gathered to recall "days spent fighting side by side with British comrades". Noting the "British cool look" upon their faces, Finchley wrote, "the great Rhodesian rebellion has been a peculiarly British affair. Bloodless. Almost gentlemanly in pace. Lots of stiff upper lips and talk of duty." Effacing a troubling history of interwar appeasement, not to mention instances of wartime class conflicts and gender antagonisms explored in the work of Sonya Rose, Finchley suggested that loyalty had been "a comparatively simple affair a generation ago" when "the menace of Nazism was something every right-minded man recognized as evil and united to put down".[64] Blithely dismissing the possibility of a British public united in condemnation of white supremacy, Finchley concluded that the conflict with Rhodesia was "much more complicated to all but the most hysterical".[65] Ultimately, Finchley's depiction of Remembrance Day in Salisbury – replete with nostalgic reveries about wartime camaraderie – combined with his derision of Smith's critics as "the most hysterical", suggested an idealized British community defined by militarism and masculinity, not to mention racial exclusivity. In a related sense, it extolled precisely the forms of self-discipline and dutiful behaviour that many Smith supporters claimed were lacking among British youth and members of the political left.

In Britain, Remembrance Day in 1965 not only evoked affirmations of historical connections and cultural affinities between metropolitan and Rhodesian whites; it also provided an opportunity for Smith's supporters to charge members of the Labour government, student radicals and black anti-colonial activists with dishonouring Rhodesian veterans. The immediate foundation for such charges was the Wilson government's decision to bar Rhodesia's High Commissioner, Andrew Skeen, from participating along with other Commonwealth representatives, in the official wreath-laying service at the Cenotaph. Sustained by a swell of public opinion, the mainstream British press made much of this decision. On November 12, the day preceding the ceremony, the *Daily Express* described a commemorative service at Westminster Abbey, devoting much attention to the presence of "Brigadier" Andrew Skeen, wearing a "bowler hat and a row of medals". After documenting Skeen's military service in both World Wars, the *Daily Express* described Skeen – ordered by Wilson to depart Britain the following day – as "the man Britain no longer wants", as he "doffed his hat to the Queen Mother" and then, with dignity, knelt to hammer a white cross into St. Margaret's Lawn.[66]

To protest Skeen's exclusion from the following day's observances, Lord Salisbury and the Anglo-Rhodesian Society planned an unofficial service to follow the ceremony at the Cenotaph. Throughout, memories of the "People's War" added a populist dimension to pro-Rhodesian sentiment. Hastily organized by the Anglo-Rhodesian Society, the *ad hoc* service fostered popular identification with Smith's reactionary regime and its metropolitan supporters by recalling the co-operation and improvisation that characterized Britain's homefront during the "People's War".

British newspapers, particularly the *Daily Express*, remarked extensively upon the differences between the official and unofficial ceremonies. Coverage of the former emphasized the decorum of Queen Elizabeth and her attendants, the solemnity of the Bishop of London and foreign dignitaries and the respectful silence of 10,000 spectators bearing poppies.[67] When the official observance ended, thousands remained to attend the Anglo-Rhodesian Society's afternoon service. "Things started off looking ragged", the *Daily Express* reported, with participants "milling about, breaking ranks without the morning's precise discipline" and "chatting" with members of the Chalk Farm

Salvation Army band, engaged at the last minute for the service. Despite its loose organization, most newspapers positively contrasted the afternoon's event to the official ceremony, the latter negatively, if accurately, described as "a set piece" by Cyril Ansley of the *Daily Express*. Of the morning's ceremony, Ansley wrote, "emotion derived from the brilliance of the Massed Bands of Guards, the splendour of the uniforms, the presence of royalty, statesmen and Commonwealth High Commissioners". By the afternoon, "the politicians and pomp" had departed. However, 2,000 marchers, "many wearing bowler hats and medals", infused the unofficial observance with dignity as they marched past Whitehall, "where purple and gold drapes still hung in empty windows filled, earlier, with the faces of politicians, ambassadors, generals, and civil servants". If the morning's procession involved individuals "guarding their emotions" and marching in tight ranks, "full-blooded cheers" accompanied the afternoon's meandering parade, which ended at the Cenotaph. After a short religious service led by the Salvation Army Commissioner, members of the Anglo-Rhodesian Society laid a wreath inscribed "To the memory of the South African and Rhodesian dead, forgotten by so many".[68]

Following the Remembrance Day observances, embittered veterans and war widows filled the editorial pages of mainstream newspapers with denunciations of the British government's seemingly callous behaviour. One London widow alleged that Wilson had "forgotten the debt" owed to Rhodesians, stating, "I am bitterly ashamed of my country and I regret that my husband gave his life for it".[69] Anger over the seemingly dishonourable treatment of war veterans often shaded into generalized attacks on an "Establishment" inattentive to the needs of "ordinary" people. The editor of the *Daily Express*, for one, lavished praise on the Salvation Army, which had always "paid attention to those about whom the Establishment just did not want to know", whether "down and outs on the Thames Embankment" or "servicemen in some hideously unpleasant spot". Describing the Anglo-Rhodesian Society's service as a "profoundly moving" tribute to veterans disregarded by "the Establishment", the editor extolled the "thousands of ordinary people" who had assembled to pay tribute to the war dead "wantonly excluded" from official commemorations.[70]

On Remembrance Day, metropolitan whites sympathetic to the Smith regime quite literally seized the unstable high ground of patriotism to attack their opponents. Following the unofficial afternoon observance, approximately 1,000 participants marched, in an impromptu demonstration, to Downing Street, where they drummed on railings outside

Number 10, shouted "Wilson out", chanted "Harold Hitler", and sang "For Smith's a Jolly Good Fellow".[71] When a group of Young Liberals coming from a "Crush Smith Rally" in Trafalgar Square entered Downing Street, a number of Smith supporters attacked several of them, seizing a sign bearing the message "Free Rhodesia from the Nazis" and smashing it over the head of one. As police intervened, shouts of "Let the Communists through" filled the air.[72]

Given their near monopoly on the most evocative and hegemonic terms of political exchange, namely those generated by memories of the "People's War", Smith sympathizers' use of the word "communist" as a term of abuse implied an association between patriotism, white racial identity and conservative politics. By invoking the memory of departed war heroes, Smith's supporters established the grounds for attacking student radicals, not only physically – on November 12, office workers in the Strand dumped jugs of water from second and third-storey windows to break up an anti-Smith march led by "hippies" – but also with accusations that the liberal "Establishment" had betrayed the memory of Britain's war dead and undermined Britain's moral fabric. In the view of many Smith supporters, the birth of consensus politics and the welfare state had inaugurated the decline of Britain's imperial power and international prestige as well as undermined the democratic and liberal values defended so dearly during the war.

Even before UDI, Smith's metropolitan supporters often criticized young radicals raised on free milk and orange juice, deemed atrophied by welfare and incapable of reversing Britain's international decline. In October 1965, as negotiations between Smith and Wilson foundered, a member of the Gascoigne Country Club in Lyndhurst wrote to the *Birmingham Post* to express his distress over a Teach-In on Rhodesia at the University of Birmingham. "Seemingly it would have been better for Africa if David Livingstone and Cecil Rhodes had never existed", he wrote, adding that "ferocious attacks on our own kith and kin portend dire consequences for what little remains of the Commonwealth, and for expanding British export trade upon which the existence of university education in Britain is wholly dependent".[73] Having "sat back" while a "crisis of the first magnitude" developed in Africa, the youth of Britain were not prepared "to educate and civilize four million Africans" in Rhodesia, or to "protect them from the constant attentions of Chinese guerillas and saboteurs" intent on using them as "puppets".[74]

Even a reporter for the *Guardian*, a newspaper by no means noted for Conservative sympathies, could remark that Rhodesian youth possessed a certain grit lacking in their English counterparts. Predicting that sanctions would fail to undermine Rhodesian resolve, he recounted the "last stand of the Shangani patrol", during which thirty-three British men had barricaded themselves against 3,000 Matabele warriors and fought "until the last man, singing 'God Save the Queen'". Their legacy, he wrote, endured in Rhodesia, where "there are no beatniks, and people dress up to go to the cinema (where they will certainly not see a French film)", and where young men "join Congolese mercenaries for a six month spell while their first cousins in Britain are probably trying to get into one of the new universities".[75]

To those concerned that Britain had lost the values that had made it an undisputed world power, corruption was rife at all levels, and most disturbingly within the upper echelons of political society. As late as July 1967, the *Daily Express'* leading political cartoonist, Michael Cummings, referenced the declining Roman Empire in depicting Wilson as a debauched and incapacitated leader, clad in a toga, reclining on a divan, smoking his trademark pipe, and staring through glazed eyes at the ceiling of "No. 10 Hippie Street". Musing, "I've been on a psychedelic trip for 1,000 days without using drugs", Cummings' Wilson imagined himself in various guises, first dispensing money from a fruit horn to a supplicant Britannia, and then imprisoning Smith, marked "RAF", in a cage.[76] In this instance and others, the conservative press suggested that by providing welfare "handouts", Labour had eroded the moral fibre of "Britons", quashing the enterprise that had driven a civilizing mission in Africa and carried Britain through the Second World War.

The evocation of wartime memories to refute social democratic values was not unprecedented, Churchill being the most iconic figure to have articulated imperial, democratic and anti-statist ideologies.[77] Smith and his supporters regularly invoked Churchill's spirit to support imperial and anti-communist agendas, effectively aligning patriotism with conservative values. Smith lost no opportunity to extol his personal hero, stating on one occasion that if alive, Churchill "would probably emigrate to Rhodesia" because the "admirable qualities and characteristics of the British we believed in, loved and preached to our children, no longer exist in Britain".[78] When speaking to the British press, he often recalled the memory of Churchill to defend his regime, and to attack "fellow travellers" in Britain and communist influences at work throughout the Commonwealth. Less than two weeks before UDI, he insisted that white Rhodesians, as Churchill had twenty-five years earlier, decided against all odds to "strive for the preservation of democracy and freedoms", even while the British government gave "full and admiring support" to those who had "pulled down the Union Jack and espoused Communism".[79]

In this instance and numerous others, Smith reworked and racialized meanings of the "People's War", linking the defence of "British freedoms" to the defence of white privilege threatened by African Communists, significantly cast in the role of fascist aggressors. He did so with the extensive help of metropolitan supporters. In late 1965, members of the Anglo-Rhodesian Society and the Monday Club distributed RF leaflets stating that "politically immature Africans", if given the vote, would invariably install a "one-party fascist regime". According to such leaflets, Rhodesians "bitterly resented" the way their British "kith and kin", with whom they had "stood in adversity and triumph", were urging them to "go the way of neo-fascist and Communist slums festering on the face of Africa".[80] The views contained in such leaflets entered into wide circulation with the assistance of the mainstream media. However critical of the RF, the BBC gave ample air time to "ordinary" Smith supporters, as when *Panorama* televised Rhodesian factory workers hanging Wilson, "the communist", in effigy, and an interview with tobacco farmers who lauded Smith as "another Churchill" embodying the values defended during the last world war.[81]

Patriotic and emotionally charged forms of identification with former "comrades in arms" in Rhodesia frequently underpinned anti-Communist screeds laced with racist suggestions about the political and intellectual "immaturity" of Africans. An individual writing to the *Birmingham Post* argued that, in Africa, "the word 'vote' is meaningless, and any form of authority outside a village headman or tribal chief is just not understood", although democratic slogans "are valuable tools to small-time Hitlers" assisted with "funds from Communist-inspired sympathizers".[82]

The belief that Labour was compromising the safety of whites threatened by Soviet-backed African nationalists gave shape to particularly virulent forms of political reaction after October 1965, when the Organization of African Unity, anticipating UDI, began pressuring Wilson to avoid a "double standard" in its relations with Rhodesia. Pointing to Britain's forceful suppression of Mau Mau, Ghana's Kwame Nkrumah and Tanzania's Julius Nyerere insisted that Britain uphold its moral obligations by either deploying troops to topple Smith's regime or allowing a UN force to install a democratic government in Rhodesia.[83] To enforce their demands, they issued an ultimatum that Ghana and Tanzania would cede from the Commonwealth if Wilson failed to restore constitutional rule in Rhodesia.[84] With Britain's leadership of the

Commonwealth in jeopardy, Michael Cummings of the *Daily Express* lost no opportunity to lampoon Wilson. In October of 1965, he depicted a sleepless Wilson in pajamas, leaning out a window to address Smith, denoted with "RAF", desperately fending off a knife-wielding black assailant, "African Nationalism". Glancing nervously over his shoulder, a harried Wilson begged Smith to "die quietly" in order to avoid waking Nkrumah and other African leaders bundled tightly together in bed and sneering malevolently.[85]

In the context of public debates about immigration, the domestic imagery was not insignificant, suggesting uncomfortable forms of interracial intimacy and a willingness, on Wilson's part, to compromise the safety of whites abroad while providing a welcome to hostile Africans "at home". In this sense, metropolitan conversations about Rhodesia were often as much about Britain as about the causes and consequences of UDI. On November 15, 1965, Conservative MP Ian Lloyd, speaking in the House of Commons, drew explicit connections between communist insurgencies throughout Britain's shrinking Empire and the alleged threat posed by immigration to British society and national security. Left-wing "politicians, journalists, clerics, broadcasters and TV interviewers, the whole sorry legion of joyless Jeremiahs", having left Rhodesians with little alternative to UDI, were punishing loyal subjects for their "civilizing efforts", and for refusing "the flaming torch" of international communist revolution, which immigration "helped to keep alive in the basements of slums of London".[86]

Throughout late 1965 and 1966, Rhodesia loomed large in public debates about immigration in Britain. Proponents of strict control often claimed the government had abrogated its moral responsibilities by ignoring the interests of Britain's "kith and kin" (and former allies) in Africa, while granting people of colour in Britain the "privileges" of social democratic citizenship, presumably at the expense of more deserving whites. Speaking to the *Daily Express* two days after UDI, a resident of Stockport described Smith as "a man, not a spineless politician, who puts the welfare of his own nation before others".[87] Interviewed by *Panorama*, another "man on the street" stated that England needed "a Britisher, Ian Smith, as Prime Minister", to do with "aliens, Greeks, Italians and coloured people", as he had done with Africans in Rhodesia. Asked whether he was "a racist", he replied, "I'm not, I'm an ex-serviceman", as if patriotism and racism were, by definition, mutually exclusive.[88]

For years following UDI, Rhodesia remained a point of reference, and indeed, a flashpoint, in debates about immigration. Far-right proponents of strict controls cast both immigration and opposition to UDI as a "betrayal" of "Britons" who had defended England in wartime. In the spring of 1966, the newly-formed Racial Preservation Society (RPS) issued its first newsletter, in which it denounced "Labour zealots" hypocritically condemning Rhodesia's unconstitutional government while lacking a "mandate from voters to commit Britain to a multi-racial society". Wilson "succeed[ed] where Hitler failed", one contributor declared, referring to neighbourhoods "denuded of their indigenous white population". In working-class areas that had "withstood the brunt of enemy bombing", he wrote, "whole streets of English families have been uprooted", and the "character and way of life have been utterly destroyed" by the forces of "world collectivism".[89] Throughout 1966 and 1967, the RPS, joined by the newly formed National Front, lobbied against immigration, sending petitions and letters to political organizations and candidates. In 1966, an RPS member wrote to the Finchley Liberal Association to warn of a "black invasion" destroying Britain's "island civilization" by creating a "burden on the Welfare State". Identifying himself as an "ex-RAF bomber pilot shot down in 1940", a former trade unionist, and an "average Englishman with a very real stake in the country", he attacked the "Establishment" press and politicians for ignoring Britain's "real natives" and privileging the views of "coloured immigrants" and communists "creeping" into CND, the BBC and trade unions.[90] Those who had "turned a blind eye" to forces undermining "England's race and civilization" included Smith's critics – those committed to the "break-up of Empire" and suffering from "the pernicious effects of the Welfare State", which was "rotting the moral fibre of the people".[91]

If right-wing extremists initiated the most radical attempts to redefine the legacies of the "People's War", linking its conduct to the defence of racial purity, mainstream politicians and pundits soon followed suit. Throughout 1968, Rhodesia continued to serve as a point of articulation between neo-liberal and racial discourses, with huge implications for working-class political culture. In March, one month before Powell's "Rivers of Blood" speech, right-wing columnist, Peregrine Worthsthorne proposed that "alien" Asian refugees from Kenya should be barred from Britain. "They are no more British citizens than Ian Smith is a genuine British traitor", Worthsthorne wrote, arguing that their admission would be an affront to working-class people who had "borne the brunt of arrogant experiments" conducted by the Labour Party and "intellectuals dreaming of a multi-racial society".[92]

Worthsthorne's message found warm welcome among the working-class whites who served as foot soldiers for Enoch Powell and, later, the

New Right. In May of 1968, Dom Moraes, the celebrated Indian poet and columnist, then writing for the *Sunday Telegraph,* interviewed Dan Harmston, a former Mosleyite and a key organizer of Powellite marches, in his London council flat. Surrounded by neo-Nazi literature, Harmston denied any fascist inclinations. As he insisted, he was merely disturbed that immigrants of a "different racial identity" had flooded Britain and stolen the "birthright" of English people by claiming social benefits and jobs belonging to whites. Harmston described himself as "an ordinary man, a Smithfield meat porter" who had organized a peaceful march, unlike the "long-haired idiots" and "communists" who threw marbles under police horses during "Vietnam and anti-Rhodesia marches".[93] In order to "become a power in the world" again, Harmston concluded, England needed to form a trading bloc with Western Europe, Rhodesia and South Africa, and to repatriate immigrants unless they "conformed to the racial identity of the English or had fought for Britain in the last war".[94] Significantly, Harmston partially qualified this open-ended concession to veterans, stating that the war had "caused all sorts of trouble" in Britain, and that "if it hadn't been for the war, the immigrants wouldn't have come". Concluding that British whites "never should have fought the war", Harmston smiled and again assured Moraes that he was "not a Fascist".[95]

As metropolitan responses to UDI demonstrate, the "People's War" left a contested legacy for the politics of race in Britain, providing the most evocative terms for expressing anxieties about immigration, as well as a rhetorical framework for denouncing members of a broadly defined left, whose values suggested a precipitous drop from the high watermark of wartime heroism, self-sufficiency and enterprise. Through skillful manipulation and sometimes sincere pronouncements, Smith's metropolitan supporters recast meanings of the "People's War" for British political culture, aligning its memory with the defence of right-wing politics and nationalist chauvinism, rather than social democratic or egalitarian values.

In May of 1968, as anti-Vietnam War demonstrations filled the streets of London, *Sunday Telegraph* correspondent Ian Waller recounted his visit to Salisbury, where he observed the effect of sanctions on Rhodesia's staggering economy. Rhodesia, Waller wrote, is a "beleaguered fortress", characterized by an "air of nostalgia, a constant reminiscing about the last war" and a "love-hate relationship with Britain".[96] A mood "reminiscent of the Battle of Britain exists in Rhodesia", he continued, noting the "tremors of excitement" that ran through Salisbury whenever the government called up reserve forces to combat Communist guerrillas operating along the northern border.[97] Sanctions "have given an added zest to life" by providing a "challenge to be overcome", Waller continued, adding that he "understood and admired the spirit" of Rhodesians. After talking to numerous Rhodesians, "for the most part ordinary, decent Englishmen", Waller flew out of Salisbury.[98] As a "green and tranquil land" disappeared beneath him, he expressed a sense that "disaster need not occur", and that Rhodesians "would point the way to a peaceful solution", as Rhodesia had "the best of British traditions".[99]

Notes

1   *Times*, 13 November, 1965.
2   *Ibid.*
3   *Ibid.*
4   *Ibid.*
5   See Bill Schwarz, "'The Only White Man in There': The Re-racialization of England, 1956–1968", *Race & Class* 38 (1996), 65–78; and Wendy Webster, *Englishness and Empire* (New York, 2005).
6   Sonya Rose, *Which People's War?: National Identity and Citizenship in Wartime Britain, 1939–1945* (Oxford, 2005).
7   Geoff Eley, "Finding the People's War: Film, British Collective Memory, and World War II", *American Historical Review* 105, no. 5 (2001): 818–38.
8   Doris Lessing, *Going Home* (London, 1957), 70.
9   *Daily Mirror*, 12 November 1965.
10 Rhodesia Political Department, Commonwealth Relations Office [hereafter CRO], The Regime's Propaganda Machine and Its Operations, 16 March 1966. National Archives, [TNA], DO 207/220.
11 *New Statesman*, 24 December 1965.
12 *Daily Mirror*, 6 November 1965.
13 Rhodesia Political Department, CRO, The Regime's Propaganda Machine and Its Operations, 16 March 1966. TNA, DO 207/220.
14 *Sunday Telegraph*, 14 November 1965.
15 *Daily Mirror*, 18 November 1965.
16 *Daily Mirror*, 23 November 1965.
17 *Daily Express*, 24 November 1965; *Zimbabwe Review*, 2 (November 1966).
18 *Soviet News*, No. 5206, 16 November 1965.
19 *Times*, 17 November 1965; *Observer*, 14 November 1965.
20 *Parliamentary Debates*, Commons, 5th ser., vol. 721, (1965), col. 1475.
21 *Parliamentary Debates*, Commons, 5th ser., vol. 720 (1965), cols. 687–872.
22 *Parliamentary Debates*, Commons, 5th ser., vol. 720 (1965), cols. 687–872.
23 *Parliamentary Debates*, Commons, 5th ser., vol. 720 (1965), cols. 687–872.
24 Martin Loney, *Rhodesia, White Racism and Imperial Response* (Harmondsworth, 1975).
25 *Parliamentary Debates*, Commons, 5th ser., vol. 720 (1965), cols. 228–438.
26 *Daily Express*, 23 November 1965.
27 *Illustrated News*, 20 November 1965.
28 *Times*, 23 December 1964.

29 *Panorama*, 15 November 1965 broadcast, Film 27, BBC Written Archives Center.

30 For excellent discussions of the historical relationship between nationalism and pseudo-scientific and popular definitions of "race", see Paul Gilroy, *The Black Atlantic: Modernity and Double Consciousness* (Cambridge, Mass., 1993); Stuart Hall, "The Toad in the Garden: Thatcherism Amongst the Theorists", in *Marxism and the Interpretation of Culture*, eds. Cary Nelson and Lawrence Grossberg (Urbana, 1988); and Robert Miles, "Recent Marxist Theories of Nationalism and the Issue of Racism", *British Journal of Sociology* 38 (1987): 24–43.

31 *Times*, 23 October 1965.

32 *Ibid.*

33 *Daily Express*, 27 October 1965.

34 Frank Clements, *Rhodesia; The Course to Collision* (London, 1969), 188.

35 Robert Blake, *A History of Rhodesia* (New York, 1978), 135.

36 Lessing, *Going Home*, 87.

37 *Observer*, 10 October 1965.

38 *Daily Express*, 21 June 1965.

39 *Ibid.*

40 *Ibid.*

41 *Punch*, 8 June 1966.

42 *Guardian*, 6 May 1965.

43 *Sunday Telegraph*, 14 Nov 1965.

44 *Parliamentary Debates*, Commons, 5th ser., vol. 721 (1965), cols. 1482–3.

45 See, for example, the *Daily Express*, 18 August 1964.

46 Webster, *Englishness*, 58.

47 *Parliamentary Debates*, Lords, 5th ser., vol. 270 (1965) col. 191.

48 Miles Hudson, *Triumph or Tragedy?: Rhodesia to Zimbabwe* (London, 1981), 27.

49 *Birmingham Post*, 11 October 1965.

50 *Times*, 13 November 1965.

51 Records of the CRO and Successors High Commission and Consular Archives, Ghana, Registered Files, 1954–1967. TNA, DO 155/33.

52 *Financial Times*, 24 June 1966.

53 *Economist*, 18 June 1966.

54 Letter to Mr. Neale from S. G. Fingland, 22 December 1965. TNA, DO 207/20.

55 Records of the CRO and Successors High Commission and Consular Archives, Ghana, Registered Files, 1954–1967. TNA, DO 155/33.

56 Circular from Foreign Office and Commonwealth Relations Office to High Commissions, July 7, 1966. TNA, DO 153/34; *Observer*, 26 June 1966.

57 *Daily Mail*, 11 November 1966.

58 *Ibid.*

59 Records of the Prime Minister's Official Correspondence and Papers, 1964–1970, Telegram from Wilson to Kenneth Kuanda, 4 January 1966. TNA, PREM 13/776.

60 *Parliamentary Debates*, Lords, 5th ser., vol. 271 (1965), col. 210.

61 *Birmingham Post*, 31 December 1965.

62 *Parliamentary Debates*, Lords, 5th ser., vol. 271 (1965), col. 140.

63 *Daily Express*, 14 January 1966; *Observer*, 3 October 1965.

64 *Daily Express*, 16, November 1965. See Sonya Rose, *Which People's War?*
65 *Daily Express*, 16 November 1965.
66 *Daily Express*, 12 November 1965.
67 *Times*, 13 November 1967.
68 *Ibid.*
69 *Daily Express*, 19 November 1966.
70 *Daily Express*, 14 November 1966.
71 *Daily Mirror*, 14 November 1966.
72 *Times*, 14 November 1965.
73 *Birmingham Post*, 16 October 1965.
74 *Ibid.*
75 *Guardian*, 12 October 1965.
76 *Daily Express*, 17 July 1967.
77 Webster, *Englishness*, 38.
78 Quoted in Webster, *Englishness*, 185.
79 *Daily Express*, 29 October, 1964.
80 Rhodesia's Case for Independence [n.d.] October 1965. TNA, PREM 13/543.
81 *Panorama*, 22 March 1966 broadcast. Film: 27, BBC Written Archives Center.
82 *Birmingham Post*, 13 October 1965.
83 Report on UN Security Council Debate, 13 November 1965. Dispatch for Foreign Office Whitehall Distribution, TNA, DO 153/34.
84 Message from Nkrumah to Wilson, 11 December 1965, Records of the Prime Minister's Office. Correspondence and Papers, 1964–1970. TNA, CAB 21/5516–17.
85 *Daily Express*, 11 October 1965.
86 *Parliamentary Debates*, Commons, 5th ser., vol. 720 (1965), 800.
87 *Daily Express*, 13 November 1965.
88 *Panorama*, 15 November 1965 broadcast, Film 27, BBC Written Archives Center.
89 *British Independent*, No. 1, Spring 1966.
90 Letter from R. Beauclaire to Finchley Liberal Association, 11 November 1966. TNA, CK 2/25.
91 *Ibid.*
92 *Illustrated London News*, 3 March 1968.
93 *Sunday Telegraph*, 5 May 1968.
94 *Ibid.*
95 *Ibid.*
96 *Sunday Telegraph*, 12 May 1968.
97 *Ibid.*
98 *Ibid.*
99 *Ibid.*

12
"Would You Let Your Daughter Marry a Negro?": Race and Sex in 1950s Britain

Elizabeth Buettner

"There are 100,000 Negroes in Britain today", the leader ran. "Hundreds more are arriving every month. Thousands of them are already married to white girls. What do relatives and neighbours think about it? How do the children suffer? What is the price in insults, hardships and tears?"

Thus began an article whose title asked "Would You Let Your Daughter Marry a Negro?" that appeared in the British illustrated weekly *Picture Post* in 1954.[1] Written by Trevor Philpott, the piece discussed one of the most central social concerns of the decade, namely the implications of the tremendous increase in the numbers of "coloured" peoples arriving from Britain's colonies and former colonies. In choosing a title calculated to provoke readers, Philpott outlined many of the forms racial prejudice took in 1950s Britain, appearing simultaneously to critique racism and fan its flames. The difficulties black migrants faced included finding housing and work, not to mention a host of other forms of discrimination that occurred in the course of their everyday lives. Philpott's focus, however, was the same as that which captured the attention of so many other social commentators: sexual relationships between white women and black men. Journalists and the people they interviewed, social scientists, playwrights, novelists and those recounting their experiences of moving to Britain from overseas territories all considered such relationships – whether legalized by marriage or taking the form of common-law cohabitation or casual sex – as among the most revealing of white attitudes towards what was commonly called the "problem" of immigration. As one representative contemporary account summarized, "the idea of mixed marriages between coloured and white people probably evokes greater antipathy than any other aspect of coloured colonial immigration to Britain".[2]

Despite the prominence of mixed-race sexual relationships within public discourse about non-white settlement, however, research done during the mid- to late-1950s suggested that their numerical extent was quite limited.[3] That social fears and hostility far outweighed actual incidences renders the public prevalence of discussions about sex, cohabitation and marriage – real or imagined – between white women and black men all the more worthy of careful analysis. Moreover, the long history of concerns about interracial sexuality in Britain, the British empire and in many other global contexts makes it essential to historicize anxieties in 1950s Britain and pay due attention to their chronological and geographical specificity. Scholars in the fields of colonial studies such as Ann Stoler, Durba Ghosh and Philippa Levine have illuminated mounting European anxieties about sexual relationships across racial lines in overseas territories since the eighteenth century.[4] Historians of metropolitan Britain including Laura Tabili have begun to explore this theme in relation to the history of colonized and other "coloured" peoples in Britain during the First World War and interwar years, while Sonya Rose's work focuses on concerns about British women and girls' interactions with African-American GIs and colonial troops on the home front during the Second World War.[5]

As this chapter examines, anxieties about interracial sex in 1950s Britain reveal similarities to and continuities with those apparent in earlier decades at home and in overseas imperial arenas.[6] Despite containing familiar features, however, they nonetheless diverge sharply from earlier as well as subsequent British concerns about race and gender. Sonya Rose's analysis of "upsurges of public commentary about sexuality as episodic rather than discrete events" is particularly pertinent here. Prior instances, she argues, inform and do much to structure subsequent expressions, but it remains essential to account for why such concerns surface at specific times and places.[7] "Outpourings of moral discourse", Rose suggests, "mark the times when questions about community or national solidarity and homogeneity become highly charged", peaking at moments of "heightened attention to questions of group or national identity" that involve challenging and reimagining them. While war provides important occasions for this, so too, she insists, do other contexts such as immigration.[8] As Stuart Hall has advanced, in 1950s Britain the "problem" of black migration had transgressive black sexuality – especially that occurring across racial lines – at its very heart.[9] During this critical decade, the gendered and ethnic demographics of the sharp increase in settlement from Britain's colonies and former colonies, the uncertainty about what place such newcomers would occupy within domestic British society and the gathering pace of nationalism and decolonization overseas worked together to under-pin the relentless focus on white women's relationships with men variously termed "Negroes", "coloureds", or "blacks".[10]

***

Although colonized peoples of different "racial" origins had been present in Britain for centuries, commentators in the 1950s were correct in their assessment that the contemporary influx of so-called "coloured" peoples from the colonies differed from what had come before. Prior to the Second World War, communities of colour existed in parts of London as well as in and around port cities like Cardiff, Liverpool and New-castle, emerging largely in connection with the shipping industry's reliance upon a colonial labour force. Alongside a non-white working-class population, colonial elites and students had long been a visible presence in London and other areas.[11] All told, however, their overall numbers remained small, particularly when compared with the post-war surge of colonial migrants following the 1948 British Nationality Act. This legislation aimed to enhance ties between Britain and its Commonwealth (which included colonies, former colonies and dom-inions) by providing a status as British subjects and a common citizen-ship for those born within the metropole and overseas. Colonial and former colonial subjects thus had unrestricted rights to enter and settle in Britain, a policy which was to last until 1962. Britain's need for manual workers at a time of full employment in the decade following the act encouraged substantial migration from many parts of the empire and former empire, with the West Indies sending the majority.[12] A study published in 1960 estimated the non-white population from the Com-monwealth then resident in Britain as approximately 210,000, includ-ing 115,000 West Indians, 25,000 West Africans, 55,000 Indians and Pakistanis, and 15,000 from other territories.[13] The vast majority had come during the peak arrival years of the mid-fifties. Most were workers, but a minority were middle or upper class. Students pursuing either university degrees or other forms of further education, for example, numbered about 11,000, with over half originating from South Asia and Africa.[14] Of equal significance was the gendered nature of Common-wealth migration, with male arrivals far outnumbering females until late in the decade.

Despite the legal rights to settle, which the "Negroes" described in Philpott's *Picture Post* article cited above possessed based on citizenship, no mention whatsoever was made of these. While deploying the terms "white", "English" and "British" interchangeably, it failed to do the same for those of other ethnic backgrounds. Instead, they were described in terms of their skin colour or their region of origin – as "Negroes", "coloured", "from Barbados", "West Indian" or "West African". They remained "Negroes in Britain" and, on one occasion only, were "British Negroes", but never simply "British". For the most part, they were depicted as devoid of nationality and reduced to pigmentation, despite holding British passports.[15]

Some commentators, unlike Philpott, took pains to remind their readers that these new arrivals were indeed citizens. As a booklet produced by the British Council of Churches about *Your Neighbour from the West Indies* put it, such people were not only Christian but also "British subjects like ourselves. They are not 'aliens' and the colour of their skin does not make them foreigners".[16] Anthony Richmond, the author of widely-circulated books such as *The Colour Problem*, went even further, juxtaposing non-white settlement in Britain with the long history of European colonization: "as a British subject the coloured colonial has every right to seek his fortune in Britain just as Europeans have a right to do so in the colonies".[17] Yet the same texts readily contradicted their own assertions, with the former contrasting *Your Neighbour from the West Indies* with "our young people" while the very title chosen by the latter revealed the extent to which "colour" continued to occupy the realm of "problem".[18] E. R. Braithwaite, who had served in the Royal Air Force during the Second World War and later found work – after considerable difficulty – as a teacher in London, described how growing up in British Guiana he had learned to value the "British Way of Life", only to discover that "it is wonderful to be British – until one comes to Britain". "I was British, but evidently not a Briton, and that fine differentiation was now very important", he recalled.[19] As another commentator summarized, "Negroes" "belong vaguely, if beautifully, to the Crown: never, unhappily, to the country".[20]

The desire to be British, to belong in Britain and to assimilate within British society was a central reason why "Negroes", and West Indians in particular, were singled out in 1950s British discourse on non-white arrivals from the Commonwealth. The larger numbers of West Indians compared with other groups only partly accounted for the relentless attention they received in scholarly studies: their perceived insistence on belonging made them considerably more worrying than other groups, namely the "self-segregating, self-sufficient Asians", as the social anthropologist Sheila Patterson summarized.[21] The author of another account published under the auspices of the Institute of Race Relations in 1958 distinguished West Indians on the grounds that they "have no separate language or dress of their own and wish to be integrated into the English pattern; they are the results of an historical upheaval, their ancestors having been transported many generations ago against their will and their whole social background having been destroyed ... misunderstandings of a more violent kind may arise because the West Indian thinks of himself as British in dress, speech and custom", and shared an adherence to the Christian faiths. Other groups, meanwhile, "do not wish to enter or to become integrated in the British system and probably mean to return to their own country. They are not hurt by rejection from a society they have no wish to enter; the chances of social misunderstandings are thus less. Among these come the Sikhs, Pakistanis, Hindus and the West Africans".[22] Other writers echoed assumptions that working-class Indians and Pakistanis did not seek assimilation on account of wishing to perpetuate religious differences and supposedly making little attempt to learn the English language; as a result, "there is less conflict, and also perhaps less integration".[23] West Indians, in short, counted as a problem *precisely because* they either believed themselves to be, or sought to become, too close for comfort, whereas others appeared content to remain outsiders throughout their stay – rendered wishfully temporary by many authors – in Britain. Patterson's description of the West Indians she studied in mid-1950s Brixton referred to their "high expectations of immediate acceptance by the English on the grounds of common British citizenship" – a hope that, considering her depiction of them as "dark strangers", she clearly dismissed as unrealistic despite their common language and Christianity.[24] Asians, on the other hand, imagined as having lower expectations, posed fewer concerns, as did other groups widely considered (rightly or wrongly) to be temporary residents rather than permanent settlers aspiring to or claiming Britishness.

Students and other middle-class or elite non-white groups in Britain for professional reasons were portrayed as similarly unproblematic by comparison, whatever their place of origin. Such persons largely counted as "expatriates": most students, one report stated, "do not intend to stay here once their courses have finished. Hence they regard themselves as representatives of the colonial countries, rather than as residents of this".[25] Because many of them returned home to assume leadership roles in colonies or former colonies, British observers hoping to strengthen what often proved to be precarious colonial and Commonwealth ties worried that any negative experiences during their time in

Britain would bode ill for Commonwealth relations long after their departure.[26] While their stay may have had implications for Britain's overseas affairs, their impact on metropolitan society and identity during what were commonly short periods of residence was seen as limited.

British anxieties about black integration indicatively revolved around the most intimate realms of private life: housing, close social relationships and – above all – sex and the family. Although hostility at and concerning the workplace certainly occurred, at a time of full employment researchers noted that white men felt differently "outside the factory" about those they "did not want 'too close to home,' especially in relation to white girls".[27] As Patterson reported of Brixton, "the receiving society may be fairly willing to open factory gates, church doors, welfare agency doors, pub doors and so on. But few of its adult members are willing to open to strangers that ultimate door, the door to their homes". Those who demonstrated some degree of tolerance, she continued, were "more willing to talk to coloured people, as indeed to all strangers, in a bar, to meet them at a sports or cultural club, to meet or even dance with them at socials, than to invite them home, have them as permanent friends, have them as in-laws or marry them and have children with them".[28] The idea of mixed marriages within their own families seemingly evoked hesitancy and often outright antagonism even among whites who otherwise proudly proclaimed their credentials as racially tolerant liberals.[29] A Gallup poll taken in late 1958 asking whether white respondents approved of marriages between white and "coloured" people revealed that 71 per cent disapproved, 16 per cent "didn't know", and only 13 per cent approved.[30]

Although interracial sexual relationships and marriages between white men and black women did occur in 1950s Britain (and certainly had predominated among mixed unions taking place overseas throughout Britain's history as an imperial power), these received scarcely any public comment and nowhere near the same level of censure. Because black men outnumbered black women by such a considerable margin, white Britons felt safe in confining their condemnation of mixed-race sexual relationships and marriages to those between white women and black men. A fundamental reason for this hostility stemmed from the inroads such relationships offered for black men's integration into British society. Michael Banton's 1955 study of "Negro immigrants" in Stepney, East London argued that marriages to white women "are of the foremost importance in the processes of adaptation and assimilation, and they show more clearly than any other feature how the immigrants are absorbed into the class structure of English society".[31] As a "coloured" man told another researcher after describing his marriage to an English girl and the birth of their baby, "Yes Sir, I'm integrated".[32]

Black male and white female sexuality were equally condemned for placing British national identity at risk. Novelist Colin MacInnes articulated what he considered common wisdom when stating in an essay that given the unbalanced gender ratio among Britain's black population, "if Africans and West Indians are to have a sex life of any kind (and one can hardly imagine them without one), most of their girls must necessarily be white".[33] Black men were widely viewed as predators, lacking sexual control and having insatiable appetites, particularly for white women.[34] Such ideas had a long colonial history, as illuminated by scholarship analysing periodic "Black Perils" in which African and other colonized men were feared as rapists and potential rapists – with little to no concrete evidence of sexual violations actually having occurred – of European women in many parts of the British empire.[35] In 1950s Britain, black men "corrupted" white women by taking them as sexual partners, and were also accused of going a step further by turning them into prostitutes. "Poncing" white girls and "living off immoral earnings" ranked high among the accusations directed against such men by many white Britons, notions that did much to bolster resentment of mixed-race sexual unions.[36]

The motives imagined for such behaviour included "natural" instincts but also, significantly, "racial revenge", as MacInnes and others put it. For black men, "acquiring a white girl" connoted social prestige, and "may also contain an element of satisfaction in that this involves paying back the white man for real or imagined slights in the past".[37] Michael Banton perhaps phrased this belief most strongly: "as the frustration he experiences is identified with white people, he may obtain compensation from the sexual possession of a woman of the same skin colour as the people whom he regards as hostile". As evidence for this, he then alluded to "the immigrant who said that he was revenging himself on the Englishmen by sending their sisters on the streets".[38]

In an era when the growing strength of West Indian and African national consciousness and anti-colonialism was irrefutable and colonial rule by white men subjected to mounting challenges, it proved an easy leap for British men to envision the empire as striking back not only in the form of nationalism overseas but also via incursions into the inter-related domestic spaces of the white British nation and white British families. In this view, sex with white women in Britain stemmed only in part from black men's untamed – and seemingly untameable – passions for the women involved; they were imagined first and foremost as directed against white men. Not only would black men prevail in the empire but at home as well, settling colonial and domestic scores alike in the process.

Whatever hostility white British society – and particularly white British men – directed against black men involved in mixed unions, far more scorn was heaped on the white women sleeping, living and bearing children with them. Such women were rarely seen as passive but rather were widely vilified as active sexual agents. As Philpott's *Picture Post* article stressed, white men blamed white women's desire as much as they pointed the finger at the imagined sexual potency and attractiveness of black men: "once a woman's had a nigger mate, she won't look at a white man again"; similarly, "lots of women are crazy about them – you see, Negroes think about nothing else".[39] Colin MacInnes' novels about 1950s London similarly portrayed white women involved with black men not simply as having been "corrupted" but as full consenting actors, desiring sex as much as their partners did.[40] By succumbing to "Negroes'" sexual charms, such women effectively had opened the door to British homes, families and the nation and thus offered black men a part to play in them. As one researcher writing in 1952 phrased it, "Everywhere the British ... resented the sight of a black man with a white woman, reacting rivalrously, sometimes violently as though to an outrage, to the thought that an alien man was being admitted to the closed society, through a woman violating her social trust".[41]

Such women became demonized in account after account. "Objective" social researchers described women who became involved with black men in terms that typically reproduced what they considered common public attitudes, taking these largely at face value. Indeed, as Chris Waters' work has demonstrated, race relations writers commonly appropriated many popular understandings and played a key role in recirculating and entrenching them through texts which reached a substantial readership.[42] Banton's description of the types of women "pre-disposed to consort with coloured men" was echoed in numerous other accounts. Most had a low socio-economic status along with "emotional insecurity and a background of personal rejection". What Banton portrayed as a downward spiral ran thus: "the girl denied affection by her parents is more likely to have an illegitimate child; the girl with an illegitimate child is more likely to be rejected by her relatives and denied the affection she needs; without the support of a family or a consort she will have difficulty in making a living". Seemingly out of desperation, Banton suggested, such women then struck up relationships with black men; moreover, some "appear to be nymphomaniacs".[43] Richmond similarly summarized that a woman in a mixed marriage tended to count as "a deviant from the norms of her own culture".[44] Even Sydney Collins, a comparatively sympathetic researcher, enumerated what he considered to be the four main causes of mixed marriage in the following order: "Firstly, premarital pregnancy may encourage a hasty marriage. Secondly, women alleged to be prostitutes may constrain colored men to marry them. Thirdly, a girl with an illegitimate child by a white or a colored, and deserted by either and forsaken by parents, may find acceptance and security by marrying a colored man. And fourthly, mutual affection may bring them together".[45]

In such renditions, white women were sexually involved with black men because they were already consigned to the category of social and sexual deviants beforehand, whether because they had been prostitutes or because they had been rejected by their parents and often by the white men who had fathered their illegitimate children. Such narratives, as will be discussed further below, worked to justify rejecting such women yet again once they had begun cohabitating with or had married black men. Yet what is revealing about Collins' account is his allusion to "mutual affection". Although this factor came last on his list and appeared almost as an afterthought, Collins did more than any other writer to illuminate the positive dimensions of mixed relationships. He portrayed such women as making active choices and asserting not primarily sexual desires for black men but, more importantly, social and emotional priorities. In the process, he shed light on some aspects of such marriages and families that most contemporary accounts neglected altogether.

Collins offset negative depictions of these white women by emphasizing the many benefits they claimed to derive from their marriages or cohabitation. His interviews suggested that many found esteem, valued companionship and socially satisfying roles as part of mixed families and communities. "Coloured" men were considered very good husbands, women repeatedly stressed. "My husband is devoted to me", one said. "The things he would be willing to do for me in the home, I doubt whether a white man would".[46] Men's devotion typically extended to their children, and many accepted their wives' previous illegitimate children conceived with different biological fathers as their own.[47] In short, of "the many cases of very happy marriages I found during these enquiries", Collins reported, "some [were] so touching in their demonstrations of affection and intimacy that I should never care to describe them in a report".[48] While other authors occasionally presented this version of mixed marriages, their accounts gave disproportionate weight to the social penalties such women and their families incurred by engaging in stigmatized behaviour. Philpott, for example, admitted that "mixed marriages *can* succeed, and, in practice, the settled marriages seem quite unusually happy".[49] Yet this assertion was largely buried beneath the lengthy account preceding it detailing the "insults, hardships and tears" that stemmed from social disapproval.

Personal fulfillment in marriage came not only from "mutual affection" but also from the power within the domestic realm white women could derive from cohabiting with black men. They were described as having much greater authority in determining how best to run their homes and raise their children than they would have enjoyed in so-called "normal" circumstances – that is, had they been married to white men.[50] What is more, such women assumed influential roles as liaisons, negotiating with their husbands' employers, their landlords and their children's schoolteachers when husbands either lacked fluency in English or simply were unfamiliar with local customs. Because they were white, they occupied a stronger bargaining position when, as Collins variously phrased it, acting as an intermediary "between her family and members of the white community", "between her family and members of the host society", and "between her family and British society".[51]

Such wording, used interchangeably throughout Collins' writings, reveals how a white woman's family became positioned as falling outside the confines of a society in which whiteness was imaginatively equivalent to Britishness – ignoring the fact that their husbands born in British colonies or the Commonwealth were British citizens, as were their children born in Britain. Collins argued, moreover, that white women in mixed marriages frequently came to count themselves as part of the "coloured" community: "They speak of themselves as 'We the coloured people', and express indignation at any instance of racial discrimination against coloured persons", he reported.[52] Like other race relations writers of the 1950s, Collins suggested that these women donned a new identity as "coloured" largely in the aftermath of having been rejected by their natal families, friends and other white associates on account of their ostracized marital choices. While white women might become "coloured", the reverse never applied: black men never became white. Exclusion from white British society was, in this assessment, the price women paid for marrying or cohabiting across racial lines. Some women clearly developed a more affirmative response to this circumstance, and may well have opted to identify themselves with, and as, "coloured" people for reasons of their own (which could include anti-racist political motivations) – not simply because white society had given them no other alternative. Yet commentators persisted in emphasizing white rejection as both the cause and the consequence of mixed marriages and family life.[53]

Children in families with white mothers and black fathers were also described as distinct from white British society. E. R. Braithwaite discussed his white pupils' attitudes towards one of their schoolmates at the east London school where he taught by emphasizing that the boy in question was "born among them, grew up among them, played with them, his mother was white, British, of their stock and background and beginnings". Nonetheless, to the other pupils he remained "a coloured boy with a white mother, a West Indian boy with an English mother. Always the same. Never an English boy with a Negro or West Indian father. No, that would be placing the emphasis on his Englishness, his identification with them".[54] Mixed-race children faced the prospect of being considered, in short, as "not belonging", indeed "belonging nowhere".[55]

Children's predicted misfortunes were deployed as a further deterrent by those counselling white women to steer clear of mixed marriages. The magazine *Woman's Friend and Glamour* printed a letter in its readers' advice column in 1951 in which "Liz from Cardiff" sought romantic guidance. "I'm very much in love with a coloured man. My parents are against our marriage, but he's the nicest, kindest boy I've ever met, and I couldn't want for a better. I know he'll be a splendid husband. Can my parents stop us getting married?", she queried. Unlike the women described by most social commentators as either desperate social misfits or as oversexed, this writer stressed love and the prospect of a solid, happy marriage as her reasons for contemplating what the magazine termed "A Serious Step". The magazine's response was revealing: "Unless you are under 21, your parents cannot prevent you from marrying", the columnist informed her. "But I hope, for your own sake, that you'll think things over very carefully. Many coloured men are fine people, but they do come from a different race, with a very different background and upbringing. Besides, scientists do not yet know if it is wise for two such very different races as white and black to marry, for sometimes children of mixed marriages seem to inherit the worst characteristics of each race".[56] Such advice indicated that scientific racism predicated upon supposed biological differences died a slow death in popular discourse after having become discredited in academic circles, with older stereotypes about the ill effects of "miscegenation" continuing to find ready expression.[57]

Despite the social stigmatization and ostracism that the women, men and children who formed mixed-race families undoubtedly faced, the fact remains that many white women went ahead and acted according to their own marital inclinations regardless of the dire consequences with which they were continually threatened. While it is impossible to know whether or not "Liz from Cardiff" chose to marry her boyfriend or heed the warnings printed in *Woman's Friend and Glamour* magazine, the wording of her letter suggested that, in her mind, the only obstacle potentially standing in the way of her happiness was her parents' possible right to prevent her from marrying the man of her choice. And, as the magazine conceded, they legally could not. Parents could attempt to hinder daughters living at home from dating black men or threaten to throw them out unless they stopped, but they could not go beyond rejection. As Philpott and other writers elaborated, white parents – significantly, their examples were overwhelmingly fathers and only rarely mothers – could rage against daughters and threaten to disown them, but do little else.[58] In actuality, "Would You Let Your Daughter Marry a Negro?" was a title calculated to mislead as much as to provoke, since, as Philpott conceded, mixed marriages were legal in Britain: "Here a man marries the woman he wants, and there's nothing to stop him. Nothing. Nothing, except the knowledge that seven British men out of ten feel their insides shrinking at the very thought of a coloured man fathering the children of a white girl".[59] With British men caught between the power and desire of unruly, independent white daughters and unruly, intrusive black men to act as they wished, mixed-race sexual relationships starkly revealed the limits of white patriarchy along with the worryingly porous nature of white British families and the British nation alike.[60]

Not only were parents unable to prevent daughters from entering into sexual relationships and family life with black men, but their will to punish them by severing contact was said by some authors to be weak and short-lived in many instances. As Sydney Collins concluded from his fieldwork, permanent estrangement from the woman's natal family was rare while either partial or complete reconciliations with parents and siblings proved far more common.[61] Philpott also admitted as much; despite his article's relentless attention to the difficulties women encountered, he included examples of forgiveness and parental rapprochement. "'Did my parents object?' says Jessie, 'I'll say. I left home over it. Dad would say I could go out, and then, when I was all ready to go, he'd stop me. He's better now and makes ever such a fuss of the children'". Having granted that mixed marriages could prove happy regardless of the social obstacles thrown in their path, Philpott concluded, "If your daughter or mine does take to bringing a coloured boy-friend home, what shall we do or say? We shall be failing in our duty if we do not tell her just how difficult a road she is preparing to tread". Given that parental discouragement was so seemingly ineffectual, however, he continued, "once she'd decided to go through with it we should be failing her if we didn't do everything in our power to help to make her husband one of the family".[62]

Attitudes towards mixed marriages and families thus revealed windows of racial tolerance among white British society and not simply denunciations and exclusion. Indeed, the very evidence of possible acceptance and happy endings may well have been a critical factor in the tendency for bigoted or sceptical commentators both to react with hostility and to threaten white women with an endless stream of negative repercussions. If often reluctantly, some Britons seemingly were prepared to count black men and children of mixed descent as part of their families. The inordinate attention and unease that sex and family life across racial lines generated among wider society, however, was inseparable from uncertainties about Britain's role within what Sheila Patterson referred to as the "new multi-racial *familia*", the Commonwealth.[63] By the late 1950s and throughout the 1960s, the Commonwealth ideal and the freedom of its black citizens to settle in Britain was increasingly perceived as a threat to a British national identity predicated upon whiteness, ultimately leading to new immigration policies and ways of perceiving Britain's black population.

***

While widespread white public condemnation of interracial sexuality and families found expression throughout the 1950s and did not disappear thereafter – opposition to black men with white women appeared prominently in accounts of the 1958 riots in Nottingham and in Notting Hill, for example – other issues gradually displaced it from centre stage.[64] A key reason was the arrival of much higher numbers of West Indian women and children starting in the mid-1950s. Some black women came to Britain of their own accord to find work, while others joined husbands who had made the journey earlier.[65] Although many white Britons expressed concern that migration seemingly showed no sign of abating, some viewed black women as a solution to the "problem" of mixed-race conjugal relations. As Sydney Collins wrote, the West Indian woman "is often welcomed by the British male who feels that she will provide a companion for the coloured male immigrant, who will keep away from British women".[66] Any such enthusiasm, however, had decided limits. After the 1950s, public attention to black men's relationships with white women and their offspring waned when compared with the growth of white social anxieties surrounding "problem families" whose members were depicted as exclusively black.[67] Asians also attracted much greater notice than before, particularly after the early 1960s when annual arrivals from the Indian subcontinent more than tripled.

The early 1960s signalled the start of a new era in other ways as well. With one colony after the next achieving independence, Britain subsequently rethought its relationships with the wider world outside of an imperial framework and placed less emphasis on the Commonwealth ideal that had remained strong in the previous decade. Concomitantly, previous nationality policies that had underscored the common citizenship and rights of settlement for all British subjects of the Commonwealth were viewed with ever declining enthusiasm. 1962 saw the first of a succession of immigration restriction acts which initially introduced numerical limits on the numbers permitted to enter Britain annually. Revealingly, however, subsequent immigration acts in 1968 and 1971 placed growing emphasis on barring persons lacking British ancestry. While race was not explicitly used as a criterion, legislation in the late 1960s and 1970s focused increasingly on "patriality" – in which the right to reside in Britain derived from having been born, or having documented ancestors who were born, in Britain. Implicitly, the vast majority meeting these requirements were presumed to be white. In this manner, white persons from parts of the "Old Commonwealth" with a history as British settler colonies such as Australia, New Zealand, South Africa and Canada remained welcome, whereas primary migrants from the "New Commonwealth" – largely Africans, West Indians of African descent and Asians – were kept out.[68]

In place of the Commonwealth "multi-racial *familia*", what prevailed was a conception of nationality in which the distinction between "race" and "nation" blurred. As Paul Gilroy has explored, this "ethnic absolutism" saw "black and white cultures as fixed, mutually impermeable expressions of racial and national identity".[69] Within this context, the reasons why sex and family life that crossed these lines within Britain were so unsettling became clearer. Britain's early postwar offer of citizenship to persons from the colonies and Commonwealth regardless of race provoked immense anxiety about the effects this might have within the domestic spaces of the nation and the homes within it. Moves to curb black incursions into the nation were preceded by discourses that condemned – but never completely contained – blacks' entry into the nation's (white) families. In the decades that ensued, versions of an implicitly white Britishness have been subjected to an ongoing stream of defences and challenges by Britons who claim a variety of ethnic identities. The contested nature and visible fluidity of British national identity that characterized the 1950s bequeathed a legacy to later generations that remains critical today.

Notes

1 Trevor Philpott, "Would You Let Your Daughter Marry a Negro?", *Picture Post*, 30 October 1954, 21.

2 Anthony H. Richmond, *The Colour Problem: A Study of Racial Relations* (Harmondsworth, 1955), 279.

3 Donald Wood, "A General Survey", in *Coloured Immigrants in Britain*, eds. J. A. G. Griffith, Judith Henderson, Margaret Usborne, and Donald Wood (London, 1960), 17; Sheila Patterson, *Dark Strangers: A Study of West Indians in London* (Harmondsworth, 1965), 251.

4 Ann Laura Stoler, *Race and the Education of Desire: Foucault's History of Sexuality and the Colonial Order of Things* (Durham, NC, 1995); Stoler, *Carnal Knowledge and Imperial Power: Race and the Intimate in Colonial Rule* (Berkeley, 2002); Durba Ghosh, *Sex and the Family in Colonial India: The Making of Empire* (Cambridge, 2006); Philippa Levine, *Prostitution, Race, and Politics: Policing Venereal Disease in the British Empire* (London, 2003). A number of essays touching on this theme appear in Philippa Levine, (ed.) *Gender and Empire* (Oxford, 2004).

5 Laura Tabili, "'Women of a Very Low Type': Crossing Racial Boundaries in Imperial Britain", in *Gender and Class in Modern Europe*, eds. Laura L. Frader and Sonya O. Rose (Ithaca, NY, 1996), 165–90; Tabili, "Empire is the Enemy of Love': Edith Noor's Progress and Other Stories", *Gender & History* 17, no. 1 (2005): 5–28; Philippa Levine, "Battle Colors: Race, Sex, and Colonial Soldiery in World War I", *Journal of Women's History* 9, no. 4 (1998): 104–30; Lucy Bland, "White Women and Men of Colour: Miscegenation Fears in Britain after the Great War", *Gender & History* 17, no. 1 (2005): 29–61; Barbara Bush, *Imperialism, Race and Resistance: Africa and Britain, 1918 to 1945* (London, 1999), chap. 8; Marek Kohn, *Dope Girls: The Birth of the British Drug Underground* (London, 1992); Sonya O. Rose, *Which People's War?: National Identity and Citizenship in Britain, 1939–1945* (Oxford, 2003), chaps. 3 and 7; Rose, "Sex, Citizenship, and the Nation in World War II Britain", *American Historical Review* 103, no. 4 (1998): 1147–76.

6 Remarkably little in-depth historical work has emerged on this theme during the 1950s. See however Wendy Webster, *Imagining Home: Gender, "Race" and National Identity, 1945–64* (London, 1998), 48–52; Bill Schwarz, "Black Metropolis, White England", in *Modern Times: Reflections on a Century of English Modernity*, eds. Mica Nava and Alan O'Shea (London, 1996), 198–200; Chris Waters, "'Dark Strangers' in Our Midst: Discourses of Race and Nation in Britain, 1947–1963", *Journal of British Studies* 36 (1997): 228–9; Marcus Collins,

"Pride and Prejudice: West Indian Men in Mid-Twentieth-Century Britain", *Journal of British Studies* 40 (2001): 405–10.

7 Sonya O. Rose, "Cultural Analysis and Moral Discourses: Episodes, Continuities, and Transformations", in *Beyond the Cultural Turn: New Directions in the Study of Society and Culture*, eds. Victoria E. Bonnell and Lynn Hunt (Berkeley, 1999), 223, 227.

8 *Ibid.*, 231–2.

9 Stuart Hall, "Reconstruction Work: Images of Post-war Black Settlement", in *Family Snaps: The Meanings of Domestic Photography*, eds. Jo Spence and Patricia Holland (London, 1991), 162.

10 Unless quoting contemporary writers, I largely avoid the terms "coloured" or "Negro" here unless using inverted commas. Instead, I refer to persons most commonly described as "coloured", "Negro", or "black" in 1950s Britain either as non-white or as black, recognizing that all racial terminology is at once constructed, historically contingent and apt to mislead. "Black", for example, became a means of referring to Britain's non-white ethnic minority communities in the 1970s and 1980s and included persons of African and Asian descent alike. This usage, however, has faced scholarly criticism for obscuring not only the differences among groups of African origin but also the distinctive identities and concerns of British Asians. Among other contributions to this ongoing debate, see Tariq Modood, "Political Blackness and British Asians", *Sociology* 28, no. 4 (1994): 859–76.

11 Laura Tabili, *"We Ask for British Justice": Black Workers and the Construction of Racial Difference in Late Imperial Britain* (Ithaca, NY, 1994); Antoinette Burton, *At the Heart of the Empire: Indians and the Colonial Encounter in Late-Victorian Britain* (Berkeley, 1998); Hakim Adi, *West Africans in Britain, 1900–1960: Nationalism, Pan-Africanism, Communism* (London, 1998).

12 Non-white arrivals in 1950s Britain were largely West Indian for several reasons. Many West Indians who might once have travelled to the United States in search of employment were unable to do so once the United States' McCarran-Walter Act imposed severe quotas on their numbers in 1952, and they more commonly turned to Britain instead. Labour shortages in Britain and the deliberate recruitment of Caribbean workers to staff London Transport, the National Health Service, textile factories and other economic sectors were equally responsible. Conversely, South Asian migration to Britain was less prominent throughout the 1950s, in part because the Indian and Pakistani governments restricted emigration and only issued a limited number of passports to its citizens prior to 1960.

13 Wood, "General Survey", 9.

14 A. T. Carey, *Colonial Students: A Study of the Social Adaptation of Colonial Students in London* (London, 1956), 11.

15 Philpott, "Would You Let Your Daughter", 21–3.

16 British Council of Churches, *Your Neighbour from the West Indies* (London, 1955), 6, 18; see also Wood, "General Survey", 4.

17 Richmond, *Colour Problem*, 290.

18 British Council of Churches, *Your Neighbour*, 30. Waters, "Dark Strangers", similarly notes how race relations writers during this era often were complicit with popular understandings of racial difference, with Michael Banton for example "collapsing his own authorial voice into that of the national community he set out to scientifically study", 227–8.

19 E. R. Braithwaite, *To Sir, With Love* (London, 1967), 38, 41.

20 Ruth Landes, "A Preliminary Statement of a Survey of Negro-White Relationships in Britain", *Man* 52, no. 184, 185 (1952): 133.

21 Patterson, *Dark Strangers*, 10.

22 James Wickenden, *Colour in Britain* (London, 1958), 19.

23 Clarence Senior and Douglas Manley, *The West Indian in Britain* (London, 1956), 9; see also Judith Henderson, "Race Relations in Britain", in *Coloured Immigrants*, Griffith *et al.*, 49.

24 Patterson, *Dark Strangers*, 72; see also 17, 200.

25 Carey, *Colonial Students*, 11–12.

26 *Ibid.*; see also *Colonial Students in Britain: A Report by P. E. P.* (London, 1956), 3–4.

27 Ruth Glass (assisted by Harold Pollins), *Newcomers: The West Indians in London* (London, 1960), 84.

28 Patterson, *Dark Strangers*, 246–8.

29 Joe Corrie, *Colour Bar: A Play in One Act* (London, 1954); Braithwaite, *To Sir, With Love*, 169, 173; Carey, *Colonial Students*, 120; Patterson, *Dark Strangers*, 249; Anthony H. Richmond, *Colour Prejudice in Britain: A Study of West Indian Workers in Liverpool, 1941–1951* (London, 1954), 77.

30 Glass, *Newcomers*, 248.

31 Michael Banton, *The Coloured Quarter: Negro Immigrants in an English City* (London, 1955), 180; see also 165–6.

32 Glass, *Newcomers*, 106.

33 Colin MacInnes, "A Short Guide for Jumbles", in MacInnes, *England, Half English* (London, 1961; originally published in *The Twentieth Century*, March 1956), 25. West Indian authors also depicted relationships between black men and white women as common in the 1950s; see for example Sam Selvon, *The Lonely Londoners* (London, 1956).

34 Patterson, *Dark Strangers*, 184.

35 Stoler, *Carnal Knowledge*; Dane Kennedy, *Islands of White: Settler Society and Culture in Kenya and Southern Rhodesia, 1890–1939* (Durham, NC, 1987), chap. 7; Jock McCulloch, *Black Peril, White Virtue: Sexual Crime in Southern Rhodesia, 1902–1935* (Bloomington, IN, 2000); Jenny Sharpe, *Allegories of Empire: The Figure of Woman in the Colonial Text* (Minneapolis, 1993); Amirah Inglis, *The White Woman's Protection Ordinance: Sexual Anxiety and Politics in Papua* (New York, 1975).

36 Glass, *Newcomers*, 261–9; Wood, "General Survey", 36; Wickenden, *Colour in Britain*, 37–8.

37 MacInnes, "Short Guide", 25; Wickenden, *Colour in Britain*, 20.

38 Banton, *Coloured Quarter*, 164.

39 Philpott, "Would You Let Your Daughter", 21–2.

40 See for example Colin MacInnes, *City of Spades* (London, 1957); MacInnes, *Absolute Beginners* (London, 1959).

41 Landes, "Preliminary Statement", 133.

42 Waters, "Dark Strangers", 222; see also 209, 217–18, 229.

43 Banton, *Coloured Quarter*, 152–3.

44 Richmond, *Colour Problem*, 280.

45 Sydney F. Collins, "The Social Position of White and 'Half-Caste' Women in Colored Groupings in Britain", *American Sociological Review* 16, no. 6 (1951): 797; see also Sydney Collins, *Coloured Minorities in Britain: Studies in British*

Race Relations based on African, West Indian and Asiatic Immigrants (London, 1957), 45.

46   Collins, *Coloured Minorities*, 163.

47   *Ibid.*, 67.

48   *Ibid.*, 60.

49   Philpott, "Would You Let Your Daughter", 23; see also Henderson, "Race Relations in Britain", 68–9; Banton, *Coloured Quarter*, 177; Richmond, *Colour Problem*, 290.

50   Collins, "The Social Position", 798–9; Collins, *Coloured Minorities*, 56, 67–8.

51   Collins, "The Social Position", 800; Collins, *Coloured Minorities*, 24, 55, 72, 202.

52   Collins, *Coloured Minorities*, 54; see also 23, 71.

53   Banton, *Coloured Quarter*, 168–9; Richmond, *Colour Prejudice*, 83; on political motivations, see Patterson, *Dark Strangers*, 254.

54   Braithwaite, *To Sir, With Love*, 164.

55   *Ibid.*, 173; Patterson, *Dark Strangers*, 239; Richmond, *Colour Problem*, 289.

56   "Between Friends", *Woman's Friend and Glamour*, 20 November 1951, 15.

57   Robert J. C. Young, *Colonial Desire: Hybridity in Theory, Culture and Race* (London, 1995); Nancy Stepan, *The Idea of Race in Science: Great Britain, 1800–1960* (London, 1982); Clifford S. Hill, *How Colour Prejudiced Is Britain?* (London, 1965), 218–21.

58   Richmond, *Colour Prejudice*, 83; Collins, *Coloured Minorities*, 23, 47, 71.

59   Philpott, "Would You Let Your Daughter", 21.

60   As Stuart Hall aptly reflected in his analysis of the main photograph accompanying Philpott's article (depicting a white woman holding a child of mixed descent), racism in England at this historical juncture involved the intertwined articulation of discourses of race, colour, sexuality, patriarchy and Englishness itself. Hall, "Reconstruction Work", 163.

61   Collins, *Coloured Minorities*, 48, 51.

62   Philpott, "Would You Let Your Daughter", 22–3.

63   Patterson, *Dark Strangers*, 357.

64   "Why Racial Clashes Occurred", *Times*, 27 August 1958; "Accused of Beating Coloured Men", *Times*, 1 September 1958; "Renewed Racial Disturbances in London", *Times*, 2 September 1958; "London Racial Outburst Due to Many Factors", *Times*, 3 September 1958. Edward Pilkington, *Beyond the Mother Country: West Indians and the Notting Hill White Riots* (London, 1988), makes frequent references to sexual themes in discussions of these events. White antagonism to interracial sexuality was a factor in earlier "race" riots in Britain, including those taking place in 1919. See Philippa Levine, "Sexuality and Empire", in *At Home with the Empire: Metropolitan Culture and the Imperial World*, eds. Catherine Hall and Sonya O. Rose (Cambridge, 2006), 133–6. On ongoing hostility to mixed marriages interspersed with some evidence of tolerance in the early 1960s see Hill, *How Colour Prejudiced Is Britain?*, ch. 7.

65   Wood, "General Survey", 11; Wickenden, *Colour in Britain*, 20.

66   Collins, *Coloured Minorities*, 253; see also Patterson, *Dark Strangers*, 255; Banton, *Coloured Quarter*, 151.

67 Webster, *Imagining Home*, xv, 60–1, 127. On black families as a "problem", see essays in Centre for Contemporary Cultural Studies, *The Empire Strikes Back: Race and Racism in 70s Britain* (London, 1982), and Heidi Safia Mirza, (ed.) *Black British Feminism: A Reader* (London, 1997).

68 Kathleen Paul, *Whitewashing Britain: Race and Citizenship in the Post-war Era* (Ithaca, NY, 1997); Zig Layton-Henry, *The Politics of Immigration: Immigration, "Race" and "Race" Relations in Post-war Britain* (Oxford, 1992).

69 Paul Gilroy, *"There Ain't No Black in the Union Jack": The Cultural Politics of Race and Nation* (Chicago, 1987), 45, 61.

13

How is the National Past Imagined? National Sentimentality, True Feeling and the "Heritage Film", 1980–1995

Geoff Eley

This essay concerns the so-called "heritage" films associated initially with the signature of James Ivory, Ismael Merchant and Ruth Prawer Jhabvala, which grew by the early 1990s into a distinct genre of recent British cinema.[1] These films affirm a strong image of Britishness through the telling of romantic stories which allegorize the wish for the wholeness of the nation. They trade on the taken-for-grantedness of a certain set of traditions, including a definite characterological heritage, a deep reservoir of cultural citation and a visual repertoire of landscape, architecture, gardens, furnishings, clothing and bodily comportment. Drawing on a dense archive of representations and cognate historical assumptions, they offer easy incitements to nostalgia in the image of an unconflicted national past. The construction of the latter, for international as well as home consumption, with all the visual pleasures of fine acting, literate screenplays and beautiful production values, laden with associated iconicities of period and landscape, promises a safe place of national identification, where the present's difficulties can be sublimated, a place where *Englishness* can imagine itself whole.[2]

Of course, in producing their effects, these films do much else besides. Any full account would register their complicated relationship to the legacies of a partially realized English modernism going back to early twentieth-century Bloomsbury. They also ambivalently recuperate some aspects of the cultural radicalisms of the 1960s and 1970s, feminism preeminently, in however reduced and depoliticized a form. The fullest account would also consider the wider heritage discourse since the early 1980s.[3] I will pick up each of these themes to some extent in the discussion below. But my main interest is to explore how these films' particular preferences and omissions might suggest some of the ways in which a consensual story of "Englishness" has been reimagined in late twentieth-century Britain.

The heritage film began strongly in the 1980s, quickening into a genre by the 1990s.[4] It dates from Hugh Hudson's 1981 Oscar-winning *Chariots of Fire*, continuing through *Another Country* (Marek Kanievska, 1984) and a string of E. M. Forster adaptations: *A Passage to India* (David Lean, 1984); *A Room With a View* (James Ivory, 1985); *Maurice* (James Ivory, 1987); *Where Angels Fear to Tread* (Charles Sturridge, 1991); and *Howard's End* (James Ivory, 1991). The sequence is completed by *Enchanted April* (Mike Newell, 1991); *Remains of the Day* (James Ivory, 1993); *Shadowlands* (Richard Attenborough, 1993); *Tom & Viv* (Brian Gilbert, 1994); and *Carrington* (Christopher Hampton, 1995). In many ways the cycle was inaugurated by Granada Television's serialization of Evelyn Waugh's *Brideshead Revisited* (Charles Sturridge and Michael Lindsay-Hogg, 1981), whose success later inspired *A Handful of Dust* (Charles Sturridge, 1987). Another prestigious Granada serial might be included, the dramatization of Paul Scott's *Raj Quartet* as *The Jewel in the Crown* (Christopher Morahan, 1982), with two other films about India, *Heat and Dust* (James Ivory, 1982) and *Gandhi* (Richard Attenborough, 1982). The list might be stretched to include films like *Orlando* (Sally Potter, 1992), or even *Angels and Insects* (Philip Haas, 1995).[5]

These were not the only filmic appropriations of British history available. In those years filmmakers were also producing class-saturated morality tales of social unease and moral decay, which explored the postwar conformities of Britain's long 1950s.[6] In another strand of 1980s cinema a strong and coherent image of British working-class masculinity was used to figure an argument about the collapse of self-consciously identified traditional values. Counterposing the consequences of Thatcherist individualism, ruthless entrepreneurialism, deindustrialization and social modernization against a seductive cultural nostalgia of ordinariness and dependable decency, in ways closely articulated with earlier moments of a long-lasting working-class representational repertoire, these films continued to evoke a fast-vanishing imaginary. Using Terence Davies' *Distant Voices, Still Lives* (1988), I have suggested elsewhere how this reflex to a postwar mythology of working-class Britishness might be changing and a different space of imagining about the contemporary working class thus opened up.[7] A further range of films, for example by Stephen Frears, Mike Leigh, Isaac Julien or Gurinder Chadha, acknowledged the disordering of previously secure identities, suggesting how else social and cultural belonging might then be conceived, engaging the possibility of "a version of Britishness that does not necessarily belong to the

English".[8] *Those* films "are set firmly in the present, away from the centers of power, in an unstable and socially divided postimperialist and/or working-class Britain, where identities are shifting, fluid, and heterogeneous".[9]

In contrast, the heritage films offer a refuge. They privilege a particular construction of the British past, running between the Edwardian years and the Second World War, sometimes extending into the 1950s, in which the English upper classes mainly people the screen. They "offer apparently more settled and visually splendid manifestations of an essentially pastoral national identity and authentic culture: 'Englishness' as an ancient and natural inheritance, *Great* Britain, the *United* Kingdom".[10] Recurring to such a ground of "pastness" throws the present into a bleaker light, but with a critical edge blunted by wistfulness. Such a vision becomes easily caricatured: "The nostalgia here is a sickening for a homeland where there is endless cricket, fair play with bent rules, fumbled sex, village teas, and punting through long green summers. British identities have been subsumed under a particular version of Englishness".[11] Even where the setting falls later (as in *Shadowlands* and *Remains of the Day*), the sensibility is unavoidably prewar. The unpleasantness of the present is managed by invoking a time apparently untroubled by the salient economic and social disruptions of the later twentieth century.

If the heritage film banishes workers to the margins, where they provide service labour for the plot, it returns blacks and Asians safely to the colonies. In contrast with more critical films of the 1980s, multiculturalism becomes effaced. Colonies are taken for granted: the Wilcoxes of *Howard's End* may owe their place to the profits of colonial enterprise, and Maurice Haigh-Wood, Vivienne's brother in *Tom & Viv*, may serve in the African colonial police service, but such details remain incidental to the Englishness portrayed, not part of its *mise en scène* and in that respect, of course, these films remain true to a lengthy literary tradition. As "race" finally began agitating the complacencies of British cultural politics during the 1980s, forcing itself through the etiological whiteness of public life to urge a "Britishness" of the present tense, the heritage film determinedly put the clock back. In the chosen period setting and its visual landscapes, blacks are back where they always used to be, "positioned as the unspoken and invisible 'other' of predominantly white aesthetic and cultural discourses".[12] As Hall says, "the black experience in British culture" didn't occur "fortuitously" at the margins, but was "placed, positioned" there, "as the consequence of a set of quite specific political and cultural practices, which regulated, governed and 'normalized' the representational and discursive spaces of English society". Given how powerfully this history became aired during the 1980s, the incorrigible *whiteness* of the heritage film's aesthetic evasions seems remarkable.

The heritage film's treatment of women effects a similar muting of contemporary complexities. These films are organized on the surface around feminist stories of female characters within a very late twentieth-century sensibility: Lucy's erotic awakening in *Room With a View*; the Schlegel sisters' divergent choices in *Howard's End*; the journey into feeling of Lotty Wilkins and Rose Arbuthnot in *Enchanted April*; or the nonconformities of the painter Dora Carrington in *Carrington*. In several other cases a strong woman is the foil to the leading man: Emma Thompson's housekeeper Miss Kenton to Anthony Hopkins' butler Stevens in *Remains of the Day*; Debra Winger's Joy Gresham to Anthony Hopkins' Jack Lewis in *Shadowlands*; and Miranda Richardson's Vivienne Haigh-Wood to Willem Dafoe's Tom Eliot in *Tom & Viv*. The films centre on love relationships and the social entanglements of romance, presenting familiar scenarios of female independence and transgression, situated in the constraining emotional landscape of a morally hidebound Englishness. Perched on the cusp of twentieth-century modernity, their protagonists strain against all the suffocating conformities that we know perdured down into the 1960s. For a knowing audience, they enact parables of an intimacy and an affective selfhood whose future has yet to come, a future which the contemporary viewer can feel satisfied to possess. The Schlegel sisters embody this scenario most perfectly. Their performance of the civilized and emancipated life, informed by a personal ethic of cultural humanism and intelligence, emotional honesty and love of the arts and the life of the mind, becomes reconciled with the more prosaic and materialistic domain of the middle-class heritage through motherhood and marriage. Wealth becomes leavened with culture, culture grounded in wealth. The older Margaret marries the dour and unimaginative capitalist widower Henry Wilcox; the younger Helen produces a son, the heir to Howard's End. In *Enchanted April*, the return of Lotty and Rose to their marriages, after fleetingly self-extending encounters with emotional freedom – back from Italy to England, exoticism to drudgery, desires to duty, sunlight to gray – reinscribes female agency within the conventional horizons of the family which the film began by wanting to surpass.

Such conformities bring us to sexuality. Some of the films feature stories of erotic awakening and sexual transgression, told as a journey of escape, whether by geography, imagining Italy as a place of exoticism, or class, as in Maurice Hall's relationship with the gamekeeper Alec Scutter in *Maurice*. In the earlier films of the cycle, notably *Room With A View* and *Maurice*, homoeroticism, gay sexuality and female desire are given their place. Yet in the films of the 1990s that textual openness has gone. Desire is redisciplined, returned into a de-sexualized construction of romantic feeling and its usually repressed pursuit. Where the earlier two films conclude optimistically, granting the homosexual protagonist a rare cinematic prospect of a happy future, that space of sexual reimagining is mainly absent from the later films, which show little trace of *Room With A View*'s "queered, gender-scrambled, deeply ambiguous celebration of female desire".[13] In *Shadowlands* and *Remains of the Day*, the most conservative possible construction of asexual romance is valourized for the love plot. Still worse, in *Tom & Viv*, female sexuality is coded misogynistically as gynaecology ("the female body as messy, uncontrollable organism"), medicalized and contained to further the husband-poet's career and reputation, themselves organized around the most austere and frigid version of counterfeit English masculinity, an aspiring and emotionless Anglo-Catholicism.[14]

This sanitizing of sexual disturbance raises again the issue of *which* past exactly gets to be represented. After all, there is ample scope in earlier twentieth-century Britain for more subversive appropriations of sexualities, not least of course from the orbit of the Bloomsbury set, whence so many of the literary and biographical materials for the heritage film are drawn. With the release of *Howard's End*, for example, *The Longest Journey* remained the only E. M. Forster novel still to be filmed. Evelyn Waugh's *Brideshead Revisited* and *A Handful of Dust*, Elizabeth von Arnim's *Enchanted April*, and Virginia Woolf's *Orlando* have all been adapted from the same years, while the biographies of T. S. Eliot, Lytton Strachey and C. S. Lewis have each been mined.[15] This extensive re-mediation of literary heritage has important implications for the cultural work of national identification.[16] But again: why one set of adaptations as opposed to another? Why some literary lives, and not others? The avoidance of more dissident sexualities – in their fraught but productive alliance with the politics of the Left – in favour of more easily assimilable stories of true feeling and personal fulfilment (or else their tragic thwarting), offers the best clue. Given the longstanding interest of feminists and bohemians, Bloomsbury lives might have provided tempting incitement to the contrary. But that makes the actual choices made in rendering the story of *Carrington*, with its heterosexualizing of the title character's life and careful de-sexualizing of her central relationship with Strachey, its *de-queering* into a form of pastoral domesticity, all the more telling.

This deafening silence, broken only by domesticated and partial recognitions, around class, around race, around gender, around sexuality, around politics, brings us to the centre of the heritage film's meaning: the telling of "private stories" set in a particular past, which simultaneously say something about England and Englishness. These are stories about the importance of feelings and expressiveness, which allegorize an argument about national character and national identity – by what is noticed, selected, and valourized, and what is not. They tell a love story, or more accurately the entry of a particular character into feelings previously contained or repressed: the young woman on the threshold of adult sexuality, or the young gay man or the repressed and cold embodiment of middle-aged male authority (usually played by Anthony Hopkins). They place that story in the earlier twentieth century to elaborate a portrait of upper-class England and its decorums. In the name of inner fulfilment and personal happiness, the films tell stories of rebelliousness and the struggle of individuals against the impairment of selfhood. They explore the capacities of their characters for a certain kind of affective integrity, for freeing their emotional lives from conformities deeply embedded in English society. The attainment of expressivity is also coded more generally as honesty, truthfulness and the integrity of personhood, sometimes linked to an aesthetics of artistic and intellectual freedom, or at least to vague and underdeveloped ideals of intellectuality. But strikingly, in one way or another and with varying severity, convention usually wins.

This becomes clearer once we move from the heritage film's women to its men. For the entry into private feeling as the truth of Britishness is only one side of what these films have to say. The resolute and successful repression of feeling is the other. In many ways, the films' discourse is organized precisely in and around this antinomy, between the foregrounding of sensuousness and expressivity, the acknowledgment of emotional needs and the virtue of acting in accordance with one's true feelings, and on the other hand the poignancy and pathology of having no feelings to express or the repression that keeps those feelings from view. This difference is highly gendered: the characters who find their emotionality and decide to live fully inside it are women (most classically Lucy in *Room With a View*), whereas the characters who deny it are men: Eliot in *Tom & Viv*, Henry Wilcox in *Howard's End*, Jack Lewis in *Shadowlands* and Stevens in *Remains of the Day*. Where Vivienne Eliot marshalls her emotional exuberance in manic rebellions against the confining conformities of family and society, Tom organizes his emotional economy into an affirmation of precisely the same decorums, which become simultaneously the idiom for a repressed and managerial Englishness. In *Shadowlands* this equation of Englishness with a particular structure of emotionality is especially clear. C. S. Lewis, in important ways an emblematic figure of postwar English middle-class culture, placed in the heritage film's typical landscape ("scenes of Oxford University ceremonial and of verdant, unspoilt countryside"), is not just an Englishman without feelings, but an academic writer on courtly love and the abstract ideal of transcendence, as well as a famous author of fantasies for children. Through the redemptive love of an American woman, he moves from dry-as-dust bookishness and arid intellectuality to the comforts of a feminized domesticity and the visual pleasures of the countryside, but still within an emotional economy of scarcity and restraint.[17]

Shadowlands' point of view in this respect is complex. In general, the heritage film oscillates between criticism of the absence of feeling and a sympathetic validation of decorum and restraint, the modalities of extreme managerialism and self-containment, which in a different construction might imply subtlety and depth of feeling. Richard Dyer makes the best case of this latter kind, identifying a strand of the British cinema – which might run, for instance, from *Millions Like Us* (Frank Launder/Sidney Gilliat, 1943) through *Brief Encounter* (David Lean, 1945) to *The Blue Lamp* (Basil Dearden, 1949), and thence eventually to its current versions – with the ability to communicate the power of emotions beneath the surface, usually in the pain of an experienced loss, like a bereavement or the end of an affair. Understatement and emotional reticence, detachment and the ability to preserve distance, re-emerge here as virtues: "Some of the great emotional moments in British cinema occur when the performance allows the pressure of feeling to be felt beneath a flatness of expression".[18] But this is surely to sentimentalize repression. The critique of emotional coldness is also mitigated by the splendour of the settings – by all the paraphernalia of lush periodicity that distracts so effectively from the substantive stories being told – and the Englishman without feelings becomes humanized against the beauties of the English countryside.[19] In some ways the prototype for this sympathetic portrayal of staid English masculinity is *84 Charing Cross Road* (David Jones, 1986), in which a New York lady bibliophile and a married London bookseller conduct a touching relationship across the Atlantic without ever getting to meet, let alone touch each other.[20]

In the heritage film we find a deliberate foregrounding of the intimacies of human relationships (sex, romance, falling in love, friendship, feelings, expressivity), within an explicit discourse of history and the nation (Englishness and its timeless authenticities), but in ways which leave the politics of its moment almost completely *out*. In the formal architecture of the films, we might even say, intimacy *substitutes* for politics, in a way which questions some gender normativities far more than others. Moreover, this separation is itself the problem, territorializing the personal into a safe and manageable ground, displacing the complexities and specificities of history – and "politics" in the conventional sense – to a space beyond the frame of the films themselves, and constituting their stories into universal and timeless texts. One way of reading this political indirection is via what I will call the Bloomsbury text of the films – the validating of a diluted version of Bloomsbury's demand for openness and honesty in personal relations, within a liberal-humanist and feminist perspective that ambiguously privileges the woman's point of view. But this pseudo-radicalism – the domesticating of Bloomsbury's incitements – simultaneously protects English *masculinity* from the call to intimacy.

In that sense, the films' discourse of personal fulfilment performs an ambivalence about modernism, where "being modern" means refusing the constraints of English tradition. But the *limits* of that engagement – with the full disconcerting subversiveness of life in its sexual and aesthetic dimensions, and the confinement of the films more generally to the romantic dilemmas of individuals, devoid of complex intellectuality and politics – remain key. That seems all the more striking because these films draw so avidly on Bloomsbury as a kind of collective text, where the double commitment to personal truth and modernist aesthetics *was* explicitly linked to a progressive politics, most clearly in the case of the Woolfs, but also in those of Keynes, Strachey and others. Yet inside the films themselves "Bloomsbury" appears simply as a coterie of famous names inhabiting a common period, with no distinctions among T. S. Eliot, Bertrand Russell and Lytton Strachey or Virginia Woolf, or any other notable intellectual or literary figure of the time. In *Tom & Viv*, Woolf becomes just another literary snob, a justified and comical target for Vivienne Eliot's rage. While the vagaries of social privilege and the class-bound insufferableness of bourgeois hauteur can be far too easily glossed over in Virginia Woolf's canonization, it is this other – political – importance that disappears from Brian Gilbert's film.

Bloomsbury itself was no simple phenomenon. It constructed an Englishness that was certainly partial and exclusionary, for all its modernist dissent. But the films rarely bring us to the point of such questioning, and reflect far more Bloomsbury's safer mainstream reabsorption into the dominant culture of post-1945 Britain. Both the painter Mark Gertler and the writer Gerald Brenan have a significant niche in British cultural history, for example, yet *Carrington* concedes to them only a comic part as walk-on lovers; their wider relevance as supporting characters remains entirely unstated. As Janet Wolff has shown, the complicated ways in which Gertler was and was not connected to Bloomsbury and its ethos (especially to Duncan Grant and Vanessa Bell, and before 1914 to Roger Fry) suggest an important argument about outsiderliness and modernism, and the relatedness of both to the understandings of Englishness of the time. In light of the 1905 Aliens Act and the preceding politics of anti-immigration, Gertler's Jewishness has the capacity to destabilize the national nostalgia around which the heritage film is built. When *Carrington* uses Gertler as a crazed and romantic caricature of the driven and tormented artist, that facile stereotype effaces both his Jewish and his working-class origins in Galicia and the East End. Such a representation colludes in the wider suppression of differences which the heritage film effects.[21] Here was a chance to ground contemporary dilemmas of cultural diversity in a deeper history, where Englishness was already being challenged from the borderlands – imperial, geographical, cultural, social, sexual – long before the latter-day eruption of postcolonial discontents occurred.[22]

The legacies of "Bloomsbury" were crucial for the public culture of the post-1945 era, but although the heritage films sometimes notice this cultural ensemble, they miss the *programmatic* presence entirely, valourizing only the liberal-humanist advocacy of emotional directness and truthfulness in personal relations.[23] The name-dropping knowingness of *Tom & Viv* is far more representative of the way in which the broader cultural history gets registered. The *specificity* of Bloomsbury, meaning both the significant radicalism of its challenge to English traditions and its longer-term successful domestication, becomes lost.

In recuperating what Peter Wollen calls Bloomsbury's "subversive residue", three important points may be made.[24] One concerns the cosmopolitan referents of Bloomsbury's modernism, whether in the Omega Workshops' debt to Parisian design, the enormous impact of the Ballets Russes or Virginia Woolf's passage from Dostoyevsky to Proust. During the critical period of 1910–40, Berlin and Paris were as important as London to Bloomsbury's imaginative geography. This has to relativize the salient categories of Englishness through which the heritage films and their literary inspirations largely work. Yet such European contexts lie entirely beyond the heritage film's horizon, except as a range of exotic locations, mainly Italian, through which the securities of national character become either threatened and destabilized, or else magically transformed. When reviewers wax lyrical about the "timelessness" of these films, projecting their anodyne and narrowly patriotic constructions deep into the past, the cultural diversity inside British society earlier in the century becomes flatly suppressed. "The peculiarly hybrid ethnicities that we reductively call Englishness" were scarcely less salient in 1920 than they were in 1996 (or remain in 2009), yet a white and ethnocentrically unselfconscious construction of the national character still somehow lives tenaciously on.[25] The novel behind *The Remains of the Day* develops a biting if poignant reflection on English sensibilities in the rapidly eroding social relations of the country-house setting between the 1920s and 1950s. But its author is Kazuo Ishiguro, an Asian-Briton actually born in Japan. Likewise, as Higson says of *Howard's End*: "It is worth recalling that 'this instant national treasure' was produced by an Indian, scripted by a Pole, directed by an American, and funded with British, American and Japanese money".[26]

Secondly, the films sidestep the challenge of feminism, whether as history or as presence. This is complicated. At one level the heritage film is entirely unintelligible without the cultural sensibility engendered by post-sixties feminism. But this enters the heritage genre in its least reflective versions, where female characters signify expressivity and feelings, whether as sensitivity or excess. The films take the woman's point of view, but in the most literal and unsubversive of ways, valourizing true romance over social propriety (*Room With a View*), regretting the tragic unmanageability of the female body (*Tom & Viv*), or translating the experimental mobility of bisexual desire into the longing for heterosexualized domesticity (*Carrington*). But Bloomsbury housed a far more radical and explicitly theorized relationship to feminist politics, which was also integrally related to how the modernist project took shape. In fact, the intellectual space of this union crystallized in that same period between 1910 and the 1920s when the Pankhursts' relentless holding of radical feminist politics to the ground of the demand for the suffrage was beginning to break down. Peter Wollen ties this to the writings of Dora Marsden, Harriet Weaver, Theresa Billington, Stella Browne, Rose Witcop and other sexual radicals in journals like the *Freewoman* and its successor, the *New Freewoman* and then the *Egoist*. These journals demanded the freeing of women in everyday life and the arts as well as from political subordination – from "all shackles of law and custom, from all chains of sentiment and superstition", as one emblematic statement put it.[27] The heritage film leaves all of this important context unsaid, an omission all the more revealing for its desire to take women's agency and desires seriously, its important but meretricious feminizing of Englishness from a late twentieth-century point of view. Sexual politics was crucial to the context in which Forster, Woolf and their contemporaries lived and wrote:

> The fact that so many Bloomsbury figures were involved in illegal sexual activities, in what Edward Carpenter called "triune" marriages, in spectacularly complicated and catastrophic love affairs and in wild infatuations with inappropriate partners is not trivial or irrelevant to the introduction of Modernism in Britain, however much Eliot – or Woolf herself – sought after distance and "impersonality" in their own art.[28]

These attenuations – beyond the limit of what the heritage film is willing to notice or represent – bespeak, thirdly, a more general exclusion of politics. In their selective telling of these self-consciously English stories, these films faced a choice over what exactly to recuperate from the early twentieth century and what to discard or leave unnoticed. In depoliticizing Bloomsbury's legacy in particular, they had to efface the wider valencies and contexts of Bloomsbury's significance. The grand events of the twentieth century are all missing from these films, from the powerful presence in English society of the Empire and the traumatizing effects of the Great War, to the crisis of the British state between the eve of the war and the 1926 General Strike, the Bolshevik Revolution and the rise of fascism in Europe and later the postwar reforms of 1945. None of these political histories ruffle the heritage film's surface. In Bloomsbury's case that omission means feminism and sexual politics, as argued above. But it also means the direct political involvements of Keynes, Leonard Woolf and others, in a wide range of arenas, including government economic policy, anti-imperialist questions, the League of Nations, the Cooperative movement and the Labour Party. Virginia Woolf too engaged with feminist questions, and (as Raymond Williams reminds us) "had a branch of the Women's Cooperative Guild meeting regularly in her home".[29] It is not that other literary models aren't available. Thus Pat Barker's ambitious trilogy specifically situates its stories of personal self-examination in the big events of the war and the 1920s, in a far richer field of class relationships, and other instances might be cited, including Nicholas Mosely's grandiose allegory of Western European history between the German Revolution of 1918 and the Cold War, or for that matter the autobiographical fictions of Raymond Williams.[30] In other words, the heritage film's determined avoidance of political histories is a conscious choice, which itself carries political meanings.[31]

Aside from the indifference to the big events, there are two dimensions to this avoidance. On the one hand, there is an unfinished public narrative of national decline in the period chosen by the heritage film concerning end of Empire, the collapse of manufacturing supremacy and deindustrialization, which Thatcherism's neo-Churchillian trumpeting of British "greatness" during the 1980s was not able to overcome. Against this, the heritage film's apolitical nostalgia for an apparently less troubled time becomes pure displacement. In other words, there could be a different way of narrating the social stabilities of upper-class life so affirmatively featured in these films, which would look beyond the country-house setting to the structures of Conservative political rule, which with the exception of the years 1940–51 (and the briefer moments of Labour rule in 1924 and 1929–31) covered forty-two years from 1922 to 1964. The genre comes closest to acknowledging this in *Remains of the Day*. That film uses the character of the butler Stevens to figure an argument about the relationship of public affairs to a particular structure of feeling, in a complicated back-and-forth between the proto-Nazi sympathies of the owner of the Hall, the disgraced Lord Darlington, and the emotionally repressed and rigidly deferential Englishness embodied by Stevens. But by its interweaving of political spectatorship and self-effacement with the unfolding of a private tragedy (the death of Stevens' father and his ensuing emotional crisis), the film moves the personal story clankingly into the foreground. In contrast, Ishiguro's novel explicitly situates itself historically, organizing its personal story of self-deception, loss and insularity, the repression of feeling, around the history of appeasement, the failures of Conservatism and the bankruptcy of tradition. Ishiguro historicizes perfectly, placing the narration in 1956, the year of Suez and the crisis of Empire, and beginning the story in 1922, the starting-point of Baldwinian Conservatism, with its rhetorics of one-nation Toryism and social harmony. The film, in contrast, loses most of that specificity – and the critical political edge – in its mixture of period nostalgia, production values and personalization.

On the other hand, the valourizing of expressivity – the importance of individual feelings and the courage to recognize them – in a modernist philosophy of personhood had an avowedly political dimension in the early twentieth century which the heritage film also evades. In its feminist form that commitment to radical personhood was at the subversive centre of Virginia Woolf's legacy, what Peter Wollen calls Bloomsbury's "unassimilable core": "The Bloomsbury fraction, and especially Virginia

Woolf, can never quite be assimilated, can never be reduced simply to English upper-class taste and values, to *boeuf en daube* or the 'Friends of Charleston' or the Laura Ashley collection or the Merchant-Ivory costume drama or the monolithic biography".[32] Over the longer term, Bloomsbury's influence profoundly changed the script of cultural value in the dominant structures of feeling in post-1945 Britain, creating a space of critique and dissidence that really endured. But beyond the Bloomsbury Set, there was a broader context of dissident sexuality, experimental living, radical feminism and sex reform, associated with figures like Oscar Wilde, Olive Schreiner, Stella Browne and especially Edward Carpenter, which creatively and courageously linked these commitments to socialism. Of course, in the mainstream archives of Englishness there is a long established contempt for Carpenter and what he represented, for which George Orwell's disreputable sneer at "that dreary tribe of high-minded women and sandal-wearers and bearded fruit-juice drinkers" may still stand in.[33] It would be perhaps too much to expect a film to be made about Edward Carpenter. But how would the life of Virginia Woolf be made into a Merchant-Ivory production?

The films discussed in this essay are also about citizenship – about who belongs to the nation, and about how that belonging is to be imagined in Thatcherized Britain's late twentieth-century public sphere.[34] By their choice of a particular period as opposed to others, by their social topography, by the visual pleasures of rustic scenery and country house settings, by the conscious play of literary reference and broader cultural citation, by evoking a familiar sensibility, by mobilizing the past as nostalgia – by all of these mediations of Britishness and its cultural archive, the heritage films restore the efficacy of a conservative and depoliticizing version of the national past, freed from any particular trace of democratic or egalitarian critique. The love stories organizing the heritage film certainly imply a modernist ideal of personhood, if we take their Bloomsbury referents seriously. But here they end by sentimentalizing the nation rather than defamiliarizing or reimagining its claims. By having women at their center, they do little for a feminist critique of nationalism, as opposed to feminizing the nation into feeling.

What might an oppositional representation of the national past using these materials entail? How might the conventionalized and canonical complacencies of "heritage" be surpassed, so that "Britishness, instead of being a secure, genetic identity, can be seen as something culturally and historically conditioned, always in the making, never made?"[35] If we are not to refuse the ground of national identification *tout court*, how might a new version of democratic patriotism begin? How might a different set of patriotic modalities, ones less exclusivist and anglocentric, less provincial and defensive, but more generous and pluralistic, more continuous with the older post-1945 ideals of the public good, more animated perhaps by the cultural radicalisms of 1968, be entertained? The heritage film reinscribes "tradition" as the central good of the national past. But the same stories might also be retold (or read against the grain) to challenge the conformities of the present – through critiques of the family, resistance to sexual repression, subversion of heteronormativity, the queering of sexualities, the claiming of feminist subjectivity and so forth. As the suppressed source of a more radical conception of personhood, moreover, and a modernism implacably hostile to the congealed normativities of the past, Bloomsbury and similar radical formations could precisely deliver such a counter-narrative, allowing a different history to be told. It would encourage other structures to be problematized too – from the reproduction of the violence and privileges of class, and the ethnocentrisms of empire, to the general oppressiveness of British traditions, including those of class inequalities and their privilege. The centrality of privacy, intimacy and love to the imagining of national wholeness so saturates the representation of the collective in the dominant forms of the heritage film, that it can be hard to see how else mass culture might mobilize history's radical alterity in contemporary Britain. For that purpose we will need very different constructions of British heritage. Rather than naturalizing the past via the reassuring pleasures of familiar repetition, bringing us back to the comforting pathways of the already known, the archive might then be drawn upon to unsettle the given forms of understanding and make them strange. If the routines of national history can become the occasion for fantasy, distortion and misrecognition in a more critical filmmaking practice, then the resulting stories might delaminate nostalgia from the nation. Britishness might be radically remapped, as a landscape where it might become possible to imagine change.[36]

Notes

1 This essay is a fragment of a larger work in progress on Cinema and the Construction of the National Past. It owes a huge amount to the readings and suggestions of colleagues, including especially Lauren Berlant, Kali Israel and Gina Morantz-Sanchez. It owes a similar debt to many conversations over the years with Sonya Rose, as well as to her own writings. See especially "Sex, Citizenship, and the Nation in World War II Britain", *American Historical Review*, 103 (1998), 1147–76, and *Which People's War?: National Identity and Citizenship in Wartime Britain, 1939–1945* (Oxford, 2003).

2 The slippage here from "Britishness" to "Englishness" is deliberate. Confusion surrounds this distinction in the politics and culture of the contemporary UK, where anglocentrism remains hardly less powerful than whiteness in the discursive and institutional machineries of British national identification. For initial help, see Leighton Andrews, "New Labour, New England?", in *The Blair Agenda*, ed. Mark Perryman (London, 1996), 125–46; Robert Colls and Philip Dodd (eds.), *Englishness: Politics and Culture 1880–1920* (London, 1986); Robert Colls, *Identity of England* (Oxford, 2002).

3 The heritage boom was framed by two National Heritage Acts (1980, 1983) and the Heritage Educational Trust (1982), preceded by the campaigning of SAVE Britain's Heritage, founded in 1975 by Marcus Binney, architectural editor of *Country Life*. Conservative politician Patrick Cormack's *Heritage in Danger* (London and New York, 1978) was a key founding tract. See Raphael Samuel, *Theatres of Memory. Vol. 1: Past and Present in Contemporary Culture* (London, 1994), 205–312. Under the Thatcher government a profusion of official and grassroots activity occurred: over 40 recognized Heritage Centres by 1990, 817 museums presenting rural history and 464 with industrial collections, half a million listed buildings, over 5,500 conservation areas and so on. See also Robert Hewison, *The Heritage Industry: Britain in a Climate of Decline* (London, 1987); John Corner and Sylvia Harvey, "Mediating Tradition and Modernity: The Heritage/Enterprise Couplet", in *Enterprise and Heritage: Crosscurrents of National Culture* , ed. Corner and Harvey (London, 1991), 45–75; Jo Littler and Roshi Naidoo (eds), *The Politics of Heritage: The Legacies of "Race"* (London, 2005).

4 The most careful and comprehensive mapping is by Andrew Higson, *English Heritage, English Cinema: Costume Drama Since 1980* (Oxford, 2003), 9–45. For current purposes my own notation is far more specific.

5 By both period setting and cultural valencies, the various Jane Austen adaptations signify very differently. See *Sense and Sensibility* (Ang Lee, 1995); *Persuasion* (Roger Michell, 1995); *Emma* (Douglas McGrath, 1996); *Mansfield Park* (Patricia Rozema, 1999); *Pride and Prejudice* (Joe Wright, 2005). Recent TV serializations have included *Pride and Prejudice* (Simon Langton, 1995), *Emma* (Diarmuid Lawrence, 1997), and an earlier cycle comprising *Pride and Prejudice* (Cyril Coke, 1980); *Sense and Sensibility* (Rodney Bennett, 1981); *Mansfield Park* (David Giles, 1983); and *Northanger Abbey* (Giles Foster, 1986).

6 E.g. *Dance with a Stranger* (Mike Newell, 1985); *Wish You Were Here* (David Leland, 1987); *Prick Up Your Ears* (Stephen Frears, 1987); *White Mischief* (Michael Radford, 1987); *Scandal* (Michael Caton-Jones, 1989); *The Krays* (Peter Medak, 1990); *Let Him Have It* (Peter Medak, 1992).

7 See Geoff Eley, "*Distant Voices, Still Lives*. The Family is a Dangerous Place: Memory, Gender, and the Image of the Working Class", in *Revisioning History. Film and the Construction of a New Past*, ed. Robert Rosenstone (Princeton, 1995), 17–43, 215–22. The older-established working-class representational repertoire was most associated with the so-called northern realist films of 1959–63. To capture its latterday evocation I used the Neil Jordan film *Mona Lisa* (1986).

8 Sarita Malik, "Beyond 'The Cinema of Duty'? The Pleasures of Hybridity: Black British Film of the 1980s and 1990s", in Andrew Higson, "The Heritage Film and British Cinema", in *Dissolving Views. Key Writings of British Cinema*, ed.

Andrew Higson (London, 1996), 214. See *My Beautiful Laundrette* (Stephen Frears, 1985); *Sammie and Rosie Get Laid* (Frears, 1987); *High Hopes* (Mike Leigh, 1988); *Life is Sweet* (Leigh, 1990); *Secrets and Lies* (Leigh, 1996); *The Passion of Remembrance* (Isaac Julien and Maureen Blackwood, 1986); *Young Soul Rebels* (Julien, 1991); *Bhaji on the Beach* (Gurinder Chadha, 1993).

9   Andrew Higson, "Re-presenting the National Past: Nostalgia and Pastiche in the Heritage Film", in *Fires Were Started: British Cinema and Thatcherism*, ed. Lester Friedman (Minneapolis, 1993), 110.

10   *Ibid.*

11   Tana Wollen, "Over Our Shoulders: Nostalgic Screen Fictions for the 1980s", in Corner and Harvey, *Enterprise and Heritage*, 182.

12   Stuart Hall, "New Ethnicities", in *Black Film, British Cinema, ICA Documents 7* (London, 1989), 27, also for the following.

13   See Claire Monk, "Sexuality and Heritage", *Sight and Sound*, 5, 10 (October 1995), 32–4. Compare Monk's argument with Higson, "Re-Presenting the National Past", which misses the radicalism of the earlier two films.

14   See Claire Monk's review, *Sight and Sound*, 4, 5 (May 1994), 57–8.

15   By the mid 1990s the heritage genre migrated backwards into the nineteenth century, embracing the novels of Jane Austen, George Eliot, Thomas Hardy, Charles Dickens and others, e.g. *Little Dorrit* (Christine Edzard, 1987); *Middlemarch* (Andrew Davies, 1993); *Jude* (Michael Winterbottam, 1996). See also *Mary Shelley's Frankenstein* (Kenneth Branagh, 1994) and *The Madness of King George* (Nicholas Hytner, 1995).

16   For the earlier literary moment of national pedagogy, see Colls and Dodd (eds), *Englishness*; Raymond Williams, *Writing in Society* (London, 1983), 177–91, 192–211, 212–26; James Donald, *Sentimental Education: Schooling, Popular Culture and the Regulation of Liberty* (London, 1992).

17   See Richard Dyer's description of the film: "An emotionally inexpressive, middle-aged, middle-class white man meets a somewhat more outgoing, somewhat younger, middle-class white woman; they marry but their contentment is cut short by her dying of cancer. The setting is an earlier period of the twentieth century, and there are scenes of Oxford University ceremonial and of verdant, unspoilt countryside. The acting is unemphatic, the direction unobtrusive and the music has something of Elgar about it". Dyer then proceeds to argue, against the grain of his own description, for the depth of feeling such a film manages to represent. Richard Dyer, "Feeling English", *Sight and Sound*, 4, 3 (March 1994), 17.

18   *Ibid.*, 17–18. See also Richard Dyer, *Brief Encounter* (London, 1993). For an interesting commentary, see Ford Madox Ford, "The Englishman feels very deeply and reasons very little", extracted from *England and the English* (1907), in *Writing Englishness 1900–1950. An Introductory Sourcebook on National Identity*, eds. Judy Giles and Tim Middleton (London, 1995), 46–52. Here "depth" means buried so deeply as to be irretrievably interred.

19   Compare the extraordinary poignancy of the final parting between Stevens and Miss Kenton (now Mrs Benn) in the novel with the filmed version's fudging of this into a visual citation of *Brief Encounter*, which crassly sentimentalizes the ending. In the book, Mrs Benn has been reflecting on the "different life, a *better* life" she might have had with Stevens, before disavowing the possibility. Stevens comments: "I do not think I responded immediately, for it took

me a moment or two to fully digest these words of Miss Kenton. Moreover, as you might appreciate, their implications were such as to provoke a certain degree of sorrow within me. Indeed – why should I not admit it? – at that moment, my heart was breaking". See Kazuo Ishiguro, *The Remains of the Day* (New York, 1993), 239. In the film, they stretch out their hands, in the dark and through the rain (in closeup), as Mrs Benn leaves on the bus.

20 Emblematically, Anthony Hopkins plays the male lead in this film, a preview of his subsequent performances.

21 See Janet Wolff, "The Failure of a Hard Sponge: Class, Ethnicity, and the Art of Mark Gertler", *New Formations*, 28 (Spring 1996), 46–64. For the 1905 Aliens Act, see David Feldman, *Englishmen and Jews: Social Relations and Political Culture, 1840–1914* (New Haven, 1994); and "The Importance of Being English: Jewish Immigration and the Decay of Liberal England", in *Metropolis – London: Histories and Representations Since 1800*, eds. David Feldman and Gareth Stedman Jones (London, 1989), 57–8. At the Whitechapel Art Gallery's 1914 exhibition on British "Twentieth-Century Art", Gertler and fourteen other Jews were quarantined in their own room. In the familiar equation of Jews with modernism, they were decried as "foreign" influences on English art. See Juliet Steyn, "Inside-Out: Assumptions of 'English' Modernism in the Whitechapel Art Gallery, London 1914", in *Art Apart: Art Institutions and Ideology Across England and North America*, ed. Marcia Pointon (Manchester, 1994), 212–31; and "Mods, Yids and Foreigners", *Third Text*, 15 (1991), 29–38.

22 For landmark discussions of the racialized discourse of Englishness: Centre for Contemporary Cultural Studies (eds.), *The Empire Strikes Back: Race and Racism in 70s Britain* (London, 1982); Paul Gilroy, "*There Ain't No Black in the Union Jack*": *The Cultural Politics of Race and Nation* (Chicago, 1987).

23 See Raymond Williams, "The Bloomsbury Fraction", in *Problems in Materialism and Culture: Selected Essays* (London, 1980), 148–69; Peter Wollen, "Wild Hearts", *London Review of Books*, 17, 7 (April 6, 1995), 28–31. Amidst the vast biographical literature, see Peter Stansky, *On Or About December 1910: Early Bloomsbury and its Intimate World* (Cambridge, MA., 1996), and Hermione Lee, *Virginia Woolf* (New York, 1997).

24 Wollen, "Wild Hearts", 31.

25 Andrew Higson, "The Heritage Film and British Cinema", in Higson, *Dissolving Views*, 48.

26 *Ibid.*

27 Wollen, "Wild Hearts", 31, quoting Billington's polemic against the Pankhursts in the *New Age*. For Teresa Billington-Greig, see Brian Harrison, *Prudent Revolutionaries. Portraits of British Feminists between the Wars* (Oxford, 1987), 45–72.

28 *Ibid.*, 31. Wollen argues that Woolf's modernist ambitions and the radical feminist "widening-out of a narrow 'votes for women' suffragism" mutually reinforced each other. See Harold L. Smith (ed.), *British Feminism in the Twentieth Century* (Aldershot, 1990); Laura E. Nym Mayhall, *The Militant Suffrage Movement: Citizenship and Resistance in Britain, 1860–1930* (New York, 2003); Sandra Stanley Holton, *Suffrage Days* (London, 1996); Lisa Tickner, *The Spectacle of Women: Imagery of the Suffrage Campaign, 1907–1914* (Chicago, 1988); also Suzanne Raitt, *Vita and Virginia: The Work and Friendship of V. Sackville-West and Virginia Woolf* (Oxford, 1993).

29 Williams, "Bloomsbury Fraction", 155.

30 See Pat Barker, *Regeneration* (London, 1991), *The Eye in the Door* (London, 1993), and *The Ghost Road* (London, 1995); Nicholas Mosely, *Hopeful Monsters* (London, 1990); Raymond Williams, *Border Country* (New York, 1962), and *Second Generation* (New York, 1964). With the exception of *Regeneration*, filmed as *Behind the Lines* (Gillies MacKinnon, 1997), these books have not been filmed. On the other hand, a rich strand of British film-making deals with the First World War, beginning with *Oh! What a Lovely War* (Richard Attenborough, 1969), and continuing e.g. with *Days of Hope* (Ken Loach, 1975), *Testament of Youth* (Moira Armstrong, 1979), *The Return of the Soldier* (Alan Bridges, 1982), and *A Month in the Country* (Pat O'Connor, 1987). This reemphasizes the selectiveness of the national past the heritage film chooses to use.

31 In screenplays that otherwise follow the novels extraordinarily faithfully, the Forster adaptations make notable omissions of dialogue. In Chapter 16 of *Room With a View* George denounces Cecil to Lucy for being incapable of intimacy, but the film modifies this indictment, omitting Cecil's denial of Lucy's personhood, making his emotional incapacity into an individual failing rather than a symptom of society's limiting gender regime. Here is the omitted portion: "He [Cecil] daren't let a woman decide. He's the sort who's kept Europe back for a thousand years. Every moment of his life he's forming you, telling you what's charming or amusing or ladylike, telling you what a man thinks womanly; and you, you of all women, listen to his voices instead of your own". See E. M. Forster, *A Room with a View* (New York, 1986), 193–7, 201–3. For a similar elision: *Howard's End* (New York, 1985), 98–101.

32 Wollen, "Wild Hearts", 31.

33 He continued: "vegetarians with wilting beards ... earnest ladies in sandals, shock-headed Marxists chewing polysyllables, escaped Quakers, birth-control fanatics, and Labour Party backstairs-crawlers". See George Orwell, *The Road to Wigan Pier* (Penguin, 1969), 160, 169. From Orwell's novels, journalism and letters Malcolm Evans compiles a fuller catalogue of these stereotypes: "'Pinks', 'pansies,' feminists, Quakers, 'shock-headed Marxists chewing polysyllables', bearded vegetarians, fruit-juice drinkers, proponents of birth control and homeopathic medicines, nudists, pacifists, 'Labour Party backstairs crawlers', people who do yoga and live in Welwyn Garden City, and those who wear pistachio-colored shirts or the ubiquitous sandals [he] so detested". See Malcolm Evans, "Text, Theory, Criticism: Twenty Things You Never Knew About George Orwell", in *Inside the Myth: Orwell, Views from the Left*, ed. Christopher Norris (London, 1984), 32–3.

34 In my usage here "citizenship" implies more than a bundle of juridical rights, also signifying a set of civic capacities, to be used in public ways, within a wider notion of political agency.

35 Raphael Samuel, "British Dimensions: 'Four Nations History'", *History Workshop Journal*, 40 (Autumn 1995), iv.

36 As markers for this more radical re-historicizing, which uses the literary heritage of the national past for critical rather than merely affirmative purposes, we might cite Sally Potter's *Orlando* (1993), Derek Jarman's *Edward II* (1991), or Richard Loncraine's *Richard III* (1995), whose retellings deliberately redesign the national stage – sometimes playfully, sometimes with dystopic bleakness and rage. So far such examples remain few and far between.

14

Afterword to *Gender, Labour, War and Empire*

Laura L. Frader

History is a field that has had an ambivalent relationship to theory and/or methodological consciousness; historically, historians' claims to operate "scientifically" have more often meant rigorous empirical investigation than conceptual or theoretical innovations or contributions.[1] Indeed, even within the field of "social science history", which took off in the 1970s in both North America and Europe, and included monumental studies of the family, labour, urban life, local and micro-studies of rural life and slavery, among other topics, with few exceptions, "social science" signified data mining and statistical analysis rather than the organization of findings according to theoretical or conceptual frameworks.[2] At the same time, within the emerging field of social history, often heavily influenced by Marxist theory, historians turned their attention to the history of under-represented groups, notably the working class, chronicling the process of class formation, organization and labour conflicts. These were in themselves tremendously important contributions that in some cases transformed understandings of the field and opened up new avenues of investigation, but they tended to assume rather than make problems for investigating the very categories of analysis that underpinned the studies themselves: categories such as class, gender, race and sexuality. At about the same time, major interventions by feminist and cultural historians also opened up new areas for research by challenging accepted definitions of their categories and analytical frameworks and pointing to how scholarly categories of analysis were themselves constituted socially and historically. Some took a post-Marxist "cultural turn", investigating how language, representations and cultural practices influenced social life; many feminist historians shifted their lens from the study of "women" as a fixed and immutable subject of analysis to consider how "women" were constituted socially and culturally in different historical contexts and to think about the instability of the category. Historians who investigated culture saw how class, gender and race were historically and socially produced as social relations, and moreover were mutually constitutive. In this context Sonya Rose's ability to practice social history (or historical sociology) with attention to the discursive dimensions of social life have made a major substantive and methodological contribution to historical scholarship. For what distinguishes Rose's work is precisely her attention to the relationship between gender, class and other forms of difference, and the politics of their intersections.

The call for historians and especially feminist historians to analyse the intersections of race, class and gender was not always matched by research that actually examined the complex intersections of these dimensions of social life. Many who shifted their lens from social history *tout court* to the social history of cultural practices as a dimension of social history, moreover, figured class as a product of language, representations or discourses, leaving aside the study of class in its political or material incarnations.[3] Whereas earlier culture appeared as epiphenomenal, now class and class politics receded into the background. This is, I believe, what Geoff Eley and Keith Nield meant when they described how "advocates of the 'discursive approach to history'" had reinstated "an older disconnection between 'politics' and 'society'".[4] This however has not been true for Rose in whose work politics appeared squarely in the foreground of the questions she asked and investigated.

Three major contributions have emerged from Rose's work. The first and most obvious is her substantive contribution to the field of British social history – from the nineteenth through the mid-twentieth centuries, spanning a period of widely diverse historical developments ranging from the process of nineteenth-century industrialization to social relations in the era of World War II and its aftermath. A second has been her contribution to debates over theory that have guided the work of historical sociologists and that have been deeply relevant to her own historical work. Rose has accomplished what relatively few scholars have achieved: combining the historian's attention to social context, materiality, culture and social change, and the sociologist's attention to theory and explanation. Third is her contribution to feminist historical studies, work that has taken seriously the broad meanings of gender to include the study of masculinity as well as femininity and that has looked at the intersecting and mutually constitutive relations of gender, class and race. These three major contributions are, of course, overlapping and intersecting and are most apparent in her books, *Limited Livelihoods: Gender and Class in Nineteenth Century England* (Berkeley, 1992); in the volume on which we collaborated, *Gender and Class in Modern Europe* (Ithaca, 1996); and *Which People's War? National Identity and Citizenship in Wartime Britain, 1939–1945* (Oxford, 2005). With these books – as with dozens of articles – her work has contributed to historical knowledge and has inspired others, among them the contributors to this volume, those who have collaborated with her and many more who have followed her work closely.

Scholars working in the field of British history – mainly historians and sociologists – had for decades attempted to make sense of the diverse social changes that eighteenth- and nineteenth-century industrialization wrought on British society. Their work reached into the private sphere of the family, examining the demographic impact of industrialization, the subtle links between family and labour and the impact of industrial change on life processes. Many, inspired by the pioneering work of Edward Thompson, teased apart the complex relationships between work, class formation and working-class culture, protest, radicalism and reformism.[5] Women, however, although they figured implicitly in stories of family structure, or even explicitly (usually along with children) as workers, did not occupy the foreground of analysis in the iconic studies of class formation, despite a substantial body of work – much of it produced in the first decades of the twentieth century – that documented the contribution of women to the project of British industrial capitalism.[6] Not, that is, until a new generation of feminist historians in the 1970s such as Sally Alexander, Catherine Hall and Leonore Davidoff, for example, began their investigations of working-class and middle-class women in British history. Within this important and indeed path-breaking literature, important questions remained. How were class interests created in nineteenth-century Britain? Why had it been so difficult for men and women to co-operate in resisting the exploitation of industrial capitalism? Why was occupational segregation so durable a feature of industrial capitalism, and why did working-class men fight so hard to maintain it?

In her path-breaking *Limited Livelihoods, Gender and Class in Nineteenth Century England* (Berkeley, 1992) Rose added a new analytical dimension to how historians looked at the class relations of British industrial capitalism. Building upon the important work of historians who had begun to make visible the crucial role of women in British history, Rose answered these questions by focusing on the centrality of gender in the class relations that marked industrialization. In this regard, she exposed how most British working-class history had ignored the fundamental fact of sexual difference. Although Rose's work departed markedly from Edward Thompson's classic *Making of the English Working Class* (not least for Thompson's lack of attention to gender as a constitutive dimension of class), it shared Thompson's attention to the relevance of culture in working-class formation. By culture Rose meant not only religion, sociability, rituals, demonstrations, newspapers, pamphlets and the work of working-class writers and poets, but the larger range of *cultural productions* that included language, discourses and visual materials, that could be read as rhetorical expressions of contest over meanings. Following the work of historians and literary critics attentive to the contributions of post-structuralism and linguistic theory, and departing from Marxist orthodox hierarchy of base and superstructure, Rose further asserted that cultural productions and practices had a formative effect on economic relations. Employers did not consistently behave as rational actors, routinely hiring women at lower wages; their perceptions of social relations, influenced by culture, shaped their strategies and behaviours. Likewise, working-class men's conflicts with women occurred not only because they feared that women would undercut their wages in some crude economic sense, but because of how their masculine work identities and their subjective sense of "respectability" shaped their ability to dominate in the workplace as well as in the home. Ideas about masculine respectability and working men's ideas about the family played a major role, for instance, in nineteenth-century British working-class men's demands for a family wage.[7] The attention to culture was critical for it was through cultural processes that gender asserted itself in material life. Thus, Rose took to heart the assertion of British scholars such as Raymond Williams that language, ideas and even feelings intersect with, and are part and parcel of, material life, not separate from it, and she weighed in on the ongoing debate among scholars, both Marxist and *marxisant* about the primacy of material/economic life versus culture.[8]

At the same time, Rose distinguished herself from feminist scholars who viewed capitalism and patriarchy as separate systems as well as from those who argued that they operated as intersecting systems (as "capitalist patriarchy" or as "patriarchal capitalism") because of how these formulations continued to "relegate gender to the realm of ideology while leaving economic relations grounded in the material world" or "see the cause of women's subordination to be their biological [material] role in reproduction".[9] Indeed the point of *Limited Livelihoods* was to explore the intersections without fixing them in a rigid structural relationship to one another. Gender, Rose argued, was everywhere – affecting "all social structures and social relations" and embedded in the very foundations of economic life.[10]

Although some were critical of her assertion that systems of meaning could shape economic and material life, Rose convincingly demonstrated how gender discourses operated in the behaviour of both employers and workers – a dynamic that should have been obvious for decades but had gone unrecognized. In discussing the paternalistic practices of employers, for instance, she showed how employers carefully structured their labour force around the gender of workers. Thus a salt manufacturer in Worcestershire in a letter to a colleague revealed an interpretation of the meanings of motherhood and family that led him to justify excluding women from his factory on the grounds that the families in which women worked lived in squalour and depravity. Other employers in paper manufacture, boot and shoe manufacture, in the hosiery industry and in the woolen textile industry likewise enforced a marriage bar on the grounds that employing married women was "bad for the home".[11] Paternalist manufacturer Edward Cadbury in Birmingham took a direct interest in the private lives and gender relations of his workers. He extended the strict gender division of labour in his chocolate factory into the recreational facilities and schools he provided on the Cadbury estate on the basis of what he perceived as the nefarious moral consequences of mingling the sexes. As Rose pointed out, because of his visibility as a model employer, these practices not only *reflected* his interpretation of gender relations, they also helped to *shape* ideas about gender and managerial practices more generally.

These dynamics were not confined to employers. Gender also proved fundamental to the conflicts between male workers and employers over who would be employed on which machines and at what rates. In case studies of competition between men and women at work, Rose skillfully demonstrated how working-class carpet weavers successfully resisted the practice of employing women on the new machines that carpet manufacturers introduced at the end of the nineteenth century. Both employers and male workers harboured a distinction between "men's machines" and "women's machines", and male workers resisted women's employment at lower rates on the former. Arguing that there wasn't enough work for men to go around, they displayed their assumption that men had priority over women in employment. Declining economic conditions and competition between manufacturers provided the context in which the fiercest battles occurred. With rare exceptions, the outcome of these labour struggles was to reinforce gender segregation.

Demonstrating culture's capacity to shape class struggles, Rose drew attention to how workers' cultural productions – letters and poems published in local newspapers – provided the symbolic ballast that helped to sustain a gender division of labour in working-class households as well as in the factory. Thus, in letters published in local newspapers, workingmen criticized those who sent their daughters into the mills as robbing men and their families of their daily bread; but women also responded to these attacks by defending their right to work "to seek my labour at any price I like, and when and where I like", refusing to accept the male breadwinner model that emerged so clearly in men's claims and cultural productions.[12]

Finally, Rose showed how gender shaped state interventions with respect to the working class, particularly through the elaboration of law and public policies. By making men responsible for the support of their families, the British Poor Law of 1834 institutionalized a male breadwinner model and assumed the dependence of women and children on male wages, belied, in reality by the high levels of female and child labour throughout the period and indeed for the entire century. Reading the language of the debates surrounding the legislation and the language of the law itself, Rose pointed to the law's symbolic consequences: by implicitly questioning the respectability of working-class men who failed to support their families adequately, it thereby "[strengthened] an association that working-class men made between manliness and independence".[13] The same proved true of subsequent protective labour legislation of the 1840s and 1870s that evoked women and children's lack of legal independence and women's maternal duties to justify limiting their working hours – something that legislators could not do for political reasons, for working-class men, for whom state regulation would have constituted interference with their freedom of contract. These ideas were expanded further in Rose's article on British protective labour legislation for our co-edited volume, *Gender and Class in Modern Europe* (Cornell, 1996), where she pointed to how arguments for protecting women and infants in legislation passed in the 1870s called on the importance of British maternity for racial quality.[14]

As *Limited Livelihoods* demonstrated, gender was not merely an ideological or discursive representation; it had the capacity to shape, in powerful ways, critical dimensions of material life. The development of a sense of working-class respectability over the course of the labour struggles of the nineteenth century was at least partially premised on the norm of a male breadwinner and the ideal of a family wage on the one hand, and on working-class female maternity and domesticity on the other hand. These distinctions, based on perceptions of sexual difference, influenced the division of labour as well as glaring and persistent inequalities between male and female wages, among other things. Nor was gender equivalent to "women". Whereas much historical work claiming to focus on gender in fact used gender as a code word for "women", one of Rose's major contributions has been to show how some of the most powerful dimensions of gender analysis lay in exposing how forms of masculinity were constituted historically. In nineteenth-century Britain, the development of working-class "masculine respectability" proved to be a forceful impetus for workingmen's claims to better material conditions of work and life. As Rose also showed, gender linked production and reproduction in fundamental ways, had the capacity to influence employers' choices, state policy and figured as a flashpoint in labour struggles, resulting in altering or confirming the configuration of jobs and wages and the contours of class. Indeed, in attempting to push the history of British industrialization beyond the story of skilled male artisans, *Limited Livelihoods* stood as a model of how the diverse meanings of sexual difference influenced economic conditions and shaped class conflict in nineteenth-century England.

Rose's contribution to our jointly-edited volume, *Gender and Class in Modern Europe*, built on the achievement of *Limited Livelihoods* to break new ground by theorizing more broadly the place of gender in the history of working-class formation. Indeed her major contribution to our jointly written theoretical introduction was to insist on the importance of unmasking the false universal of the "quintessential worker" that had for over a century constituted the object of working-class political mobilization as well as historians' scholarship on class formation. The volume (indeed its very *raison d'être*) owed a tremendous debt to how Rose had demonstrated the centrality of sexual difference to class formation in her own research on Britain. The challenge was to demonstrate that this was not merely a nationally specific phenomenon, but that it extended to a range of European countries throughout the nineteenth and twentieth centuries. Rose's own article, "Protective Labor Legislation in Nineteenth Century Britain: Gender, Class and the Liberal State", expanded on her earlier study of state policy to argue that the enactment of gender-specific legislation was possible within the framework of the bourgeois, liberal state, because of how reformers and legislators conceived of women and children's lack of legal personhood. Gender proved central to the state's ability to legitimate its legislative reach. Some of these same questions about the relationships of state to people, and how gender legitimated diverse aspects of state policy, arose in subsequent research.

Which People's War? constituted another brilliant example of the use of theory in historical writing to understand how issues of gender, class and race came together in the process of working out the meanings of nationality and citizenship. Once again, Rose turned her lens on language and cultural representations to understand how ordinary British citizens interpreted the meanings of nationhood and citizenship during the war. How did ordinary Britons experience the war, and in particular how did they understand their belonging to the nation? In some larger sense, Rose was concerned to illuminate how culture shapes historical subjectivities. *Which People's War?* took as its point of departure the myth of national unity in Britain during World War II. Although other scholars had studied the stresses and strains of the war years, Rose attempted to show that even as the British government called upon the British people to unite in wartime solidarity, the very call to unity produced fractures along the already existing fault lines of gender, sexuality, race and class. This was particularly striking in the case of efforts to mobilize working-class support during the war, but which partially backfired in working-class unrest and other expressions of class resentment in the popular press, for example. Especially interesting was the new "social problem" created by the evacuations from British cities to rural areas in the West, the South and to Scotland and Wales, that threw urban poor and rural folk into contact, leading to a "Conference on Problem Families" at the war's end. Not only did the evacuation reveal the existence of a divided Britain, but also in a manner strikingly reminiscent of nineteenth-century moralists' approach to protective measures for women and children, those who defined the "social problem" did so from the standpoint of mothers' failings. The new awareness of urban poverty that the evacuations brought may well have fuelled postwar reforms designed to relieve social and economic inequalities.

The myth of the self-sacrificing unified nation at war was also disrupted in other ways, notably by the allegedly immoral behaviour of young women who consorted with soldiers, especially African-American soldiers stationed in Britain. As Rose pointed out, "Wartime is an especially prime historical moment, not only for demarcating the national self from that of the enemy, but also for identifying and excluding those who do not exemplify particular national virtues" (72). Using Richard Rorty's theoretical insights on morality ("the voice of ourselves as a community"), Rose pointed to how moral discourses acquired new importance in wartime when "national identity becomes a crucially powerful mode of identification" (73). Like young pleasure-seeking women who defied moral and racial conventions to date African-American soldiers, Jews were identified as another "enemy within" by virtue of their alleged profiteering on the black market and their wealth in the midst of wartime sacrifice. Rose asserted that even as these internal enemies disrupted the notion of a nation united against a common enemy, critiques of moral impropriety and alien status also helped to mark the boundaries of citizenship and reinforced the "civic myth" of "Britishness". But as Rose argued, even these boundaries proved elusive.

Rose showed how gender complicated that evolving concept of citizenship as the gender inequality embedded in women's status as economic persons (their lack of property rights, their occasional loss of employment if they married, in additional to wage inequality, for example) surfaced during the war. If women were considered to be bad citizens when they enjoyed relationships with American servicemen, even when they performed their expected obligations in munitions production or civil defence activities, they were accused of taking on male responsibilities in civil defence work (they were excluded from becoming regular members of the Home Guard, a position that men fought to preserve) or "diluting" British industry in ways that would ultimately deprive men of jobs. Accusations of the "loose morals" of women serving in the armed services further undermined the "good citizenship" of women who participated in the war effort. And there was no "equality of sacrifice" for women who continued to suffer from a gender-based wage gap for war-related work, even though equal pay became a significant wartime issue. Finally, the popular representations of women varied widely from those promoting maternity and the sexually neutral or relatively asexual mother, on the one hand, to a glamorous, "sexualized femininity" on the other. As Rose wrote, "The very status of 'woman' in the context of the 'Peoples' War' was full of contradictions. Regardless of the nature of her patriotic contribution or how she enacted femininity, she was problematic. Gender difference was both essential to the nation and disruptive of its imagined unity" (149).

Masculinity, Rose argued, in contrast, was invisible – that is, it was an "unmarked category", normal, and therefore assumed. At the same time, as Rose stated, the tales of heroism that peppered the popular press, wartime iconography of the valiant soldier, and the focus on the strength and health of male bodies seen in advertisements, cartoons and letters in the popular press all contributed to the construction of hegemonic masculinity during the war, and provided tropes that endured long after. Military service, after all, was a quintessentially masculine activity and men who did not serve were "tarred with the brush of effeminacy or were considered sexually suspect" (176). The masculine military hero likewise became the quintessential British citizen.

Race was fundamentally divisive of the myth of wartime unity. In an exceptionally interesting chapter, Rose demonstrated how, despite Britain's attempt to portray itself as a well-intentioned empire, a combination of metropolitan and colonial racism tarnished that image. Colonial subjects who came to Britain to assist in the war effort found themselves subject to a colour bar and routinely discriminated against by the British as well as subject to racial insults and treatment by white Americans. And despite the fraternization of African-American soldiers with white British women, soldiers of colour were strictly segregated in separate units – a situation that the British did not question. The government supported the colour bar in refusing the possibility of military commissions for men of colour. Racism in the colonies, long a tool of colonial rule, hardly stopped during the war. Rose pointed to how during the war the notion of an "imperial citizenship" came into more regular usage as a way of extending the fiction of national belonging to colonial subjects. But as Rose asserted, colonial subjects were hardly fooled by the fiction that they were "citizens of the Empire", and the racism and discrimination that became more visible in a war fought against fascism undermined British pretensions not only to unity on the home front but to the values for which it claimed to be fighting.

In the end, *Which People's War?* contributed to a major re-thinking of British notions of national identity and the meanings of citizenship as they were inflected by gender and sexuality, race and class. Indeed the sacrifices, tensions and uneasiness that Rose has described may well have bolstered the crashing success of the Labour Party at the war's end along with its important social reforms. The picture she has painted is hardly one of the united Britain that has emerged in so much of the literature. Indeed, the fractured understandings of nationhood and citizenship that emerged constituted a provocative portrait of the "people" – a category that Rose repeatedly deconstructs – and adds enormously to the wider literature on the social history of war.

In these works as in many of her articles, Rose, while showing how the theoretical contributions of gender, class and race can illuminate historical problems and processes, has not been wedded to theory as a totalizing or universalizing map for historical analysis. Rather, her work has incorporated a notion of theory close to what Iris Marion Young meant when she wrote that feminists needed a "pragmatic orientation to our intellectual discourse. By being pragmatic, I mean categorizing, explaining, developing accounts and arguments that are tied to specific practical and political problems, where the purpose of the theoretical activity is clearly related to those problems".[15] Examples of how Rose has used theory in this way appear in numerous forms throughout her work from her use of the insights of gender analysis to illuminate the problem of class formation to her theoretical discussions of gender and citizenship, citizenship, race and nationality as well as British identity in wartime. As Rose wrote in her 1998 essay, "Resuscitating Class", published as part of a roundtable in the journal *Social Science History*, "I do not think we are going to be able to come up with a theoretical model for how race, class, gender, and ethnicities fit together in the abstract. I don't think we can afford to look for an epistemologically pure way to combine discursive analysis of texts with assessments of their cultural, social, and political contexts. The best we might be able to do is to specify heuristic devices and questions that we could bring to the study of the changing constitutive aspects of economic inequality and forms of contestation".[16] Rose proposed Sartre's concept of "seriality" as one such heuristic device to re-orient the historical study of class, a concept that Sartre used to refer to the shared situation of people who are linked by a logic external to them – in the case of class, the logic is their economic position. At the same time political identities create boundaries and involve inclusions and exclusions. Understanding the dynamics of inclusion and exclusion is critical to understanding the potential and the limits of political struggles. If Rose attempted to use the notion of seriality in her own work as a way to get beyond the universalizing concept of the "quintessential [read male] worker", a new notion of materiality also runs throughout her work – a notion of materiality that incorporates culture, discourses, symbols and representations as rooted in social relations and constitutive of the politics and political consciousness that ultimately emerge from everyday life. This creative imagining of the relationships between theory and historical explanation, between culture and material life, between life and politics, constitutes a model of scholarly practice and a lesson from which we can all learn.

Notes

1 On the scientific bases of historical investigation, see Peter Novick, *That Noble Dream: The Objectivity Question in the American Historical Profession* (Cambridge, 1988).

2 For scholarship in North America, see for example, the work of the Philadelphia Social History Project, the work of family historians such as Tamara Hareven, Herbert Gutman's work on the black family, American labour

history. Much of this work was published in the *Journal of Interdisciplinary History*. In Britain, the work of demographers Peter Laslett, Richard Wall and others in the Cambridge Social History group are examples; in France the numerous local and regional studies of historical demographers and social historians associated with the Ecole des hautes études en sciences sociales, and the important work of Hans Medick and Franklin Mendels on protoindustrialization.

3 I explored some of these questions in my essay, "Dissent Over Discourse: Labor History, Gender, and the Linguistic Turn", in *History and Theory* 34 no. 3 (1995): 213–30. See also Carole Turbin, Laura L. Frader, Sonya O. Rose, Evelyn Nakano Glenn and Elizabeth Faue, "A Roundtable on Gender, Race, Class, Culture and Politics: Where Do We Go From Here?" in *Social Science History* 22, no. 1 (Spring, 1998): 1–45.

4 See Geoff Eley and Keith Nield, *The Future of Class in History. What's Left of the Social?* (Ann Arbor, 2007), 10. I am necessarily oversimplifying these developments, which are addressed more closely by Eley and Nield.

5 Edward Thompson, *The Making of the English Working Class* (Harmondsworth, 1963). The work of Neil Smelser, *Social Change in the Industrial Revolution* (Chicago, 1959); Michael Anderson *Family Structure in Nineteenth Century Lancashire* (Cambridge, 1971); John Foster, *Class Struggle in the Industrial Revolution* (New York, 1974); Patrick Joyce, *Work, Society, and Politics* (London, 1980); David Levine, *Reproducing Families: The Political Economy of English Population History* (Cambridge, 1987); and Levine, *Family Formation in an Age of Nascent Capitalism* (Cambridge, 1977); Eric Hobsbawm, *Labouring Men* (London, 1974) and Hobsbawm, *Workers. Worlds of Labour* (London, 1984); Gareth Stedman Jones, *Languages of Class: Studies in English Working-Class History (1832–1982)* (Cambridge, 1983) are but a few examples of this pathbreaking work.

6 Alice Clark, *The Working Life of Women in the Seventeenth Century* (London, 1919); Ivy Pinchbeck, *Women Workers and the Industrial Revolution 1750–1850* (London, 1930); Wanda Neff, *Victorian Working Women: an Historical and Literary Study of Women in British Industries and Professions, 1832–1850* (New York, 1929); Clementina Black, *Sweated Industry and the Minimum Wage* (London, 1907) and Black, (ed.) *Married Women's Work, Being the Report of an Enquiry Undertaken by the Women's Industrial Council* (London, 1915) for example.

7 I discussed some of the literature with which Rose engaged on this question in my article, "Engendering Work and Wages: the French Labor Movement and the Family Wage", in Laura Frader and Sonya Rose, (eds.) *Gender and Class in Modern Europe* (Ithaca, 1996), 142–64.

8 *Limited Livelihoods*, 12; Williams, *Marxism and Literature* (Oxford, 1977).

9 *Limited Livelihoods*, 12.

10 *Limited Livelihoods*, 11.

11 *Limited Livelihoods*, 44–7.

12 *Limited Livelihoods*, 121 and 123.

13 *Limited Livelihoods*, 53.

14 Rose, "Protective Labor Legislation in Nineteenth Century Britain: Gender, Class, and the Liberal State", in *Gender and Class in Modern Europe*, 205.

15 Iris Marion Young, "Gender as Seriality: Thinking About Women as a Social Collective", *Signs: Journal of Women, Culture, and Society* 19, no. 3 (1994), 717–18.

16 Rose, "Resuscitating Class", in Turbin *et al.*, "A Roundtable on Gender, Race, Class, Culture and Politics: Where Do We Go From Here?", 21. Rose's comments in the roundtable were developed more thoroughly in her article, "Class Formation and the Quintessential Worker", in John Hall, (ed.) *Reworking Class* (Ithaca, 1997), 133–66.

Index